BOOKS BY CLAUDIA DREIFUS

Radical Lifestyles

Woman's Fate

SEIZING
OUR BODIES

SEIZING OUR BODIES

THE POLITICS OF WOMEN'S HEALTH

EDITED AND WITH AN INTRODUCTION BY

Claudia Dreifus

VINTAGE BOOKS

A Division of Random House / New York

A VINTAGE ORIGINAL, January 1978

First Edition

Copyright © 1977 by Claudia Dreifus

Library of Congress Cataloging in Publication Data
Main entry under title:

Seizing our bodies.

  Bibliography: p.
  1. Women's health services—United States.
2. Women's health services—Political aspects—
United States. 3. Feminism—United States.
4. Women in medicine—United States. I. Dreifus,
Claudia. [DNLM: 1. Gynecology—United States—
Collected works. 2. Quality of health care—
United States—Collected works. 3. Women—
Collected works.
RG14.U6S53   362.1′9′80973   77–76554
ISBN 0–394–72360–0

Grateful acknowledgment is made to the following for permission to reprint previously published material:

Deborah Baker: "The Class Factor" reprinted from *Win* and *Mountain Life and Work.*

Baywood Publishing Company, Inc.: "Women and Health Care: A Comparison of Theories" by Elizabeth Fee, reprinted from *International Journal of Health Services*, Vol. 5, No. 3 (1975). Copyright © 1975 by Baywood Publishing Company, Inc.; "Women Workers in the Health Service Industry" by Carol A. Brown, reprinted from *International Journal of Health Services*, Vol. 5, No. 2 (1975). Copyright © 1975 by Baywood Publishing Company, Inc.

The Feminist Press and Barbara Ehrenreich and Deirdre English: Excerpts from "Complaints and Disorders: The Sexual Politics of Sickness" by Barbara Ehrenreich and Deirdre English. Copyright © 1974 by Barbara Ehrenreich and Deirdre English. Reprinted by permission of The Feminist Press, Box 334, Old Westbury, N.Y. 11568.

Forum: The Journal of Human Relations: "Breast Cancer No Longer Has to Mean Mastectomy" by Rose Kushner (May 1977).

vii : : Acknowledgments

Harper & Row, Publishers, Inc.: Selections from *The Horrors of the Half-Known Life: Male Attitudes Towards Women and Sexuality in Nineteenth-Century America* by G. J. Barker-Benfield. Copyright © 1976 by G. J. Barker-Benfield.

Health Policy Advisory Center: "The Birth Controllers" by Jean Sharpe. Reprinted from Health/PAC Bulletin (April, 1972).

HealthRight: "The Women's Health Movement—Where Are We Now?" by Rachel Gillet Fruchter, Naomi Fatt, Pamela Booth, and Diana Leidel of the HealthRight Collective.

Majority Report: "What My Doctor Didn't Tell Me about Menopause" by Rosetta Reitz. Copyright © 1974 by *Majority Report.*

Helen Marieskind: "The Women's Health Movement: Past Roots and History" by Helen Marieskind.

Mother Jones: "A Case of Corporate Malpractice" by Tracy Johnston and Mark Dowie.

New Times Magazine: "The Epidemic in Unnecessary Hysterectomy" by Deborah Larned was previously titled in the December 1974 *New Times Magazine* "The Greening of the Womb." Reprinted by permission of the *New Times Magazine* and Deborah Larned.

New York News Magazine: "Building a Hospital Workers' Union: Doris Turner, The Woman from 1199" by Claudia Dreifus.

W. W. Norton & Company, Inc.: "The Theft of Childbirth" by Adrienne Rich, reprinted from *Of Woman Born.* Copyright © 1976 by W.W. Norton & Company, Inc.

Off Our Backs: "What Medical Students Learn about Women" by Kay Weiss, reprinted from *Off Our Backs* (April/May, 1975).

Playgirl Magazine: "The Dangers of Oral Contraception" by Barbara Seaman (June 1976); "The Dangers of Sex Hormones" by Barbara Seaman (July 1976).

The Progressive, Inc: "Sterilizing the Poor" by Claudia Dreifus. Copyright © 1975 by *The Progressive,* Inc., 408 West Gorham Street, Madison, Wisconsin 53703; "The Pushers" by Amanda Spake. Copyright © 1976 by *The Progressive,* Inc., 408 West Gorham Street, Madison, Wisconsin 53703.

Quadrangle/The New York Times Book Co.: "Vaginal Politics" by Ellen Frankfort. Copyright © 1972 by Ellen Frankfort.

Science for the People: "Have You Ever Wondered about the Male Pill?" by Rita Arditti was previously titled "Male Contraception" in the July 1976 issue of *Science for the People.*

MANUFACTURED IN THE UNITED STATES OF AMERICA

To the memory of my mother,

Marianne Wildorff Dreifus Jorjarian,

an early health feminist
who knew that a woman's right
to her body
was
a woman's right
to her life

ACKNOWLEDGMENTS

The thank-you list is long. Very long. Thank you to Erwin Knoll, editor of *The Progressive,* the man who encouraged me to write about a little-known case of forced sterilization of Mexican-American women out in Los Angeles. Thank you, too, to Howard Bray and the Fund for Investigative Journalism for financing my research for that article. To Bray and the fund, special appreciation must be offered: they believed, as few in the journalistic world do, that the violation of a woman's body is as important a "story" as a war or an economic crisis. My research into coercive sterilization was, in fact, the genesis of this anthology.

Warm thanks to my sisters in the women's health movement for their generous advice—to Barbara Carress of Health/PAC, Ellen Frankfort, Sharon Lieberman, Judy Norsigian of the Boston Women's Health Collective, Barbara Seaman, Naomi Fatt and Carla Cassler of HealthRight. Thank you to Helen Marieskind, who served as consultant, soothsayer and friend during the long months this volume was in preparation. Thanks to Beatrice Dreifus, Janet Stone, Celine Hertzman, Carol Botwin, Peter Kelsh, Helen Gary Bishop and Janet Page for their loving support. Thank you to Jean Pohoryles, a brilliant editor with good instincts and a fine soul. Thanks to Betsy Amster of Vintage Books for her good work. And thank you, of course, to Elaine Markson, my literary agent, a sister who cares deeply about women's health and who makes free space for all those unpopular ideas that would never see print without her energy and effort.

CONTENTS

Part Five: Taking Our Bodies Back: The Women's Health Movement

INTRODUCTION

This book begins with the premise that health care is an expensive and hazardous necessity for man and woman alike in the United States. Consider these economic statistics: In 1975, medicine rivaled only defense as the largest single sector of the American economy;[1] that year, citizenry and government jointly expended more than $118.5 billion dollars in the quest of longevity and good health;[2] that same year, while the United States per capita income was $5,843, the per capita expenditure for health was $476.22.[3] Americans were spending more money for medical services than any other nation in the world.[4]

But were Americans getting good value for those tens of billions? And are they now? Is the United States—with its high-powered medical technology, empire-sized hospital centers and massive quantities of miracle drugs—the healthiest nation in the world? Statistics say no. The United Nations' *Demographic Yearbook* for 1973 indicts the United States for having one of the highest infant mortality rates in the industrialized world—we are only fifteenth from the top,[5] a certain indicator of widespread malnutrition and poor prenatal services; the United States ranks fifth, not first, on low maternal death rates[6] for similar reasons. Despite all the scientific advances of the postwar era—the kidney machines, the open-heart surgery—life expectancy for Americans who reach the age of 65 has not gone up since 1940; indeed, the life span of American men is shorter than that of men in fifteen other countries, and American women do not live as long as their sisters in five other countries—all of them spending less per individual on medical needs.*[7]

Where does the money go? For the most part, it is misappropriated and squandered in a system whose planners seem never to have heard the words *preventive medicine.* Money is spent on unregulated doctors' fees, which skyrocket year after year and give physicians a median reported annual income of $44,580.[8] Money is spent on unnecessary surgery: We have a system that graduates too many surgeons, who in turn do too much cutting; Britain has half the surgeon–patient ratio of the United States, and half the surgery-per-patient rate.[9] Money is wasted on unnecessary inpatient hospitalizations because hospitals have empty beds they must fill, and because most health insurance plans do not pay for home care. The fee-for-service basis of medical practice gives doctors and hospitals a vested interest in illness, not health. All of this results in Americans being overtreated for maladies that are profitable, and undertreated for the everyday problems that make them sick.

But if all Americans suffer from the organization of the medical system, women are especially jeopardized. By virtue of their reproductive functions, women use medical facilities 25 percent more frequently than their male counterparts.[10] Designated by sex-role division as nurturers, it is the American woman who takes her children, husband and parents to the doctor when illness strikes.[11] More likely than not, the physician employed will be a man.** Organized medicine has a long, bitter history of discrimination against women practitioners. Yet within the health service indus-

---

*For an excellent rundown on the failure of the American health care system, see *Prognosis Negative: Crisis In the Health Care System,* edited by David Kotelchuck of the Health Policy Advisory Center (New York: Vintage, 1976).

**Some of this is changing, though. Medical schools, prodded by threats of feminist lawsuits, have opened up admissions to female students; entering classes in 1977 are reportedly as high as 30 percent female at some institutions. Still in 1970, according to Health/PAC, only 7 percent of all American doctors were women. In 1977, that figure has doubled—though 14 percent is hardly equity. Discrimination against women entering surgical specialties remains strong.

try, women make up the bulk of the workforce, toiling at low-pay, no-control, no-prestige ancilliary jobs. As Dr. Carol Brown writes in "Women Workers in the Health Service Industry" (page 235), 85 percent of all employees in the health field are women; the vast majority are nurses, nurses' aides, housekeepers and laundresses. Men, with a few publicized exceptions, run the hospitals, the research institutes, Blue Cross, the pharmaceutical firms. It's a male monopoly almost all the way, but it is with the practice of obstetrics–gynecology, that medical specialty having female reproduction as its unique territory, that sexism is most apparent.

Ninety-four percent of all Board-certified gynecologists are male. This is no accident. Though all of organized medicine shows a record of discrimination against women practitioners, obstetrics has been particularly virulent in barring females. Obstetrics, it seems, is a surgical specialty, and the gentlemen who decide such things have long felt females too frail for the labor of cutting.* Even now, in 1977, when greater numbers of women are gaining admission to American medical schools, female doctors are finding themselves excluded from all specialties but those deemed properly feminine: pediatrics and psychiatry.[12] What we have is patriarchal rear-hegemony of technology, information, medicine and facilities affecting female reproduction. And who exactly are these men who dominate female reproductive lives? They are males raised, as we all have been, in a society steeped deep in woman-hatred. Only these men have unique on-the-job opportunities to act out their misogyny. A gynecologist in a small town who abhors abortion— the only practitioner in the area—can withhold his services, forcing young women with no other options into motherhood. An obstetrician—aided by a hospital system, medical technology and the vulnerability of pregnant women—can remove from a mother the very basic experiences of childbirth. Collectively, gynecologists can,

---

*I have a private theory on this, one that I like to apply to all areas of economic discrimination: If an occupation pays well, women are likely to be barred from it. Surgery is the most profitable of all areas of medical practice.

through their medical societies, affect important issues of public health. Throughout the dark years of illegal abortion, a time when women died of self-mutilation and fear, the professional societies were near-mute in the campaigns for abortion law repeal.

It's not a pretty picture. Nor is the reality that obstetrics–gynecology is a surgical specialty, and surgical medicine, while sometimes necessary, tends on the whole to be highly aggressive against patients. One does not need a surgeon to fit a diaphragm, to clear up a vaginal infection, or even, in many cases, to deliver a baby. Yet the surgical bent of the specialty, I suspect, gives its practitioners special opportunities for unnecessary but socially sanctioned hacking away at female genitalia.* The frequency with which unnecessary hysterectomies are performed has become a national scandal. (See Deborah Larned's piece "The Epidemic in Unnecessary Hysterectomy," page 195). Surgical intervention into the natural process of childbirth, as Adrienne Rich writes in "The Theft of Childbirth," (page 146) is an ever-growing problem.

Gynecologic oppression, having as it does roots in social psychology, differs vastly from other forms of medical malpractice. Health care, it must be repeated, is a very different proposition for women than it is for men. Females, are, after all, the means of reproduction of the species—and on this matter, at least, Freud may have been right: biology, uncontrolled, is destiny. When women have dominion over their biologic functions, only then, I'm convinced, is liberation possible. Surely the great struggle between men and women has been the historic battle over who controls female fertility; women have sought to control it in order to free themselves of the vicissitudes of nature; men, wanting to maintain patriarchal dominance, have, over and over again, moved to usurp that control. History is littered with examples of women devising means of contraception and men creating laws against their use.

---

*This is not to say that all gynecological surgery is unnecessary or motivated by deep unconscious feelings of woman-hatred; it is to suggest that the specialty tends to look to surgical solutions as the answer to most medical problems. It makes functional sense: what else is a surgeon to do, but cut?

Think of Margaret Sanger, hauled off to jail in 1919 for the crime of dispensing birth control. As Dr. Helen Marieskind explains in her opening article, "The Women's Health Movement: Past Roots" (page 3), masculine attempts at pushing women out of any independent role in healing practices are rife in medical history. That drive, I suspect, came from a male fear that female healers would provide their sisters with instruments of biologic liberation. Birth control is not a modern phenomenon—spermicides and pessaries were used by the ancient Greeks, Egyptians and East Indians.[13] Some medical historians have suggested that in Europe, during the Middle Ages and later, when Church-promulgated misogyny reached hysteric proportions, tens of thousands of female peasant lay healers and midwives were burned as witches.* The crime of these women was often nothing more than the fact that they were keepers of traditional knowledge about childbirth, abortion and contraception. The witch-burning handbook of the time, *Malleus Maleficarum* (Hammer of Witches), written by two Dominican priests, Reverends Heinrich Kramer and Jakob Sprengler, makes this motive abundantly clear:

> Now there are, as it is said in the Papal Bull, seven methods by which they infect with witchcraft the venereal act and the conception of the womb: First, by inclining the minds of men to inordinate passion; second, by obstructing their generative force; third, by removing the members accommodated to that act; fourth, by changing men into beasts with their magic act; fifth, by destroying the generative force in women; sixth, by procuring abortion; seventh; by offering children to the devils, besides other animals and fruits of the earth with which they work much harm . . .[14]

Patriarchal antagonism toward women healers has not been based solely on the fear that women might teach each other contraception; it also can be linked to ancient feelings of womb-envy. Childbearing, after all, is the one thing women do that men cannot.

---

*All manner of non-conformists were subject to witch burning, including some males. But female lay healers were a particular target.

The mere idea of this exclusivity of function has for much of history incited male intervention. The much abused witch/midwives of Europe were very different from the upper-class, Church-approved, male physicians of their day: they understood female anatomy, they had a time-tested body of knowledge, they defied the Church by performing abortions, they did not believe in the myth of feminine evil and the biblical necessity for female suffering in childbirth. Many midwives were burned for offering herbal pain-killers to laboring patients.

Barbara Ehrenreich and Deirdre English in their pamphlet, *Witches, Midwives and Nurses: A History of Women Healers,* argue that four centuries of witch-burning led to modern patriarchal medicine:

> So throughly was she [the midwife] discredited among the emerging middle classes that in the 17th and 18th centuries it was possible for male practitioners to make serious inroads into that last preserve of female healing—midwifery. Non-professional male practitioners— "barber-surgeons"—led the assault in England, claiming technical superiority on the basis of their use of the obstetrical forceps. (The forceps were legally classified as a surgical instrument, and women were legally barred from surgical practice.) In the hands of the barber-surgeons, obstetrical practice among the middle-class was quickly transformed from a neighborly service into a lucrative business, which the real physicians entered in force in the 18th century.[15]

How much better it would have been for womankind if child-birth had remained in the hands of the midwives—for though the midwife lacked "professional" training (women were excluded from most universities), she provided comfort and support for the birthing mother, and she often was cleaner, if only by virtue of her limited functions, than the general physician. Suzanne Arms, a journalist and childbirth crusader whose book, *Immaculate Deception,* is reviewed as part of Adrienne Rich's essay, describes the immediate effect of the destruction of midwifery:

> The first hospitals were not only centers of disease and disorder but disseminators of infection, and the effect on laboring women was catastrophic. For many centuries women lived with the fear that even

if she survived the terrible agony of birth, a mysterious disease known as childbed fever might overtake her body a few days later, causing delirium, high fever, convulsions and death. . . . "Physicians" of all kinds—students, barbers, butchers and (in some areas) shepherds and hog-gelders—worked on women in labor as part of medical training. Often, they would arrive with their hands bloody from dissecting cadavers or diseased patients and would then insert their hands far into the birth canals of laboring women, infecting one and all with germs that remained on unwashed skin. So the "doctor" himself, sporting a bloodied apron as a badge of his profession, became the carrier of the very disease he was supposed to cure, and childbed fever became the scourge of Europe for more than two centuries.[16]

From this cruel history emerged the childbirth of today: an unnecessarily frightening experience where technology is over-employed, where women are turned into passive birth-objects from whom male obstetricians seize infants. Babies are no longer born, they are delivered.

If the men of obstetrics had merely wanted to interpose themselves on feminine life because they found it pleasurable to deliver babies or help women in pain, then their motives might have been more acceptable. Professional doctoring, however, has a nasty history. G. J. Barker-Benfield, in his essay, "Sexual Surgery in Late-Nineteenth-Century America" (page 13), details the extent to which American gynecology in the last century expressed Anglo-Saxon male fears of women. Dr. Barker-Benfield illustrates how emerging gynecology worked to counter the political force of the first feminist wave; a cult of biologic inferiority and sex-hatred fostered by some of the nation's first gynecologists resulted in tens of thousands of "deviant" women being castrated and, in much smaller numbers, being cliterectomized and circumcised. Jean Sharpe's "The Birth Controllers" (page 57) updates the picture, telling us just who the forces behind population control are. In the past, patriarchal institutions sought to make most women into mothers; today a new technology can determine who will be allowed to breed. There are many forces, as Sharpe illustrates, anxious to play popular eugenics with women's lives.

Not all calls for birth control, we are learning, are calls for women's liberation. We now have societal forces prompted by valid concerns with population growth, who are moving for invalid social policies that would encourage some women to have families (albeit small ones) and others to have none at all—but the decision would not remain with the woman. Male domination of science, medicine and social planning—coupled with a national heritage of racialism—would pressure white affluent women into motherhood, while indigent black and brown females would be actively discouraged. Orwellian signposts of danger are already visible (see "Sterilizing the Poor," page 105). Beyond fears of eugenic engineering is the reality that women's bodies must bear the brunt of population control campaigns. As Rita Arditti writes in her article, "Have You Ever Wondered about the Male Pill?" (page 121), the gentlemen of science have not concentrated their research efforts on male contraception, although birth control for women is often hazardous and life-threatening. Never mind, say the scientists, it's all for the greater good. John Peel and Dr. Malcolm Potts, authors of the widely read *Textbook of Contraceptive Practice,* are telling medical students that women's lives are not particularly valuable when they write: "Contraception is not merely a medical procedure; it is a social convenience, and if a technique carried a mortality several hundreds of times greater than that now believed to be associated with the Pill, its use might still be justified on social, if not medical grounds."[17] Dr. Frederick Robbins, a Nobel Laureate and the dean of Case Western Reserve Medical School, went one step further in a 1969 speech to the Association of American Medical Schools: "The dangers of over-population are so great that we may have to use certain techniques of conception control that may entail considerable risk to the individual woman."[18]

Women, individually and collectively, have in recent years refused to accept this doctrine of female expendability. An extraordinary social movement has developed around the idea that women should control their own bodies. It's a remarkable thing, this women's health movement: females of all ages, races and classes, brought together by a unanimity of negative experience with the American health-care system. Radical, anarchic, sometimes leaderless, sometimes not, the women's health movement cannot be defined as one set thing. Health professionals staff the movement, and nonprofessionals, too, including housewives, mothers, students, writers, lesbians, socialists, herbalists, and even some women who consider themselves witches. What unites these women is their common femaleness, their distrust of organized medicine, their belief that self-knowledge of anatomy and bodily functions can be liberating, their insistence that women control the means of reproduction—and thus their lives. Large segments of the movement believe that health care for both sexes is a highly political problem, that none of us can be healthy in a system that creates sickness out of normal life-functions and that profits from illness. The scope of the movement is enormous. A 1973 study conducted by Health-Right, a New York-based collective, found over a thousand active projects from coast to coast (see page 271).

This movement was born in a half-dozen cities during the late 1960's, coinciding with the rebirth of the second wave of American feminism. In those consciousness-raising groups that were the core of the early women's rights organizations, women sat together and shared knowledge of past and present oppression.[19] It was a rare CR group that did not devote sessions to frightening tales of illegal abortions and manipulative gynecologists. In no time, the women's rights movement had identified gynecologic oppression as a major target. Abortion seemed the most obvious grievance, because abortion, at the time, was still illegal. During the first feminist march down Fifth Avenue in New York in August of 1970, banners flew high demanding, "FREE ABORTION, NOW."

By the early 1970's, coalitions of feminists, clergy and populationists were working together for national legalization. New York State in 1970 had passed a liberal abortion law, permitting pregnancy termination almost on demand; California, Hawaii and Washington, D.C. had liberal statutes also. But elsewhere, abortion was strictly prohibited, and feminists organized counseling services to shuttle pregnant women into legal areas. In Chicago, a women's liberation collective questioned the value of cross-state shuttling. It was expensive, they said, and of limited value since only well-to-do women could afford transportation costs and fees at New York's high-priced clinics. After much debate, the collective decided to try a new tactic: they approached a nurse who'd been performing abortions illegally for many years. Would she teach them her craft? Yes, she said, gladly. From there, the feminists set up their own underground clinic and contact system. Women in need would call an answering service and ask for "Jane." Naomi Fatt, of the HealthRight Collective, a participant-historian of the women's health movement, feels that the moment the "Jane" group moved outside the scope of law and official medicine, a basic step in radical health-feminism was taken. "Out of their training," she says, "the group went on to provide abortions for thousands of mid-western women who lacked the necessary money to buy abortions from local hospitals or to travel to areas where it could be obtained legally.* In the four years before abortion became legal in Illinois 'Jane' provided 11,000 abortions."

In Los Angeles in 1970, Carol Downer, a thirty-nine-year-old housewife, the mother of six, was doing part-time abortion counseling.[20] Downer wanted a better sense of the politics of abortion, and so she founded a consciousness-raising group with several other abortion counselors. There she met Lorraine Rothman, mother of five, and the vice-president of the Orange County NOW chapter. A friendship and partnership grew. "What we were trying to do in the CR group," Downer recalls, "was to find safe and reasonably priced places for abortion. As soon as we started talking about it, we realized we didn't even know how to judge what a good abortionist was, who was safe, what was considered a reasonable cost. We realized, too, that women need to know a lot more about health care and women's anatomy." While inspecting local abortion clinics, Downer and Rothman observed what they considered poor medical practices. "The most common type of abortion we saw was

---

*Even during prohibition, wealthy women could always buy a "therapeutic" abortion at regular hospital facilities. It involved a certain amount of bribery, deception and degradation, but it was possible.

the D and C [dilation and curettage]. Most of the physicians were dilating the opening of the cervix more than necessary," Downer continued. In no time, Rothman and Downer were reading, observing, learning everything they could about abortion and gynecology. They watched as many kinds of gynecological procedures as they were permitted. Like the "Jane" sisters, Downer and Rothman found actual medical practice simple enough for the lay person to understand. Downer recalled:

> After seeing doctors do abortions I was amazed to learn that the operation is fairly simple, that there is nothing mystical about entering the uterus and removing its contents. I was especially amazed to see a cervix. After having six children and two abortions, it was amazing to see this organ that had such significance in my own life, and that I had no knowledge of. I figured that few women knew much about their internal organs, either. The point wasn't that I saw a cervix and that was it! Nurses and doctors see cervixes all the time and it doesn't create change. But what I saw was the importance of women understanding and having access to the parts of our bodies so tied up in reproduction.[20]

Thus the idea of self-help clinics was born. Carol Downer and Lorraine Rothman began holding meetings with feminists around Los Angeles where women with flashlight, speculum and mirror in hand would view each other's internal organs. For the participants, these early self-help meetings were world-changing experiences Society had always considered a woman's inner parts to be dark, foul mysteries. Women had been discouraged from touching themselves. What the self-help pioneers saw when they looked at their cervixes was a beautiful universe that had been there all the time. It was *their* universe, and they were clean, and their bodies were understandable, and they were *good.* The more Downer and Rothman performed self-examination clinics, the more they began to understand how easily diagnosable some gynecological problems are. Soon they could recognize a yeast infection, a displaced IUD. Why should a woman go to a gynecologist every time she developed monilia, why couldn't she learn to recognize the symptoms and use simple home remedies for their cure? With friends, Downer and Rothman assembled an illustrated lecture on self-examination, and set out on a national tour to promote this new frontier of liberation. Ellen Frankfort, then a health columnist for the *Village Voice,* wrote her famous "Vaginal Politics" article (see page 263) about one of their early demonstrations. Reader response to the article was so enthusiastic that for months afterwards Frankfort found herself deluged with letters requesting self-help information and speculums. Returning to Los Angeles after their tour, Downer and Rothman formed the Los Angeles Feminist Women's Health Center, a full-service gynecological clinic run, staffed and controlled by women. The Los Angeles Center later spawned several dozen others, including clinics in Tallahassee, Florida; Orange County, California; and Detroit, Michigan. The clinics, which have varying policies, often employ staff physicians, but uniformly have women, often nonprofessionals, doing the bulk of the medical service; their emphasis, always, is on patient involvement in diagnosis and treatment, on deprofessionalization of services.

Organized medicine, as expected, has been hostile to these new lay practitioners. Some doctors fear competition. Others suspect quackery. Either way, physician-fear has led to a series of legal confrontations. Carol Downer was arrested in 1972 for the crime of illegal unlicensed yogurt insertion into a woman's vagina. She was tried and later acquitted for her peculiar crime. In 1974, undercover police swooped down on the Santa Cruz (California) Birth Center, a clinic offering midwife services to birthing mothers. Santa Cruz nurses and lay midwives were charged with unlicensed medical practice. A drawn-out court battle resulted, draining the Center of its resources; in the end, the Santa Cruz Birth Center disbanded, though many of the midwives remain as individual practitioners serving their community. In Florida, local doctors have been fighting the Tallahassee Feminist Women's Health Clinic over abortion. The feminists wanted to organize and advertise a low-cost abortion service. Local doctors, fearing economic competition, retaliated by blacklisting any physician who worked for the clinic. Since by law an abortion can only be performed by a licensed doctor, this action was aimed at putting an end to the clinic. For over a year, the feminists imported doctors from as far away as Miami Beach. On a second front, they went to federal court and charged the local doctors with violations of antitrust laws and restraint of trade. However, on November 30, 1976, U.S. District Court Judge William Stafford ruled in favor of doctors, saying: "The State of Florida has adopted the policy that the health and welfare of its citizens are best protected by making the medical profession largely self-disciplining."

Embattled and controversial, self-help is only one part of the women's health movement. From the beginning, health feminists have been highly political, focusing much effort on lobbying to counter the weight of the AMA and the pharmaceutical companies. In 1969, when the movement was still in its infancy, Senator Gaylord Nelson (D–Wisconsin) held hearings on the safety of oral contraception. Doctors and scientists were invited, as usual, to give their expert testimony—but no women. Washington, D.C. feminists and Barbara Seaman, the author of the just-then-published muckraking best seller, *The Doctor's Case Against the Pill,* did the unprecedented: they disrupted the Nelson hearings and demanded that women, the true "experts," be allowed to speak. The incident made national television and raised national consciousness on the dangers of the Pill. Seaman herself was radicalized by the demonstration and went on to devote the next nine years of her life to a crusade against hazardous estrogen drugs. She was instrumental in pressuring the Federal Drug Administration into ordering the pharmaceutical companies to insert warnings into birth control pill containers. Seaman, along with others, also helped form the National Women's Health Network, which does extensive lobbying in Washington for female health interests.

Experimental, activist, unorthodox, the women's health movement is also a constant source of printed material; it's as if its organizers travel the country with speculum in one hand and typewriter in other. HealthRight in New York publishes a professional-looking newsletter six times a year. *The Journal of Women and Health,* edited by Helen Marieskind, publishes academic research.

Self-help news is printed in *The Monthly Extract: An Irregular Periodical,* a broadside published by Lolly Hirsh, a Connecticut housewife and mother. Books. Pamphlets. Mimeosheets. They all proliferate. In the early seventies, a Boston feminist group decided to publish a small underground pamphlet giving basic gynecological information—the facts of life that doctors never tell their patients. The collective called their effort *Our Bodies, Ourselves,* and it became an underground best seller. A New York publisher offered them a fat advance to expand the booklet. In no time, the Boston Women's Health Collective found themselves with an *overground* best seller. *Our Bodies, Ourselves* has gone into two editions, sold hundreds of thousands of copies, and made everyday medical information instantly accessible to women everywhere.

Prodded by the demands of this insurgent movement, organized medicine is showing signs of change. Suddenly doctors are attending seminars on how patients respond to *them*—modern courses in bedside manners. Physicians also are discovering that the sexual composition of their profession is changing. Medical schools, spurred by the specter of feminist lawsuits, have begun admitting more than just the token female. A decade from now, perhaps 20 percent of all doctors will be women —a reform that offers only slight comfort to health radicals. Why should women doctors, members of the higher social classes, graduates of the same old dehumanized medical training, be all that different from their male counterparts? Actually, the great success of the women's health movement has come with the creation of a new, aggressively informed class of consumer. Moreover, health feminism, in its challenge to organized medicine, has rendered both genders a service: It has destroyed the Marcus Welby myth of Doctor-As-God; it has demanded that a very basic part of human life—health—be democraticized. This book, *Seizing Our Bodies,* is an examination of the feminist complaint. In editing the collection, I've asked the question, "Who controls a woman's body—and why?" Moreover, I've sought to tell the story of the women who call themselves health feminists, these pioneers of self-knowledge and self-determination. *Seizing Our Bodies* is meant as a guidebook to a social revolution: It is not factories or post offices that are being seized, but the limbs and organs of the human beings who own them. This anthology is meant to be a small part of that effort.

PART ONE

HISTORY/
HERSTORY

Helen I. Marieskind, Dr., P.H.

THE WOMAN'S HEALTH MOVEMENT: PAST ROOTS

Conflict and activism centered around women's health care has a long tradition. Palmer Findley shows in *Priests of Lucina* that in Egypt as early as 3500 B.C. conflicts existed between two types of midwives, the *maiai* and *jatromaiai;* the former was only able to attend to matters strictly obstetrical, the latter was entitled to do surgery and internal medicine as well.[1]

Many women in ancient Greece were skilled physicians, but their performance of abortions, the influence of Hippocrates and the growth of the Pythagorean school had combined by the third century B.C. to cause their disbarment from practice. Perhaps apocryphally, history relates that disbarment ended when Greek women "picketed the courthouse" to win the acquittal of their favorite gynecologist, Agnodice. Pliny, Martial and Celsus, Greek and Roman writers, tell us she had been arrested for practicing medicine under false pretences because she had disguised herself as a man.[2]

With the growth of Christianity and the deepening conviction by

Christian men that women should keep out of public and religious affairs, major conflicts over women's role in health-care delivery and in the nature of health care began in earnest. At first the Christian brothers condoned women's medical practice as an occupation befitting their inferior status. Wrote Saint Augustine:

> . . . educated women should take care of the sick and wounded at home, attend women in confinement, bleed or cauterize all who request it and gather herbs for medicines.

By the end of the sixth century, however, the brothers were asking if women "were reasoning animals or soulless brutes," and by 660, we learn from Canon III of the Council of Nantes that they had decided women were, indeed, "soulless brutes." Thus began centuries of denying education to women, a situation that paved the way for male dominance in medicine, male definition of medical skills and indeed of medicine itself, and male control over the right to practice.

Only a few women—usually the wealthy, nobility or clerics—were educated. But there were no positions for them in a male-oriented world, so many sought refuge in the monastic life, which rapidly increased in popularity during the seventh and eighth centuries. Monastic women became medical missionaries and their monasteries were centers of healing. For example, the English princess Walpurga (c. 710–777), who is always depicted with a flask of urine in one hand and bandages in the other, founded a monastery at Heidenheim, Germany, where she treated the poor.

Hildegard of Bingen (1098–1179) was nobly born and entered monastic life at the age of eight. When thirty years old she succeeded her aunt as abbess of the convent of Disibodenburg. Throughout her earlier years, Hildegard experienced visions from an undetermined cause, although migraine is suspected.

In 1147, when she was about fifty, Hildegard and approximately fifty nuns built a new convent at Rupertsberg, across from Bingen, where the Rhine joined the Nahe. Although it was a relatively small convent, Hildegard wielded great power; Kate Campbell

Hurd-Mead notes in her history of women healers that she corresponded with "four popes, five emperors and kings, among them Conrad III and Frederick Barbarossa, and the kings of England and France."[3] Fiery and prophetic, she was widely regarded as the most important medical writer of the Middle Ages. Marks and Beatty in *Women in White* list among Hildegard's many insights theories on the circulation of the blood, the causes of contagion and autointoxication, nerve action originating in the brain and the chemistry of the blood.[4]

Such brilliance makes it all the more ludicrous that the Church continued to deny formal education to women. The learned role of medical men had been reinforced by the Council of Trent in 1125 and the Lateran Council of 1139, in which the Church decreed that monks should not let blood or perform surgical operations. Forced to rely on their "uneducable" sisters for basic medical care, women (along with the barber-surgeons) became the providers of direct care—the treatment of wounds and infections and the setting of bones. This dichotomy laid the groundwork for what was eventually to limit women healers to mere nursing tasks, with male practitioners taking an elite, specialist role.

But with an increase in the power and prestige of medical men came an increase in their determination to even more effectively exclude women from the ranks of general practitioners. By means of licensure dependent on educational qualifications that women could not possibly meet, by sexist regulations, by harassment and murder and by pitting one type of female practitioner against another, women's participation in the healing arts was radically reduced.

The case of Jacoba Félicie de Almania illustrates the point. Brought to trial in Paris in 1322 under a licensure law of 1220 with which she had not complied, Jacoba was confronted, not with incompetence, but with a detailed reading of her medical practices. These, and the witnesses who willingly testified on her behalf, showed her to be both practical and knowledgeable. She argued that the licensure law of 1220 was made for idiots and ignorant persons who knew nothing of the art of medicine and from which groups she was excluded because of her skill and expertise. Her eloquent pleas for the need for women to be treated by other women are recorded in the Charter of Paris, II:

> . . . it is better and more honest that a wise and expert woman in this art visit sick women and inquire into the secret nature of their infirmity, than a man to whom it is not permitted to see, inquire of, or touch the hands, breasts, stomach, etc. of a woman; nay rather ought a man shun the secrets of women and their company and flee as far as he can.[5]

Intense conflicts over women's health raged during the witch hunts of medieval Europe, when thousands of people were slaughtered. Most of the women were "old wives" who served as midwives and other lay women healers. This is an important distinction, because while accusations of witchcraft were also at times leveled at more recognized midwives, some provisions were made for them to be distinguished from the "old wives." In England, for example, the Archbishop of York provided that curates should teach midwives the sacrament of baptism so that they could perform it in the course of their duties, should this be necessary. Licenses were given to these midwives by the Church. Eleanor Preade, for example, was licensed in 1587 to perform the functions of midwife, including baptism, and there is an entry in the records of St. Mary's Church, Lichfield, England, dated 1591 and cited by Sophia Jex-Blake in *Medical Women,* that a child had been "baptised by the midwife, and not yet broughte to ye Church to be examined [for signs of devilry]."

Essentially, female witches were accused of sexual powers magnified to proportions terrifying to a celibate male clergy—and careful clerical propaganda made it terrifying to the lay populace as well. Witches were accused of being an organized group and of having magical powers that could both heal and hurt. The burning of Agnes Simpson in 1591, a woman who had been consulted by a lady of rank and who had provided her with successful methods of relieving pain in childbirth, indicates that an element of professional jealousy was probably involved in such accusations.

But as Thomas Szasz points out in *The Manufacture of Madness,* what was probably more important was that healing witches, the majority of whom were women, violated the Church's liaison with the State in their prohibition against unlicensed practitioners.[6] They did dissect—even if for nonmedical purposes; they did experiment with herbal cures and relied on common sense. They treated the poor, thus challenging the Church's doctrine that "suffering on this earth brings rewards in the life hereafter."

In an age where those with an academic or clerical education were the only accepted sources of knowledge, such enterprising self-help as shown by these lay healers was unacceptable. "If a woman dare to cure without having studied, she is a witch and must die," declared the Church in the fourteenth century.[7]

While all Europe was captivated by the *idea* of witchcraft until well into the eighteenth century, the *belief* in witchcraft was not universal. The Italian philosopher Giordano Bruno (1548–1600), who was burned at the stake as a heretic, openly said that many of these so-called witches were simply psychologically disturbed old women. Szasz states that this is also the modern psychiatric view, and illustrates that whenever medical "science" is challenged, the challenger is declared mad. He offers the example of Ignaz Semmelweiss, who in 1848 was declared mad and imprisoned in an insane asylum for demonstrating that physicians were contributing to the staggering mortality from childbed fever among parturient women.

In England the last witchcraft trial occurred in 1712, in Scotland the last official burning was in 1727, in Germany one of the last and most famous trials took place in 1628 and in France, Louis XIV's edict of 1682 rapidly ended witchcraft trials.

In spite of this decline, the witchcraft trials had a lasting effect on women's place as healers. The remaining areas where women could practice unlicensed had become so fraught with danger that few women risked practicing for fear of being accused. The poor lost their village healers, and the professional control by Church and State became firmly entrenched. The increasing corruption in the monasteries led to a decreased interest in the medical and charitable aspects of clerical life, while the exclusion of women from the universities continued to effectively bar the participation of even upper-class women from medical practice. Finally, by licensing some midwives and not others, stratifications and divisions formed amongst women healers, preventing a unified protest.

Surprisingly, some outstanding midwives and women physicians did survive this period. Universities in Italy were not closed to women, and important female physicians were still emerging from there at a time when England and France were persecuting them. One such physician was Dorothea Bocchi, who in 1390 was appointed professor of medicine and moral philosophy at Bologna, where she taught for forty years; one of her contemporaries was Costanza Calenda of Naples, whose lecturing in medicine won her high honors.

In France in particular, outstanding midwives practiced from the sixteenth century to the nineteenth. Louyse Bourgeois (1563–1636) laid down rules for the handling of each of the varied fetal positions, and although it is generally credited to the French obstetrician La Motte, it was she who originated the delivery of the shoulders in a head presentation by inserting the fingers of both hands under the armpits. Angèlique Marguerite le Boursier du Coudray (1712–89) invented a dummy of the female torso, an invaluable object that was to become the mother of the modern "gynny" model. Du Coudray was ordered by Louis XVI to travel throughout the French provinces, giving free instruction to all "unenlightened midwives." Yet even in France, England and Germany, where all highly accomplished midwives had their skills well rewarded, their discoveries published, and their talents utilized by the noblest and humblest of citizens, conflict still surrounded their licensure and their entry into universities. "The midwives of the Academy have no desire of me,"[8] mocked Madame Boivin (1773–1847), midwife, decorated by the French crown and awarded an honorary M.D. degree by Germany in 1827, upon being denied entry into the (male) French Academy of Medicine.

By the end of the eighteenth century conflicts over female physicians, particularly midwives, were highly institutionalized throughout Europe. In France and Germany, although the status of some was diminished, the training programs organized led to an overall increase in competence and respect. This finally resulted in the incorporation of the midwife into modern health-care systems.

Midwives in England did not fare as well. Hampered by their lack of organization, by their assignment to only obstetric as opposed to general medical skills, by competitiveness among various types of female health personnel each striving for respectability, by a wealthy and well-organized onslaught from the male physicians backed by Church, State and licensure and by an ever-expanding technology from which they were excluded, the ceaseless struggles of midwives such as Mrs. Elizabeth Nihell,[9] Mrs. Sarah Stone,[10] and Mrs. Elizabeth Cellier[11] were ultimately useless. By the end of the eighteenth century in England the opposition of the midwives to male control of obstetrics and their influence in the profession had subsided to a low ebb. So low, in fact, that Martha Mears, practitioner in midwifery, could in 1797 write glowingly of Harvey, Smellie, Leake and Denman, all leading male obstetricians:

> It would with heartfelt rapture strain my feeble voice to swell the note of public praise which they have so justly deserved. I would put their books into the hands of every midwife in the Kingdom, and say to her, in the words of the Poet—"Day and night read them—read them day and night!"[12]

It was not until the Midwives Institute was founded in 1881 by Rosalind Paget that the midwife once more became an integral part of the English health system.

In the United States, too, the midwife gradually lost her status, as did practicing female physicians—generally for the same reasons as in England. Women physicians, such as Dr. Mary Lavinder (1776–1845), who set up a pediatric and midwifery practice in Savannah, Georgia, in 1814, and Dr. Sarah E. Adams (1779–1846), also a practitioner in Georgia, were highly popular and successful even if not given equal status. It took another hundred years before the Georgia Medical Society would admit its first woman member. Similarly, Harriet K. Hunt (1805–75) set up medical practice in Boston, where she gained a large following despite the fact that she had no degree. Supported by Oliver Wendell Holmes in seeking admission to Harvard Medical School, the faculty found nothing in the statutes to deny her admission, but would make no commitment to grant her a degree.

Bertha L. Selmon records in her *History of Women in Medicine* that the students, however, resolved:

"That no woman of true delicacy would be willing in the presence of men to listen to the discussions of subjects that necessarily come under consideration of the subject of medicine;"

and

"That we object to having the company of any female forced upon us, who is disposed to unsex herself, and to sacrifice her modesty by appearing with men in the lecture room." Miss Hunt was forced to withdraw her application.[13]

But the greatest conflicts around women's health care in the United States arose during the Popular Health Movement of the 1830s and 1840s and continued well into the twentieth century. Richard Shryock, in his *Medicine in America: Historical Essays,* identifies a current of liberal democratic thinking that was hostile to all professionalism as being conducive to the growth of the Popular Health Movement. This manifested itself by lax or nonexistent licensing laws, by a broadly encompassing recognition of bodily states that could be treated domestically, and by a generally held belief that anyone who demonstrated healing skills should be permitted to practice medicine.[14]

Feminists, women practitioners such as Harriet K. Hunt and working-class radicals joined together in the Popular Health Movement to reject the perceived general arrogance and incompetence of most doctors. A total redefinition of health care was demanded by the various sects encompassed in the Movement.

Their common focus was that the body and mind were one, and that a harmonious balance between the two produced personal well-being.

Whether they espoused herbalism, hydropathy (water cures), animal magnetism or homeopathy, these groups were known as the irregulars, as opposed to the regulars or allopaths. The allopaths —who eventually evolved into the American Medical Association —revered book learning as opposed to the family-centered medicine of the irregulars. The regulars relied on "heroic" measures such as bleeding, surgery, or powerful emetics. With only a rudimentary knowledge of anatomy and almost no understanding of the germ theory, their acts frequently harmed their patients, whereas the healing properties (even if unrecognized at the time) of the more natural cures of the irregulars were obviously beneficial.

During and following the mid-nineteenth century, women were widely regarded as sickly, and this condition was commonly attributed to their general ignorance regarding health. To help protect themselves, Ladies' Physiological Reform Societies were formed as part of the Movement and women lectured on elementary anatomy, sex and general hygiene. Female sectarian medical colleges established by branches of the Popular Health Movement offered courses to women to improve both their own health and that of their families, while women graduates frequently taught through the Societies.[15]

Lydia Folger Fowler (1822–79) was one such teacher. On November 5, 1849 Fowler entered a nonconformist medical school, the Central Medical College of New York, which taught eclecticism and homeopathy. After graduating in 1850, Fowler was appointed professor of midwifery in 1851 at one of the Colleges' splinter schools, the Rochester Eclectic Medical College. She thus became the first woman to hold a professorship in a legally authorized medical school in the United States.

The Ladies' Physiological Reform Societies promoted sensible— yet radical—ideas such as frequent bathing, preventive care, loose-fitting female clothing (whalebone corsets worn by women of fashion disastrously cramped their internal organs), temperance, the importance of a healthy diet, including whole-grain cereals, and even birth control. Birth control, and woman's right to it, continued to be highly controversial even up to the repeal of the last of the Comstock Laws in 1965 in Connecticut.

Many of these topics and much of the historical issues of women's health care remain central to the Women's Health Movement today. We are still struggling over the questions of licenture, of women's entry into medical schools and whether the technological intervention of specialists is superior to the more natural healing methods of general practitioners and midwives. Given our more advanced technology the complexities may have changed, but the fundamental conflicts surrounding women's health care remain the same. This does not invalidate today's issues in any way, but rather should teach us that to find solutions we will need to learn from past struggles and find even more radical measures than we have at present. Today's Women's Health Movement is a positive beginning.

G. J. Barker-Benfield

SEXUAL SURGERY IN LATE- NINETEENTH- CENTURY AMERICA

In spite of an interlude of pioneering efforts in the "moral treatment" of the insane (that is, emphasizing what we would call psychotherapy and environmental factors) before the Civil War, the "whole movement of modern medicine inclined towards somaticism in the narrow sense—a sort of mechanical materialism" (1, 2).* In 1848, the year of the first Woman's Rights Convention, Dr. Charles Meigs (3) had indicated the direction that post-Civil War gynecologists would take. He advised his pupils that their study of female organs would command an understanding of woman's whole being. Woman's "intellectual and moral perceptivity and forces . . . are feminine as her organs are. Beyond all these, you shall have to explore the history of those functions and destinies which her sexual nature enables her to fulfill, and the

*Dain describes the new theory of local pathology as a "weapon" developed in the 1850s in the attack on moral treatment. It became common after 1865, and clues to insanity were sought "on the dissecting table" (2, p. 86). It should be noted that this account means some men attacked other men indirectly, by means of someone else's body.

strange and secret influences which her organs, by their nervous constitution, and the functions, by their relation to her whole life-force, whether in sickness or health, are capable of exerting, not on the body alone, but on the heart, the mind, and the very soul of woman. The medical practitioner has, then, much to study, as to the female, that is not purely medical—but psychological and moral rather: such researches will be a future obligation lying heavily on you. . . ." Meigs's analysis here was consistent with that of his contemporary "alienists," i.e., doctors who supervised asylums. They emphasized woman's especial liability to insanity by way of her body's peculiar dominance. Amariah Brigham (4), Edward Jarvis (5), and Isaac Ray (6) were three of the most prominent of these alienists. In 1866 Dr. Isaac Ray stated expressly that all women hovered on the verge of hysteria, insanity, and crime. "With woman it is but a step from extreme nervous susceptibility to downright hysteria, and from that to overt insanity. In the sexual evolution, in pregnancy, in the parturient period, in lactation, strange thoughts, extraordinary feelings, unseasonable appetites, criminal impulses, may haunt a mind at other times innocent and pure" (6). It was woman's sexuality that made woman mad. It was, perhaps, because the maddening pressure on men was a given of civilization, that the experts said or assumed that man's insanity was harder to cure, and, conversely, that woman's was easier. (For the assumption that male madness was a given risk, see references 2, p. 89; 6, pp. 228–229, 284; and 7.) And, until midcentury, the experts had concentrated on programs for the support of man's physique and mentality (two such programmers were Ray and the Reverend John Todd (8, 9)).

After the Civil War men increasingly emphasized woman's contribution to society's sickness, and implemented programs to restrain women. Once modern medicine settled on medical materialism (consistent with a generally more materialistic society—as de Tocqueville (10) had anticipated), it was logical that those beings whose insanity had long been held traceable to material causes— their female organs—should receive the benefits of the most up-to-date surgery. Obstetricians and gynecologists (which obstetricians became as they claimed more and more territory and social importance) shared the anxieties of other doctors. They devalued women as most men did. The gynecologic crescendo in the latter part of the century was part of the tendency Donald Meyer (11) has called a "special pathology." "The repression being imposed in the 50's and nailed down in the 70's was a special pathology, not the disciplined, long-practised style, but a defensive, emergency ideology. . . . Men had their own passion, and at the prospect of emancipated women recoiled with that fright special to those addicted to an obsession."

The men pursuing "somaticism," that is, focusing on the physicality of the body, were "disenchanted" and "pessimistic" (2, pp. 132–143), moods which seem to have run through American society generally in the late 1860s and 1870s. Robert Wiebe's account (12) of the social breakdown following the Civil War can be taken as a frame of reference for the rise of gynecology. Among the identifiable symptoms of the breakdown were the failures and corruption of Reconstruction, the longest depression in American history, insatiable business trusts, swarms of what were held to be sexually potent and racially inferior immigrants, and a government discredited at all levels. According to Wiebe, people responded to these changes with a reassertion of the "old bedrock values." These values were laced with the paranoia endemic to American history. The Civil War had perhaps dramatized the crudest source of identity, the sexual distinction between fighting men and nonfighting women. That line had already been sharpened as a reaction to the women's rights movement. Even before the war that movement had been "overborne by the high tide of visionary masculine democratic morale" (11). In 1852 Dr. Augustus Kinsley Gardner (13) had lashed out at disorderly women, lumping together women's rightists, Bloomer wearers, and midwives. "At the present time there is a proposition mooted—springing from the same high source which advocates woman's rights, the Bloomer costume, and other similar nonsensical theories—to give again the portion of the healing art, if not the whole domain of medicine, to the females," that is, to midwives.

Doctors were in no wise apart from the postwar apprehensions Wiebe identifies. One change which seemed to them to affect the constitution and health of the social body was the nature of mass immigration. In 1872 there was, according to Gardner (14), "more necessity to direct our attention to cleanliness, because this country is being filled up with various nations of foreigners, some whole classes among them are essentially and entirely dirty." Another and, perhaps, more profoundly felt, apprehension was what doctors perceived as the increasing disorderliness of women. Their professional concern with the body may have made doctors even more sensitive to the sexual line than other men. But women challenged doctors professionally too. By the mid-1870s women had arrived in medicine: the first woman member of the American Medical Association (AMA) sat silently through attempts to oust her at the annual meeting of 1876 (15, 16).

Doctors at the pinnacle of their profession revealed an abysmal sense of vulnerability. The president of the AMA in 1871, Dr. Alfred Stillé, warned that certain "women seek to rival men in manly sports and occupations, and the 'strong-minded' ape them assiduously in all things, even in dress. In doing so, they may command a sort of admiration toward a higher type than their own" (17). Stillé assumed only two characterological slots: if woman was changing roles, she could only be becoming a man. Moreover, he construed this disorderliness on a vertical scale. Woman moved up from under, from a position beneath man, naturally closer to the animal. The " 'strong-minded' ape them" phrase included that scale and its values: in spite of its direction, woman's upward motion could only be simulative, as men conceived an ape to be simulative of themselves. The quotation marks indicated the irony of a woman so much more animal, more ape-like, pretending to have a strong mind. The relations of men and women on such a scale exposed the pedestal rhetoric for what it was, although characteristically Stillé reiterated that form of the scale in the same speech. "If, then, woman is unfitted by nature to become a physician, we should, when we oppose her pretensions, be acquitted of any malicious or even unkindly spirit. We may admit that she is in some sense a perfected man, and was created a little less lower than the angels. . . ." (17). Seen at that elevation, the difference between man and woman was woman's greater perfectedness; and, conversely, man's distinction from woman (defined by sex organs), his penis and testicles, was a degrading imperfection. One must allow here the possibility of an element of admiration or envy, even a desire to emulate woman—after all, such angels were spared the ordeal of perplexing and sordid traffic with the world.

On the other hand, Stillé shuddered at the idea of man perfecting himself according to such a standard. Following a sentence referring to man-rivaling women as "monstrous productions," Stillé said "a man with feminine traits of character, or with the frame and carriage of a female, is despised by both the sex he ostensibly belongs to, and that of which he is at once a caricature and a libel" (17). Emulation or horror, either sentiment implied castration, even at a level that was not "ostensible."

While Stillé compared each sex to the other, he asserted an intransigent distance between them. The ambiguity represented his fear that the gap was closing, and democracy was heading toward that "preposterous medley of the works of nature" against which de Tocqueville (10, Vol. 1, p. 222) had warned. In Stillé's view, women were characteristically uncertain in rational judgment, capricious of sentiment, fickle of purpose, and indecisive of action. Men excelled women even in activities "essentially feminine" including cookery, hairdressing, and dressmaking: if the line was to be maintained, women must be confined to a diminishing compass. Yet such an assertion of the expansion of male competence clearly had a dangerous aspect for Stillé, given his horror for feminine men. To have it that men were already like women revealed a combination of defense and the danger against which the defense was erected: men did not have to castrate themselves after all; but that could also mean that they were already castrated. The attempt to pull men out of the frightening cracking open and jumbling together of the old sexual molds restated the conditions that made such an attempt necessary. Woman was responsible for those conditions. She "breaks" man's particular strength (moral sense, mental perception, the capacity to contract an "engagement"), as if it were "a rope of sand." She destroyed this "binding force . . . with a serene unconsciousness that anything was broken, or that there was anything to break": Stillé's blaming woman in this way for the erosion of male power seems to have compressed together both a wish for castration (in order to become perfect), and a fear of it, and, of course, a deflection of the origins of such feelings in himself. At that point Dr. Stillé's presidential rhetoric seems to have embodied the assertive, even phallic, heroine fantasy of his contemporary dime novels (18). And the somatic reemphasis in medical theory (applied by men to the bodies of women) was coordinate with the male view of woman's upward thrust.

The following remarks by Senator George Vest (19) of Missouri made in 1887 should be compared with Stillé's remarks and with my interpretation of them: "For my part I want when I go to my home—when I return from the arena where man contends with man for what we call the prizes of this paltry world—I want to go back, not to be received in the masculine embrace of some female ward politician, but to the earnest loving look and touch of a true woman."

The 1872 president of the AMA was prepared to give "the people" women doctors "if they wanted them." Medical schools would have to be sexually segregated and unequal in what could be taught, and he hoped such women doctors "would never embarrass us by a personal application for seats in this Association" (17). In 1900 the editor of *The Journal of the American Medical Association* continued to assert that the "whole question of woman's place in medicine hinges on the fact that, when a critical case demands independent action and fearless judgement, man's success depends on his virile courage, which the normal woman does not have nor is expected to have" (17, p. 218).

Dr. Gardner's rhetoric against the entrance of women into medicine in 1870 indicates the reinforcement war had given to the notion of the separation of the sexes. In this case he was attacking the New York Medical College for Women. He began an argument which he saw himself taking to "the people" in the pages of *Frank Leslie's Illustrated Newspaper* (20), by associating women doctors with the whole subversive range of feminism, the "efforts made to equalize the social and political position of the sexes." Woman's separation from the horrors of medicine was both a privilege and (rather awkwardly) the inevitable result of her psychology.

> More especially is medicine disgusting to women, accustomed to softnesses and the downy side of life. They are sedulously screened from the observation of the horrors and disgusts of life. Fightings and tumults, the blood and mire, bad smells and bad words, and foul men and more intolerable women [i.e. midwives] she but rarely encounters, and then as a part of the privileges of womanhood, is permitted, and till now, compelled, to avoid them by a not, to her, disgraceful flight.

The rest of this article was irony founded on the assumption of woman's innate shrinking delicacy. Furthermore, Gardner implied, white women who chose to enter the body business would have to consort with black women. Gardner concluded with the suggestion that women would finally encroach on the most exclusively male bastion, taken by Melville as microcosmic of nineteenth-century American enterprise: "The day will come when . . . you will find women on the high seas." This of course was the other side of Stillé's version of role diffusion, men taking over hairdressing and dressmaking. The assertion of male supremacy seems to have been a response to fears of female encroachment.

The Reverend John Todd turned his most passionate guns against women at the same time, having concentrated during his earlier career on the behavior of young men. Immediately after the Civil War (and the Emancipation Proclamation) he attacked the emancipation of women directly, linking it with the heinous sins of contraception and abortion, for which Todd, like Gardner, made woman almost entirely responsible. Todd (21) detected among "the other sex [women] . . . a wide-spread uneasiness,—a discontentment with woman's lot, impatient of its burdens, rebellious against its sufferings, an undefined hope of emancipation . . . by some great revolution, . . . propagating theories, weak, foolish and criminal." Abortion, according to Todd, was "a direct war against human society, the best good [sic] of the country, [and] against the family order. . . ." Gardner's tract against women's masturbation, contraception and abortion, *Conjugal Sins* (1870) (22), was written, he said, to "arrest the rapid extinction of the American people." Rebellious women threatened the United States with disintegration on the scale of the fall of the Roman Empire. Moreover, since women were held to be creatures at the mercy of their physiology, the problem required physiological experts.

The emergence of modern gynecology must be seen in this context (even if, in some senses, it may be construed to have advanced medicine). In 1853, Dr. L. P. Burnham of Lowell, Massachusetts, performed the first successful hysterectomy in America (23). In 1857 the American Medical Association formed a "Special Committee on the Present State of Science as Regards the Pathology and Therapeutics of the Reproductive Organs of Females" chaired by Dr. Fordyce Barker, a collaborator of Gardner (24, 25). In 1868, Dr. T. Gaillard Thomas (26) observed that "the specialty of Gynecology is being rapidly separated from its sister branch, Obstetrics," and two years later, Gardner (22, pp. 13–14) said that the "numerous new class of specialists" (gynecologists) had arisen in the period 1845–1870, precisely as they discovered women generally were "deteriorating" to that condition where they needed them. The absence of an equivalent medical specialty for men should be placed in the same context as the emergence of gynecology—and compared with the argument that man's anxiety about woman's potential anarchy, disorder, was a deflection of his own. The editor of the *Journal of the American Medical Association* correctly predicted the abortive future of those urologists who, in 1891, attempted to constitute an "Andrology" specialty, in contrast to gynecology (17, p. 150).

The "deterioration" of women which, according to Gardner, called gynecology into existence was moral in both senses, woman's nervous complaints the results of her sexual transgressions. Doctors placed greater and greater emphasis on the physio-

logical origins of woman's mental disorders, of which sexual transgressions—masturbation, contraception, abortion, orgasm—were
held to be symptoms. They cited woman as a major source of
society's ills, when she should have been the fountain of society's
healthy, male future. If, as came to be generally held, women's
insanity and nervous disorders were finally functions of faulty
sexual organs, why not destroy the sickness at its source? In the
late 1860s and early 1870s, gynecologists, following this Meigs-
style logic, began to practice the surgical treatment of the psychologic disorders of women. Dr. Horatio Storer (27), advocate of
such treatment, said in 1871 that woman "was what she is [sic] in
health, in character, in her charms, alike of body, mind and soul
because of her womb alone." Post-Civil War pressures revealed
that "old bedrock" of American identity more clearly as physiologic and male. Excision of the clitoris (clitoridectomy) and extirpation of the ovaries (female castration; also called oophorectomy
and normal ovariotomy) were two out of an array of new gynecologic operations. Gynecologists' case histories are suffused with
male anxieties over, and attempts to deal with, women out of their
place (28).

Operations provided the material for the inauguration of specialized publications and institutions. J. Marion Sims had published
his successful treatment for vesicovaginal fistula, the "stumbling-
block of gynecology," in 1852 (17, p. 1094), and he established the
first hospital for a specific physiologic group, women, in New York
in 1855. In 1866 Sims published his *Clinical Notes on Uterine
Surgery* (29). In his eulogy at the time of Sims's death in 1883,
W. O. Baldwin (30) said of Sims's *Clinical Notes:* "There has been
no work published on uterine surgery within the last century that
has been as full of original thought and invention, or that has
contributed so largely to the advance of gynecology as this book
has done." Baldwin had been president of the AMA in 1869.

Sims's achievements are generally credited with "raising gynecology . . . to a respected medical specialty." *The American Journal
of Obstetrics and Diseases of Women and Children* was founded in
1869. The AMA constituted an authoritative "Section" on obstet-

rics and the diseases of women and children in 1873, the year of the publication of Battey's invention of female castration. The American Gynecological Society was founded in 1876, while Sims was president of the AMA.

Dr. James Chadwick (31), the first secretary of the American Gynecological Society, suggested that the new obstetric and gynecologic periodicals and societies were gauges of "the degree of interest taken in this branch of medicine," and tabulated both. Between 1876 and 1881 American periodicals increased 100 percent, to double the number of the nearest competitor, France; and there were a greater number of contributions to these periodicals than in any other country. In the years 1876–1880, the number of American gynecologic societies increased from six to eleven, a total higher than those in Britain, Germany, Spain, France, and Russia put together. Chadwick described a particular psychologic style behind these figures. Inevitable vicissitudes in the popularity of certain topics did not "dampen the ardor" of gynecologists seeking "immortality by propounding new theories, devising new operations, and above all, by inventing new instruments." Dr. Chadwick gave an account of the typical "life history" of a new operation after its first publication. "Immediately it is tried by many practitioners, who hasten to publish their results, particularly if favorable, when they expect to derive renown or practice from being early identified with the operation." After this novelty wore off, the published life of the operation continued by way of its unfavorable results, until the operation was adopted, or forgotten. Typical of American operative procedures in Sims's view was the "éclat of sudden success," which he admitted was more dangerous than the more cautious British surgery (27). The spate of gynecologic activity in America was characterized by flamboyant, drastic, risky, and instant use of the knife.

One factor linking gynecology with other more familiar aspects of American social history was male psychology. Gynecologists exhibited the same mad impatience and ferocious competitiveness with other men—and a paradoxical dependence upon them for judgment of success in becoming "self-made men." Their anxiety over identity, their measurement of themselves in terms of what I have called the "spermatic economy" and "proto-sublimation" (9, 32), and the consequent and interactive responses to women, were typical of democratic American men as de Tocqueville had described them in the first half of the century, and as they continued to be in the second half. They thought of themselves and the world as John Todd and the other popular authors of advice manuals had assumed and advised. Self-making was a particularly literal (and self-defeating) reproductive goal in the hands of gynecologists.

So there is a weight of American history behind the striking appearance of American gynecologists on to an international stage, from which other American medical specialists were notable by their absence. Nineteenth-century American gynecology's originality lay in sheer operative daring, not in theory or laboratory research. Some of the operations which Americans pioneered or improved upon, ovariotomy, hysterectomy, and the repair of the vesicovaginal fistula, were hazarded under the most primitive conditions. American triumphs in this particular area of medicine are all the more intriguing in that research facilities were almost nil at the time of the operations. No American city was a research center in the way that Paris, London, or Vienna was. Yet by the second half of the century, New York was a gynecologic leader, exchanging teachers, practitioners, and discoveries with Edinburgh, Paris, and London (9, Ch. 8).

While I have described some of the new operations to cure woman's mental disorders elsewhere (32), it is appropriate to repeat the following unfamiliar information here. Clitoridectomy was the first operation performed to check woman's mental disorder. Invented by the English gynecologist Isaac Baker-Brown (33, 34) in 1858, it was first performed in America in the late 1860s, continued to be performed in the United States at least until 1904, and perhaps until 1925. After publishing his results in 1866, the English inventor was severely censured by his profession; he died two years later and the performance of clitoridectomy in England died with him (35). Analysis of Baker-Brown's cases shows a significant incidence of female hostility toward men and the role men demanded women play, and suggests that he regarded woman's sexual independence, whether construed to have stemmed from nymphomania or from misandry, as a sickness to be treated. The cases suggest, too, that he drew his clientele from a wide social spectrum, although it is probable that it came largely from the middle class which was associated by employment with the upper class; this group was traditionally concerned with distinguishing itself clearly in the matter of sexual morality from both upper and lower classes. For an account of Baker-Brown's theory and of an American precursor, see reference 28, Ch. 2.

In the United States, however, clitoridectomy coexisted with and then was superseded by the circumcision of females of all ages up to the menopause (it removed all or part of the "hood" of the clitoris); circumcision continued to be performed until at least 1937. Both clitoridectomy and circumcision aimed to check what was thought to be a growing incidence of female masturbation, an activity which men feared inevitably aroused women's naturally boundless but usually repressed sexual appetite for men. Men needed to deploy their sperm elsewhere for social and economic success—in the gynecologic curbing of female sexual appetite, for example. There is, by the way, ample evidence that gynecologists saw their knives' cutting into women's generative tract as a form of sexual intercourse.

Female castration, or oophorectomy, or normal ovariotomy, was a much more widespread and frequently performed operation than clitoridectomy. Invented by Robert Battey of Rome, Georgia, in the U.S. in 1872, it flourished between 1880 and 1910, then slackened its pace in the 1910s; women were still being castrated for psychologic disorders as late as 1946. One estimate in 1906 was that for every one of the 150,000 doctors in the United States there was one castrated woman; some of these doctors boasted that they had removed from 1500 to 2000 ovaries apiece. Female castration was largely superseded by other similar operations, including hysterectomy, which had coexisted as an alternative and auxiliary to castration since about 1895. And of course there is evidence today of "excessive," "promiscuous," and "careless" surgical treatment in America, particularly that accorded women and children. The examples frequently cited include hysterectomy, mastectomy, tonsillectomy, infant circumcision, hemorrhoidectomy, and oophorectomy, the latter indicated by apparently physical conditions. Such emphasis on surgical therapy perhaps sustains the argument that the operations reflect beliefs especially true of American psychology. The operations (performed overwhelmingly by men) are distinct from those performed in other countries in frequency and in concentration. For example, in America in 1965, 516 hysterectomies and 278 breast operations were performed for each 100,000 of the female population. The respective figures in England and Wales in 1966 were only 213.2 and 171.7. The contrast should be compared to the relative positions of midwives in each country. They have been driven out by doctors, obstetricians, and legislators in the United States, whereas in England (as in most countries in the world), babies are frequently delivered by midwives (9, 36–42).

Women were castrated and clitoridectomized in England, Germany, and France although both operations seem to have ceased earlier in England and France than in America. There was continual interpenetration of ideas between Europe and America, although Americans tended to receive rather than to give; and, of course, there was a fundamental historical relationship between the new world and the old. American attitudes toward Europe embodied a constellation of powerful feelings, including guilt, hostility, and a sense of cultural and historical inferiority. The factor with which I have been concerned, and which I have in some sense isolated from that skein, is the effect of the social pressures on men on male attitudes toward women. The history of female castration in European countries must be woven into the fabric of those societies' histories, including the effects of the progress of democracy in each place.

From one perspective, the castration of women starting in the 1870s (performed overwhelmingly on noninstitutionalized outpatients, and only later—in the 1890s—on inmates of mental institutions) was part of the general anxiety about the racial future of white America. Jefferson had suggested a racial-improvement breeding program in *Notes on Virginia* (43). From the post-Civil War period until World War II there was an accelerating eugenic program in the United States, carried out on the bodies of the insane and epileptic. In the period I have been studying, such sterilization was actually implemented on the bodies of women, not men. Ruth Caplan (1) has described how late-nineteenth-century treatment of the insane combined sterilization, isolation, and dehumanization. Perhaps the same can be said for a growing number of Americans' experiences of urban and industrial life. The purging of criminals, paupers, deaf mutes, the retarded, and so on (the period is remarkable for its bizarre and vast compendia of physiologic curiosities and abnormalcies) was a major contribution to the process of dehumanization (44).

Social leaders and molders—doctors, clergymen, popular novelists, and politicians—saw America as a beleagured island of WASP righteousness, surrounded by an encroaching flood of dirty, prolific immigrants, and sapped from within by the subversive practices of women. Their masturbation, contraception, and abortion were exhausting society's procreative power. These males saw society as a body invaded by foreign germs, its native blood corrupted and used up from outside and within. These metaphors emerge in the work of Todd, Gardner, and a myriad of their contemporaries (see references 9, parts 3 and 4; 14; 21; 22; 45; 46).

Whatever its metaphor, this vision was shared by gynecologists attempting to purge midwives away from the perverted sources of new life, snipping off the clitorises of girls and women addicted to masturbation and removing the ovaries of women deemed unfit to breed, or too rebellious in themselves to be tolerated. The anxieties intensified toward the end of the century, the critical zenith of the "search for order." The separation and subordination of blacks was formalized at a national level in 1896, and their segregation, castration, and lynching coincided with the growing nativism, the lynching of immigrants, the extirpation of resistant Filipinos and Indians, and the peak of the castration of women (47, 48). Such treatment manifested the aggrandizement of the white skin and penis, a process manifesting the hypostasis of physiologic identity in lieu of other forms of identity (dynastic, class, craft) stripped from men by industrialism and by democracy: the stripping went on less extremely and more slowly in Europe. The only source of identity remaining to men other than body was the less certain form of money, with which body was confused. (For the argument that body—and money—were the only sources of identity left because of democracy, see references 9; 10, Vol. 2, pp. 239–240; 32.)

Advocates and modifiers of wholesale female castration saw themselves reimposing order, of the kind conventionally expected of female behavior. Woman was supposed to be dependent, submissive, unquenchably supportive, smiling, imparting an irrelevant morality, regarding sex as something to be endured, and her own organs as somehow a dirty if necessary disease. Above all she was supposed to be entirely predictable. It was a role geared to man's behavior in, and apprehensions of, the ceaseless strife of the world outside home. The overriding importance attached to physiologic identity entailed a rigid asseveration of the sexual distinction (9; 10, Vol. 1, p. 315, Vol. 2, pp. 209–242, 256–262; 32). Hence any attempt by women to break out of their circumscription signified to men that such disorderly women wanted to become men. Female castration was designed to take care of such a threat. Accordingly, cure was pronounced if a woman was successfully stuffed back into her appropriate slot. An 1893 proponent of female castration claimed that "patients are improved, some of them cured; . . . the moral sense of the patient is elevated . . . she becomes tractable, orderly, industrious, and cleanly." While in the vast majority of cases castration failed of its purpose, in that it tended to make a woman's symptoms much worse, there were cases of cure. Doctors claimed success for castration when it returned woman to her normal role, subservient to her husband, her family, and household duties. Her disorder lay in her deviation from that role, a broad enough characterization to explain the bewildering and suspicious variety of indications. Opponents of wholesale castration applied the same yardstick—they criticized the operation because it failed to restore woman to her standard role (49).

Membership of the body politic had always been limited by sex organs. The assumption of woman's special liability to mental sickness by way of her characteristic menstrual and reproductive functions pushed all women close to the criminal category: "an insane woman," in the words of Dr. William Goodell (50), Professor of Clinical Gynecology at the University of Pennsylvania, "is no more a member of the body politic than a criminal." If women were only sex organs, and female sex organs were by nature a menace to health unless run to earth by pregnancy, then women were by nature sick; and if woman's sickness was construed as intolerable social disorder, then to be a woman was a crime. For Gardner (14, 22), menstruation was an "infirmity." He held that "it was a crime to be sick." Women, then, were criminals by nature.

Men's growing sense of vulnerability after the Civil War—their notion of social crisis and the concomitant gynecologic crescendo —cannot be disassociated from the increasing vociferousness of women at the same time, most noticeably on the suffrage front. Doctors, like other men, also displayed persistent anxiety over the growing numbers of the new, conspicuously consuming, fashionable life style of city women, their style dangerously attractive to all women (9, Ch. 25; 28, Chs. 5 and 7).

Between 1870 and 1910, women ran 480 campaigns in 33 states, trying to put women's suffrage before the male voters. Women most active in the suffrage movement and related consumer organizations came from the same social background from which gynecologists drew their patients—those new women left workless by the industrial revolution's change in work patterns, and reenslaved as possessions for display in the way described by Donald Meyer (11). In the light of evidence supplied by men in gynecology, it seems inaccurate to suggest, as Eleanor Flexner (51) does, that woman's suffrage was felt as less of a threat in the 1890s than it had been before. Women's organizations may have become more conventional and conservative in their views toward immigration and race. Moreover, they confined their base to richer women, drawing back from the poor and alien. In this women shared the beleagured antipathy of their male peers. Nonetheless, WASP women supplied the largest proportion by far of the bodies that were sterilized. John Higham (46, pp. 143, 147–148) has described WASP male anxieties over "race suicide." But while Engelmann castrated women (62), he ignored castration as a cause of sterility among WASP women in his later article (45).

It may be noted that for nearly all of the 150,000 castrated women (53) (a number corresponding to that of castrating doctors estimated to have existed in 1906) there was a custodial male—husband, father, or other relative who had given permission for the castration, in consultation with wives, mothers, friends, and general practitioners, as was so frequently reported. One is talking here of a considerable number of people—say half a million. Examples of the extensive involvement of parents, friends, and other doctors are in Meyer (54) and Brockman (55). A large number of the detailed case reports given in reference 28 include reference to custodial relatives and encouraging friends.

The women on whom these operations were performed were rich enough, or in rich enough hands, to afford the new gynecologic care (56). It is true that the poorest class of women in America had played a crucial part in launching gynecologic surgery and the careers built upon it. Sims was the inventor of the first successful operation for the cure of the vesicovaginal fistula; his greatest influence in medical history was the encouragement of an extremely active, adventurous policy of surgical interference with woman's sexual organs in the interest, above all, of making woman produce babies. He also castrated women. (Castration and impregnation were both regarded as ways to control woman's dangerous sexuality.) Early in his career Sims bought a number of slaves suffering from vesicovaginal fistula expressly for his surgical experiment, housing them in a private hospital in his backyard. With the support of some of the wealthiest and most influential men and women in New York City he later established the Woman's Hospital there. It maintained the supply of human material upon which Sims, his colleagues, their pupils, and guests, could experiment. Most of the first patients were destitute Irish immigrant women, whose fistulae and general health were so bad that they allowed

Sims and his fellows to keep them there indefinitely, even as the slaves' medical and social condition enabled Sims to make them literally "his" patients. One of the first of these Irish indigents, Mary Smith, endured 30 operations between 1856 and 1859, precisely the number the slave Anarcha had endured between 1845 and 1849. Like his contemporaries—and rivals—Sims constantly devised new operations and instruments, discarding them when they caused too many accidents. The Hospital's patients were treated free. Sims and other gynecologic surgeons made their money by applying the hospital discoveries in private practice, where they charged "stupendous" fees. The conclusion is inescapable that the Hospital was instituted for the same reason that Sims garnered diseased black women into his backyard: to provide guinea pigs before he and the others could convincingly offer care to the wives of the wealthy (9, Ch. 10). It may be that the fact that the first American clitoridectomy patient I have come across (57) was the only working-class one (she was a seamstress) can be explained in the same way.

But the chief targets of gynecologic surgery aimed specifically at sexual discipline were the wives and daughters of rich, or at least middle-class, men. These women might also be guinea pigs. Battey's first castration (58) was of a young private patient who seems to have been of the same leisured class that supplied the rest of his patients. According to Dr. Palmer Dudley (56) in 1900, "the hardworking, daily-toiling woman is not as fit a subject for gynecologic surgery as the woman so situated in life as to be able to conserve her strength and, if necessary, to take a prolonged rest, in order to secure the best results." If her sick condition derived from postindustrial worklessness, it also depended on it for cure. The greatest amount of sexual surgery was performed on the nonworking female dependents of men economically "well situated in life." The operations were performed throughout the country in urban centers small and large where gynecologists practiced, from Ottumwa and Keokuk in Iowa, to New Orleans, from Young's Crossroads, South Carolina, to New York, Philadelphia and Boston, to Los Angeles, San Francisco, and Portland, Oregon.

According to Dr. Gardner (59), it was wealthy modern woman's freedom from the necessity of work, her assumption of the new, or newly democratic, roles of display and consumption as the marks of her husband's success that caused her peculiar ills. He realized that the fashion-conscious, leisured woman was becoming the model for all women. "What Fifth Avenue does, the girls who can earn their living by dress-making, book-folding, shop-keeping or the like . . . do." Ultimately the trend was not limited to urban women. Gardner's father, like so many other men caught up in the extreme vicissitudes of the nineteenth-century American economy, had failed financially, and Gardner had gained his medical education at the cost of hardship and privation. Analysis of the language of other men, including doctors, demonstrates that status anxieties were wrapped up with sexual anxieties, and in the cases of men like Gardner, came to be focused on the wives of the newly rich. Gynecologic careers embodied deep social and sexual resentments. Nineteenth-century gynecologic surgeons liked to regard themselves as self-made men, although they came from a range of economic circumstances. They were WASP males, and nearly all allopaths (although such definitions were essentially insecure). I am arguing that it was the social and psychologic pressures of being male in America (reflected and reinforced in the family) that led to the surgical discipline of women deemed deviant, rather than simply considerations of class. Indeed, it was the belief in social fluidity and the consequent vulnerability of a status subject to competition that created the greatest pressure on sexual identity.

From the beginning, woman's "right to motherhood" had given the castrators pause in "unsexing" her. Robert Battey listed "loss of procreative power" as one of the chief objections to the operation. Men assumed women shared this view of their own significance. Battey finessed the issue by asking rhetorically, of what value was reproduction to a 30-year-old woman (the average age of his reported castratees), all her life an invalid, and "hopelessly incurable excepting by the change of life which itself implies the loss of this function?" In any case, a candidate for castration was, he said, "in all probability sterile." Battey's followers extended the rationale by arguing that even if she did give birth, a woman disordered enough to warrant castration would bear defective children anyway (56, 60). Castration, like controlled pregnancy in the right kind of women, helped implement the vision of a healthy body politic for which women simply supplied the material.

A second definition of "unsexing" was the obliteration of woman's sexual desire. If castrators found it impossible to argue that castration did not destroy a woman's reproductive power, they could and did contend that it left her her sexual feelings. But desire was regarded as a symptom indicating castration (for examples of the assumption of "positive amorous signs" as disorder, or symptoms of disorder, see references 61–65); so men redefined her "aphrodisiacal power," her "sexual feeling," to be the signals of her attraction which men wanted to receive. One of them was her absence of desire. In taking up this prickly issue, the castrators were as elusive in their evidence as they were over the success of the operation. Dr. E. W. Cushing (64) of Boston declared, "As to the loss of sexual desire, I have heard my patients frankly answer that they have not suffered in that direction." In one of his earlier cases of castration, Cushing had demonstrated his belief that orgasm was disease, and cure was orgasm's destruction. In 1897, Cushing said that gynecologic anxieties over "unsexing" represented the projection of male feelings: "we must not impute to a woman feelings in regard to the loss of her organs which are derived from what we, as men, would think of a similar operation on a man. A woman does not feel she is unsexed, and she is not unsexed" (61). Cushing's assumption was that "the sex's" sexuality did not lie in its sex organs as man's did. It was irrelevant to woman's feelings whether she had sex organs or not. Cushing went on, "I have questioned more than 200 of them on that point." Another doctor, Henry Carstens, questioned 400 castratees on the score. Such questions about woman's desire were put by medical authority, male and castrating, to the nonmedical, powerless, female and castrated, both sides sharing precepts of what constituted being male and being female. One woman who had been castrated for the "sexual perversion" of masturbation, wrote back to her castrator to report, "My condition is all I could desire. I know and feel that I am well; I never think of self-abuse; it is foreign and distasteful to me."

In effect, male gynecologists without exception revealed a profound anxiety about female sexual appetite. Opponents of wholesale castration agreed with proponents on the need to castrate women manifesting uncontrollable desire. Dr. Archibald Church (66) attacked castration where there were no "underlying pathological changes clinically discoverable." But he fell back on just such questionable ground when he came across willful sexual promiscuity in woman. "Certain women especially at the menstrual epoch are so overcome by the intensity of sexual desires and excitement that they practically lose self-control and all modesty. Here social relations enter into the argument." In Church's view the implicit inner struggle must be weighted by the intervention of the surgeon's knife on the side of the woman's modest self. Consideration of woman's right to sexual appetite is entirely absent from the medical record (66, 67).

The case histories of the 1890's and the years following paid lip service to other kinds of rights—the patient's right to express a preference for "conservative" or extirpative surgery, for example, provided the surgeon judged such a preference to be consistent with his notion "of domestic happiness." Female circumcision was advocated on the grounds that depriving infant females of it was denying their equality with boys (68). In the final analysis, the physician was supposed to know what was best for the patient (56). If "rights" rhetoric reflected awareness of feminist demands, or of contradictions in democratic practice, it was usually pressed into the service of the reimposition of the male order. So it was with Dr. Cushing's allowing woman's "being ready" to have some opinion: he interpreted the readiness and the opinion as symptoms for which he castrated her. Similarly, Dr. W. P. Manton (69) found it appropriate to describe his advocacy of the castration of "demented" women in terms of their "right to relief from bodily suffering." If woman had a voice, doctors attempted to control it, scaring woman into choosing what the doctor chose, just as obstetricians persuaded women after 1910 that naturally safe childbearing was unnatural (9, Ch. 7), that parturient women would need expert, male, therapeutic attendance; and just as de Tocqueville's typical American male (10, Vol. 1, pp. 209–214) provided his young woman with the illusion of freely choosing the course (marriage) he presented it to her as the one on which her social existence depended.

There was another way in which woman's participation in the therapeutic relation seemed to expand late in the century. The gynecologists' limited awareness of woman's voice (only to adjust their techniques in quelling it) coincided with a resuscitation of "suggestive therapeutics" in the 1880s and 1890s, and the years following, a precursor of psychosomatic medicine (11, pp. 69–71, 96–98; 70). Suggestive therapeutics was one aspect of the renewed interest on the part of a few gynecologists in their patients' wholeness. They acknowledged that their patients had an entire nervous system, a background, an environment, and a mind.

Mind and body were construed to be interdependent throughout the nineteenth century. What changed were the ideas of the relation between them, the relative weight of each in health and sickness, and whether mental disease originated in mind or body. The tendency toward medical materialism had been an expression of the imbalance in democratic medicine after the Revolutionary period, and was perhaps an expression of the physiologic residuum democracy left identity; that is, in theory, at least, men were denied the given status of class, dynasty, and inherited work role (9, 32). Gynecologic materialism was symbolized by the removal or modification of woman's sexual organs on account of her mental disorder. Yet castrators and clitoridectomists persistently presented their work as an attempt to get woman to control herself. They demanded woman's collusion. As we saw in the case of Church, gynecologists assumed the existence of a will, a "modest" self, which their treatment seemed to deny, even as men separated themselves from women on whom they depended—for order, for reproduction, and to know who they were.

In America, the acknowledgment of the part played by the

patient's mind in therapy derived largely from gynecologists' difficulties with the iatrogenic effects of female castration—it drove women insane (61, 71–73). Postoperative insanity manifested the existence of mental disease apart from ovarian cause to all but the most dedicated of castrators: the latter argued removal of the ovaries was not enough, and moved on to extirpate uterus and Fallopian tubes. But a Dr. Warner (74) had disputed Cushing's claim in 1887 to have cured a woman by means of castration. Warner believed that the favorable result of Cushing's operation, performed on a woman driven by masturbation to melancholia, came from the psychologic impact. Dr. Symington-Brown (75) agreed with Warner on the same occasion, saying that any shock would have had a comparable effect, since the brain was involved in nymphomania, not the ovaries (76).

Some of these critics were led to a view of disease, treatment, and cure, as an interactive process between doctor and patient. But these same critics shared many assumptions with the castrators they opposed. Moreover, awareness of castration's effectiveness as "shock" treatment could and did lead all the way back to Battey's original (1873) advocacy of castration for nonovarian conditions. The suggestive rationale was adopted by the wholesale castrators —they performed the operation precisely on the grounds for which Warner and Symington-Brown had attacked it (61, 71).

Emphasis on mind and wholeness led in several other directions: to the advocacy of a general examination of the patient by the gynecologist, starting with her mouth or eyes; and to consultation with the proliferating neurologic and psychologic experts (coexisting with the accelerating experiments with the therapeutic transplanting of ovaries) (77, 78). Acknowledging the significant existence of the patient's mind, doctors found they had to diversify to compete with nonmedical experts. Dr. Robert Edes (73) said in 1898 that castration stood "on the same basis as regards its immediate effect on the patient as any of the popular forms of faith cure." Some gynecologists realized that their patients and the devotees of the new mind cures were the same category of disordered women. The imparting of confidence and suggestion were among the brands of orthodox medicine having to compete with Christian Science. Donald Meyer (11) points out that among the reasons doctors had to compete with mind cure was that their intrusive, "gross masculinity" embodied the world that female patients yearned to escape. In a sense, such women were over-avid believers in the separated world of Victorian delicacy, the ones whom gynecologists were not able to persuade that the new kind of encroachment was necessary. There had been, at mid-century, some considerable dispute in gynecologic ranks between the pedestal subordinators of women and the more intrusive ones (9, Ch. 7). Meyer's magnificently subtle *The Positive Thinkers* (11, pp. 72, 93, 123) presents the predominantly female-supported Christian Science and other mind cure sects as reactions to the aggressive, masterful, self-sufficient, and obsessively masculine life-style. Yet the alternative, feminine style's sick helplessness was dependent on the achievement and character of such a "tunnel vision of the straining world of male ego," in the same way that women generally were dependent on men. (Ironically, that male vision was dependent on the distinct dependence of women.) Meyer points out the spiralling metapsychology of mind cure, its dependency projecting "upon that on which it was dependent, the same closed self-sufficiency it dared not claim for itself." More than that, the "deliberate drill" Christian Science imposed during its class instruction was for the "maintenance of order," specifically over body. Mind cure shared the ambition of the nineteenth-century crypto-Franklins (32) for the young men they claimed to teach; and mind cure shared the gynecologic ambition to reimpose order on the same sort of women flocking to doctors' offices, women whose novel lives were created by the sort of men whom women wished to escape (66, 73, 79).

The voluminous and extraordinarily explicit evidence supplied by medical journals, together with Meyer's account of mind cure, suggest that the variety of symptoms focused on woman's sex organs can be explained as an expression of female anxiety shaped by conventional role expectations. The sound of mass complaint which rises ceaselessly from these case histories may be added to the other kind of female voice protesting political discrimination. Both kinds harmonized with a large part of the register sounded by male voices. In Dr. Manton's phrase of 1909 (80), castratable women were mentally alienated. But all women were supposed to be alien from the democratic norm. It was male. Men wanted women to be shrinking, withdrawn, and separate from the sordid traffic of the world. But if the ebullient, masterful male was the standard of social health, then anyone different from it ran the danger of being labeled sick. Such associations were a long-standing tradition within and without medicine, from 1820 to 1920, and later. J. Marion Sims's newly discovered and labeled cases of "vaginismus" reported in 1866, and Battey's candidates for castration between 1872 and 1891 exhibited "exquisite tenderness" in organs shrinking from the male touch—precisely the response women were supposed to make, in bed and in general (9, Ch. 10; 28, Ch. 5).

Doctors in the nineteenth century claimed to direct society morally, and exhorted ministers and politicians to do so according to medical precepts. Women were being orderly in asking the appropriate social authorities to help. After Cushing's castration of her, that woman "previously sunk into a state of profound melancholia on account of her belief that her masturbation eternally damned her, told him that 'a window has been opened in heaven.'" Gynecologists were answering women's prayers. But their sexual values condemned gynecologists to sustain the belief that being female was a disease. Doctors' attempts to restore to women a measure of will power was a sisyphean rock of their own making. As men generally (including doctors) confined women to the butterfly existence that made them sick, more demanding, in need of more confinement (to bed, asylum, or both) and so on, so doctors created symptoms they attempted to cure, their therapy expressing the same assumptions of the male identity which found it necessary to exclude and subordinate women (as they excluded the "feminine" in themselves). Doctors and gynecologists prescribed addictive drugs for displaced and disordered women; if drugs did not work, the same doctor, or another one, castrated the patient, deeming her drug addiction a symptom of her sick condition; if that operation did not work, she was put back on drugs. If only one ovary was extirpated at first, or both ovaries but not the tubes, or ovaries and tubes but not the uterus, the cycle of drugs and operations could drag on and on. It was extended when surgeons began to cure castrated women by transplanting other women's ovaries into them. This kind of circle permitted men to ignore the commitment to male insanity they believed their competitive and obsessive life style entailed. Castration destroyed woman's one remaining thread of identity, her hope for motherhood, in the way critics of the operation described. Many castrated women were left hopeless, sunk into despair on a scale almost beyond imagination (9, Ch. 9; 28; 81).

But by the same standard of social beliefs generating disease, castration could and did work. If the nature of the doctor's authority, and its expression in his treatment, and the nature of the patient's belief, and its expression in her disorder, were all pitched just right, then she might be restored to an "order" she would be willing to accept. Clearly the missing factors in all of these cases could have been crucial. Perhaps one reason for the success of a few cases was the gynecologic surgeon's necessary decisiveness, which made him more likely to conform to the putatively authoritative role of the male than the dreadfully pressured democrat, unsupported by such expertise. Disorderly women were handed over to the gynecologists for castration and other kinds of radical treatment by husbands or fathers unable to enforce their minimum identity guarantee—the submission of woman. The handed-over woman then underwent a period of intense discipline by anesthesia and knife, or the S. Weir Mitchell kind of discipline, developed concurrently with castration (which Mitchell also performed). Mitchell's "rest-cure" consisted of the patient's descent to womblike dependence, then rebirth, liquid food, weaning, upbringing, and reeducation by a model parental organization—a trained female nurse entirely and unquestioningly the agent firmly implementing the orders of the more distant and totally authoritative male, i.e., the doctor in charge. The patient was returned to her menfolk's management, recycled, and taught to make the will of the male her own (82).

Some women refused castration, standing on their right to motherhood, and the value of maternal identity which they shared with men, whatever the difference in their reasons. On the other hand, many women went much further than simply allowing their men to submit them to the knife. By and large, women share beliefs about roles and social order: if such beliefs drove them inevitably to disorder, they went to the proper authorities. One "maiden lady" in 1877 demanded of William Goodell and Weir Mitchell that they remove her womb and ovaries, once they had told her of such operations (52, 83).

The sequence of such a gynecologist-patient dialectic is clear: men invented, or heard of, the new operations, and decided to try them; they informed women, or women's menfolk. The news got abroad. So some proponents of castration could declare innocently that the patient came in to beg to be castrated. Edes (73) said in 1898 that such pleas reflected the "professional medical errors of a previous medical generation." In 1897 B. Sherwood-Dunn (61) considered the doctor's responsibility in such cases: "The fact ... that women come to us pleading to have their ovaries removed, a thing which happens to every man in practice, is all the more reason why we should stand between them" and the deleterious results. On the same occasion, Dr. Henry Carstens admitted that (61) "... a woman does not always come to us to have [her ovaries] removed, but because she has some morbid condition which causes her to apply to the physician, and the doctor, thinking it is the tubes and ovaries that are at fault, removes them. In many cases a wrong diagnosis is made." Gynecologists remained convinced that they knew best, and either tortured the notion of the participation of the patient's will, or simply reneged on a preoperation agreement if a woman managed to extract one—not to remove both ovaries, for example—once the patient was unconscious under the knife (73).

The conflict in a woman confronted with the Hobson's choice of castration must have been a terrible one, torn as she was by the differing male demands on her. She was troublesome enough to her husband or father (with his persistent apprehensions of her sperm-sucking propensities (32) and the menace of her menstruation) to have him present her for castration. At the same time, she would have been aware of the male demand for race preservation, his woman's-ovaries man's-route to the future of the WASP nation. Gynecologists accused WASP women of undermining that future by aborting and contracepting. And as a corollary, woman would have been aware of the social calumny that followed her castration; castrated women were commonly known as "its" (56, 84). To paraphrase Freud, what did men want? And woman would have been torn, too, by her own lifetime's interiorization of such feelings. They were hers, together with her feelings about her body's submission to the doctor's surgical appetite.

In 1904 one doctor noted the power of social beliefs in spreading these operations. Female patients were "fully convinced that directly or indirectly, all their grief emanates from the pelvis, and oftentimes this idea is fostered and materially augmented by their friends" (77). Women were "the sex." The gynecologic phenomena herein described were symbiotic between patient and doctor, reflecting and refracting the largest contours of social beliefs and expectations. Another doctor, this time in 1906, reported a case where a patient had repeatedly requested that the right ovary and the uterus be removed. She was refused because no conditions existed warranting such a procedure. But usually friends, relatives, and doctors would confirm a woman's tracing her trouble to her sex organs. In the words of this 1906 doctor, Ely Van de Warker (53), "the sociological relations of the mistakes about the ovaries have been brought into the daily life of the woman. So constantly have they been held up before her as the one evil spot in her anatomy, that she has grown to look with suspicion on her own organs." "The sex" naturally associated identity problems with that part of themselves deemed by men, and women, to be their *raison d'être*. According to Robert Edes (73), "tradition, popular prejudice and accident play no inconsiderable parts in giving that bad eminence to the pelvic organs." While he condemned the carelessness and ignorance of doctors, Van de Warker included women in his account of the "sociological reflex" of pelvic surgery. Another doctor had laid part of the responsibility for the almost automatic mutilation of woman's sexual organs to women's own appropriation of such operations as a "fashionable fad," and as a "mark of favor," an image suggesting that some women understood and responded to the surgeon's invasion of their bodies as a form of courtship and copulation (85). It may be noted that clitoridectomists and castrators tested women for indications of the disease of desire by inducing orgasm, manipulating clitoris or breasts. Some women considered their scars "as pretty as the dimple in the cheek of sweet sixteen," and so adopted the views of Goodell and other gynecologists that castration made women more attractive sexually. Van de Warker placed the major portion of responsibility for the operations on the medical profession, but he also described the collaboration of passive, careless, and wealthy women. A man of his times, he bewailed the destruction of what he regarded as nationally owned ovaries.

Nonetheless, one cannot help being moved by the critically distinct perspectives supplied by the handful of radically thoughtful doctors like Van de Warker. Historical change seems to come about, as William James remarked somewhere, by adding as little as possible of the new onto as much as possible of the old. Van de Warker was ashamed that medical reform had always come from outside medical ranks. But given the symbiotic nature of the relation he described, given gynecologic persistence in castration in the face of massive evidence against the operation, and given its significance as the prominent tip of an iceberg of social beliefs, it was reasonable to assume that the iron circuit could only be broken from outside.

Barbara Ehrenreich and Deirdre English

COMPLAINTS AND DISORDERS: THE SEXUAL POLITICS OF SICKNESS

As a businessman, the doctor had a direct interest in a social role for women that encouraged them to be sick; as a doctor, he had an obligation to find the causes of female complaints. The result was that, as a "scientist," he ended up proposing medical theories that were actually justifications of women's social role.

This was easy enough to do at the time: no one had a very clear idea of human physiology. American medical education, even at the best schools, put few constraints on the doctors' imaginations, offering only a scant introduction to what was known of physiology and anatomy and no training in rigorous scientific method. So

Ed.'s note: Excerpted here is Barbara Ehrenreich and Deirdre English's examination of class factors in the sexual politics of sickness. Ehrenreich and English write of the United States from the Civil War period through the turn of the century, yet many of the attitudes they cite remain part of current gynecologic ideology today.

Complete copies of *Complaints and Disorders: The Sexual Politics of Sickness,* available for $2.50 from The Feminist Press, Box 334, Old Westbury, N.Y. 11568.

doctors had considerable intellectual license to devise whatever theories seemed socially appropriate.

Generally, they traced female disorders either to women's inherent "defectiveness" or to any sort of activity beyond the mildest "feminine" pursuits—especially sexual, athletic, and mental activity. Thus promiscuity, dancing in hot rooms, and subjection to an overly romantic husband were given as the origins of illness, along with too much reading, too much seriousness or ambition, and worrying.

The underlying medical theory of women's weakness rested on what doctors considered the most basic physiological law: "conservation of energy." According to the first postulate of this theory, each human body contained a set quantity of energy that was directed variously from one organ or function to another. This meant that you could develop one organ or ability only at the expense of others, drawing energy away from the parts not being developed. In particular, the sexual organs competed with the other organs for the body's fixed supply of vital energy. The second postulate of this theory—that reproductivity was central to a woman's biological life—made this competition highly unequal, with the reproductive organs in almost total command of the whole woman.

The implications of the "conservation of energy" theory for male and female roles are important. Let's consider them.

Curiously, from a scientific perspective, *men* didn't jeopardize their reproductivity by engaging in intellectual pursuits. On the contrary, since the mission of upper- and upper-middle-class men was to be doers, not breeders, they had to be careful not to let sex drain energy away from their "higher functions." Doctors warned men not to "spend their seed" (i.e., the essence of their energy) recklessly, but to conserve themselves for the "civilizing endeavors" they were embarked upon. College youths were jealously segregated from women—except on rare sexual sprees in town—and virginity was often prized in men as well as women. Debilitated sperm would result from too much "indulgence," and this in turn could produce "runts," feeble infants, and girls.

On the other hand, because reproduction was woman's grand purpose in life, doctors agreed that women ought to concentrate their physical energy internally, toward the womb. All other activity should be slowed down or stopped during the peak periods of sexual energy use. At the onset of menstruation, women were told to take a great deal of bed rest in order to help focus their strength on regulating their periods—though this might take years. The more time a pregnant woman spent lying down quietly, the better. At menopause, women were often put to bed again.

Doctors and educators were quick to draw the obvious conclusion that, for women, higher education could be physically dangerous. Too much development of the brain, they counseled, would atrophy the uterus. Reproductive development was totally antagonistic to mental development. In a work entitled *Concerning the Physiological and Intellectual Weakness of Women,* the German scientist P. Moebius wrote:

> If we wish woman to fulfill the task of motherhood fully she cannot possess a masculine brain. If the feminine abilities were developed to the same degree as those of the male, her material organs would suffer and we should have before us a repulsive and useless hybrid.

In the United States this thesis was set forth most cogently by Dr. Edward Clarke of Harvard College. He warned, in his influential book *Sex in Education* (1873), that higher education was *already* destroying the reproductive abilities of American women.

Even if a woman should choose to devote herself to intellectual or other "unwomanly" pursuits, she could hardly hope to escape the domination of her uterus and ovaries. In *The Diseases of Women* (1849), Dr. F. Hollick wrote: "The Uterus, it must be remembered, is the *controlling* organ in the female body, being the most excitable of all, and so intimately connected, by the ramifications of its numerous nerves, with every other part." To other medical theorists, it was the ovaries that occupied center stage. This passage, written in 1870 by Dr. W. W. Bliss, is, if somewhat overwrought, nonetheless typical:

Accepting, then, these views of the gigantic power and influence of the ovaries over the whole animal economy of woman—that they are the most powerful agents in all the commotions of her system; that on them rest her intellectual standing in society, her physical perfection, and all that lends beauty to those fine and delicate contours which are constant objects of admiration, all that is great, noble and beautiful, all that is voluptuous, tender, and endearing; that her fidelity, her devotedness, her perpetual vigilance, forecast, and all those qualities of mind and disposition which inspire respect and love and fit her as the safest counsellor and friend of man, spring from the ovaries—*what must be their influence and power over the great vocation of woman and the august purposes of her existence when these organs have become compromised through disease!* Can the record of woman's mission on earth be otherwise than filled with tales of sorrow, sufferings, and manifold infirmities, all through the influence of these important organs?

This was not mere textbook rhetoric. In their actual medical practices, doctors found uterine and ovarian "disorders" behind almost every female complaint, from headaches to sore throats and indigestion. Curvature of the spine, bad posture, or pains anywhere in the lower half of the body could be the result of "displacement" of the womb, and one doctor ingeniously explained how constipation results from the pressure of the uterus on the rectum. Dr. M.E. Dirix wrote in 1869:

> Thus, women are treated for diseases of the stomach, liver, kidneys, heart, lungs, etc.; yet, in most instances, these diseases will be found, on due investigation, to be, in reality, no diseases at all, but merely the sympathetic reactions or the symptoms of one disease, namely, a disease of the womb.

If the uterus and ovaries could dominate woman's entire body, it was only a short step to the ovarian take-over of woman's entire personality. The basic idea, in the nineteenth century, was that female psychology functioned merely as an extension of female reproductivity, and that woman's nature was determined solely by her reproductive functions. The typical medical view was that "The ovaries . . . give to woman all her characteristics of body and mind. . . ." And Dr. Bliss remarked, somewhat spitefully, "The influence of the ovaries over the mind is displayed in woman's artfulness and dissimulation." According to this "psychology of the ovary," all woman's "natural" characteristics were directed from the ovaries, and any abnormalities—from irritability to insanity—could be attributed to some ovarian disease. As one doctor wrote, "All the various and manifold derangements of the reproductive system, peculiar to females, add to the causes of insanity." Conversely, actual physical reproductive problems and diseases, including cancer, could be traced to bad habits and attitudes.

Masturbation was seen as a particularly vicious character defect that led to physical damage, and although this was believed to be true for both men and women, doctors seemed more alarmed by female masturbation. They warned that "The Vice" could lead to menstrual dysfunction, uterine disease, and lesions on the genitals. Masturbation was one form of "hypersexuality," which was said to lead to consumption; in turn, consumption might result in hypersexuality. The association between "hypersexuality" and TB was easily "demonstrated" by pointing to the high rates of TB among prostitutes. All this fueled the notion that "sexual disorders" led to disease, and conversely, that disease lay behind women's sexual desires.

The medical model of female nature, embodied in the "psychology of the ovary," drew a rigid distinction between reproductivity and sexuality. Women were urged by the health books and the doctors to indulge in deep preoccupation with themselves as "The Sex"; they were to devote themselves to developing their reproductive powers, their maternal instincts, their "femininity." Yet they were told that they had no "natural" sexual feelings whatsoever. They were believed to be completely governed by their ovaries and uteruses, but to be repelled by the sex act itself. In fact, sexual feelings were seen as unwomanly, pathological, and possibly detrimental to the supreme function of reproduction. (Men, on the other hand, *were* believed to have sexual feelings, and many doctors went so far as to condone prostitution on the grounds that the lust of upper-middle-class males should have some outlet other than their delicate wives.)

The doctors themselves never seemed entirely convinced of this view of female nature. While they denied the existence of female sexuality as vigorously as any other men of their times, they were always on the lookout for it. Medically, this vigilance was justified by the idea that female sexuality could only be pathological. So it was only natural for some doctors to test for it by stroking the breasts or the clitoris. But under the stern disapproval, there always lurked the age-old fear of and fascination with woman's "insatiable lust" that, once awakened, might be totally uncontrollable. In 1853, when he was only twenty-five years old, the British physician Robert Brudenell Carter wrote (in a work entitled *On the Pathology and Treatment of Hysteria*):

> . . . no one who has realized the amount of moral evil wrought in girls . . . whose prurient desires have been increased by Indian hemp and partially gratified by medical manipulations, can deny that remedy is worse than disease. I have . . . seen young unmarried women, of the middle class of society, reduced by the constant use of the speculum to the mental and moral condition of prostitutes; seeking to give themselves the same indulgence by the practice of solitary vice; and asking every medical practitioner .. . . to institute an examination of the sexual organs.

(Did Dr. Carter's patients actually smoke "Indian hemp" or beg for internal examinations? Unfortunately, we have no other authority on the subject than Dr. Carter himself.)

Uninformed by anything that we would recognize today as a scientific description of the way human bodies work, the actual practice of medicine at the turn of the century was largely a matter of guesswork, consisting mainly of ancient remedies and occasional daring experiments. Not until 1912, according to one medical estimate, did the average patient, seeking help from the average American doctor, have more than a fifty-fifty chance of benefiting from the encounter. In fact, the average patient ran a significant risk of actually getting worse as a result: bleeding, violent purges, heavy doses of mercury-based drugs, and even opium were standard therapeutic approaches throughout the nineteenth century, for male as well as female patients. Even well into the twentieth century, there was little that we would recognize as modern medical technology. Surgery was still a highly risky enterprise; there were no antibiotics or other "wonder drugs"; and little was understood, medically, of the relationship between nutrition and health or of the role of hormones in regulating physiological processes.

Every patient suffered from this kind of hit-or-miss treatment, but some of the treatments applied to women now seem particularly useless and bizarre. For example, a doctor confronted with what he believed was an inflammation of the reproductive organs might try to "draw away" the inflammation by creating what he thought were counterirritations—blisters or sores on the groin or the thighs. The common medical practice of bleeding by means of leeches also took on some very peculiar forms in the hands of gynecologists. Dr. F. Hollick, speaking of methods of curing amenorrhea (chronic lack of menstrual periods), commented: "Some authors speak very highly of the good effects of leeches, applied to the external lips [of the genitals], a few days before the period is expected." Leeches on the breasts might prove effective too, he observed, because of the deep sympathy between the sexual organs. In some cases leeches were even applied to the cervix despite the danger of their occasional loss in the uterus. (So far as we know, no doctor ever considered perpetrating similar medical insults to the male organs.)

Such methods could be dismissed as well intentioned, if somewhat prurient, experimentation in an age of deep medical ignorance. But there were other "treatments" that were far more sinister—those aimed at altering female *behavior*. The least physically destructive of these was based, simply, on isolation and uninterrupted rest. This was used to treat a host of problems diagnosed as "nervous disorders."

Passivity was the main prescription, along with warm baths, cool baths, abstinence from animal foods and spices, and indulgence in milk and puddings, cereals, and "mild sub-acid fruits." Women were to have a nurse—not a relative—to care for them, to receive no visitors, and as Dr. Dirix wrote, "all sources of mental excitement should be perseveringly guarded against." Charlotte Perkins

Gilman was prescribed this type of treatment by Dr. S. Weir Mitchell, who advised her to put away all her pens and books. Gilman later described the experience in the story "The Yellow Wallpaper," in which the heroine, a would-be writer, is ordered by her physician-husband to "rest":

> So I take phosphates or phosphites—whichever it is, and tonics and journeys, and air, and exercise, and am absolutely forbidden to "work" until I am well again.
>
> Personally, I disagree with their ideas.
>
> Personally, I believe that congenial work, with excitement and change, would do me good.
>
> But what is one to do?
>
> I did write for a while—in spite of them; but it *does* exhaust me a good deal—having to be so sly about it, . . . or else meet with heavy opposition.

Slowly Gilman's heroine begins to lose her grip ("It is getting to be a great effort for me to think straight. Just this nervous weakness, I suppose.") and finally she frees herself from her prison—into madness, crawling in endless circles about her room, muttering about the wallpaper.

But it was the field of gynecological surgery that provided the most brutally direct medical treatments of female "personality disorders." And the surgical approach to female psychological problems had what was considered a solid theoretical basis in the theory of the "psychology of the ovary." After all, if a woman's entire personality was dominated by her reproductive organs, then gynecological surgery was the most logical approach to any female psychological problem. Beginning in the late 1860s, doctors began to act on this principle.

At least one of their treatments probably *was* effective: surgical removal of the clitoris as a cure for sexual arousal. A medical book of this period stated: "Unnatural growth of the clitoris . . . is likely to lead to immorality as well as to serious disease . . . amputation may be necessary." Although many doctors frowned on the practice of removing the clitoris, they tended to agree that this might be necessary in cases of "nymphomania." (The last clitorectomy we know of in the United States was performed twenty-five years ago on a child of five, as a cure for masturbation.)

More widely practiced was the surgical removal of the ovaries —ovariotomy, or "female castration." Thousands of these operations were performed from 1860 to 1890. In his article "The Spermatic Economy," G. Barker-Benfield describes the invention of the "normal ovariotomy," or removal of ovaries for non-ovarian conditions, in 1872 by Dr. Robert Battey of Rome, Georgia.

> Among the indications were a troublesomeness, eating like a ploughman, masturbation, attempted suicide, erotic tendencies, persecution mania, simple "cussedness," and dysmenorrhea. Most apparent in the enormous variety of symptoms doctors took to indicate castration was a strong current of sexual appetitiveness on the part of women.

Patients were often brought in by their husbands, who complained of their unruly behavior. When returned to their husbands, "castrated," they were "tractible, orderly, industrious and cleanly," according to Dr. Battey. (Today ovariotomy, accompanying a hysterectomy, for example, is not known to have these effects on the personality. One can only wonder what, if any, personality changes Dr. Battey's patients really went through.) Whatever the effects, some doctors claimed to have removed from fifteen hundred to two thousand ovaries; in Barker-Benfield's words, they "handed them around at medical society meetings on plates like trophies."

We could go on cataloging the ludicrous theories, the lurid cures, but the point should be clear: late-nineteenth-century medical treatment of women made very little sense as *medicine,* but it was undoubtedly effective at keeping certain women—those who could afford to be patients—in their place. As we have seen, surgery was often performed with the explicit goal of "taming" a high-strung woman, and whether or not the surgery itself was effective, the very threat of surgery was probably enough to bring many women into line. Prescribed bed rest was obviously little more than a kind of benign imprisonment—and the prescriptions prohibiting intellectual activity speak for themselves!

But these are just the extreme "cures." The great majority of upper-middle-class women were never subjected to gynecological surgery or long-term bed rest, yet they too were victims of the prevailing assumptions about women's "weakness" and the necessity of frequent medical attention. The more the doctors "treated," the more they lured women into seeing themselves as sick. The entire mystique of female sickness—the house calls, the tonics and medicines, the health spas—served, above all, to keep a great many women busy at the task of doing nothing. Even among middle-class women who could not afford constant medical attention and who did not have the leisure for full-time invalidism, the myth of female frailty took its toll, with cheap (and often dangerous) patent medicines taking the place of high-priced professional "cures."

One very important effect of all this was a great increase in the upper-middle-class woman's dependence on men. To be sure, the leisured lady of the "better" classes was already financially dependent on her husband. But the cult of invalidism made her seem dependent for her very physical survival on both her doctor and her husband. She might be tired of being a kept woman, she might yearn for a life of meaning and activity, but if she was convinced that she was seriously sick or in danger of becoming so, would she dare to break away? How could she even survive on her own, without the expensive medical care paid for by her husband? Ultimately, she might even become convinced that her restlessness was itself "sick"—just further proof of her need for a confined, inactive life. And if she did overcome the paralyzing assumption of women's innate sickness and begin to act in unconventional ways, a doctor could always be found to prescribe a return to what was considered normal. In fact, the medical attention directed at these women amounted to what may have been a very effective surveillance system. Doctors were in a position to detect the first signs of rebelliousness, and to interpret them as symptoms of a "disease" which had to be "cured."

It would be a mistake to assume that women were merely the

passive victims of a medical reign of terror. In some ways, they were able to turn the sick role to their own advantage, especially as a form of birth control. For the "well-bred" woman to whom sex really *was* repugnant, and yet a "duty," or for any woman who wanted to avoid pregnancy, "feeling sick" was a way out—and there were few others. Contraceptive methods were virtually unavailable; abortion was risky and illegal. It would never have entered a respectable doctor's head to advise a lady on contraception (if he *had* any advice to offer, which is unlikely). Or to offer to perform an abortion (at least according to AMA propaganda). In fact, doctors devoted considerable energy to "proving" that contraception and abortion were inherently unhealthy, and capable of causing such diseases as cancer. (This was before the Pill!) But a doctor *could* help a woman by supporting her claims to be too sick for sex: he could recommend abstinence. So who knows how many of this period's drooping consumptives and listless invalids were actually well women, feigning illness to escape intercourse and pregnancy?

If some women resorted to sickness as a means of birth—and sex —control, others undoubtedly used it to gain attention and a limited measure of power within their families. Today, everybody is familiar with the (sexist) myth of the mother-in-law whose symptoms conveniently strike during family crises. In the nineteenth century, women developed, in epidemic numbers, an entire syndrome which even doctors sometimes interpreted as a power grab rather than a genuine illness. The new disease was hysteria, which in many ways epitomized the cult of female invalidism. It affected upper- and upper-middle-class women almost exclusively; it had no discernible organic basis; and it was totally resistant to medical treatment. For those reasons alone, it is worth considering in some detail.

A contemporary doctor described the hysterical fit this way:

The patient . . . loses the ordinary expression of countenance, which is replaced by a vacant stare; becomes agitated; falls if before standing; throws her limbs about convulsively; twists the body into all kinds of violent contortions; beats her chest; sometimes tears her hair; and attempts to bite herself and others; and, though a delicate woman, evinces a muscular strength which often requires four or five persons to restrain her effectually.

Hysteria appeared, not only as fits and fainting, but in every other form: hysterical loss of voice, loss of appetite, hysterical coughing or sneezing, and, of course, hysterical screaming, laughing, and crying. The disease spread wildly, yet almost exclusively in a select clientele of urban middle- and upper-middle-class white women between the ages of fifteen and forty-five.

Doctors became obsessed with this "most confusing, mysterious and rebellious of diseases." In some ways, it was the ideal disease for the doctors: it was never fatal, and it required an almost endless amount of medical attention. But it was not an ideal disease from the point of view of the husband and family of the afflicted woman. Gentle invalidism had been one thing; violent fits were quite another. So hysteria put the doctors on the spot. It was essential to their professional self-esteem either to find an organic basis for the disease, and cure it, or to expose it as a clever charade.

There was plenty of evidence for the latter point of view. With mounting suspicion, the medical literature began to observe that hysterics never had fits when alone, and only when there was something soft to fall on. One doctor accused them of pinning their hair in such a way that it would fall luxuriantly when they fainted. The hysterical "type" began to be characterized as a "petty tyrant" with a "taste for power" over her husband, servants, and children, and, if possible, her doctor.

In historian Carroll Smith-Rosenberg's interpretation, the doctor's accusations had some truth to them: the hysterical fit, for many women, must have been the only acceptable outburst—of rage, of despair, or simply of *energy*—possible. But as a form of revolt it was very limited. No matter how many women might adopt it, it remained completely individualized: hysterics don't unite and fight. As a power play, throwing a fit might give a brief psychological advantage over a husband or a doctor, but ultimately it played into the hands of the doctors by confirming their notion of women as irrational, unpredictable, and diseased.

On the whole, however, doctors did continue to insist that hysteria was a real disease—a disease of the uterus, in fact. (Hysteria comes from the Greek word for uterus.) They remained unshaken in their conviction that their own house calls and high physician's fees were absolutely necessary; yet at the same time, in their treatment and in their writing, doctors assumed an increasingly angry and threatening attitude. One doctor wrote, "It will sometimes be advisable to speak in a decided tone, in the presence of the patient, of the necessity of shaving the head, or of giving her a cold shower bath, should she not be soon relieved." He then gave a "scientific" rationalization for this treatment by saying, "The sedative influence of fear may allay, as I have known it to do, the excitement of the nervous centers. . . ."

Carroll Smith-Rosenberg writes that doctors recommended suffocating hysterical women until their fits stopped, beating them across the face and body with wet towels, and embarrassing them in front of family and friends. She quotes Dr. F.C. Skey: "Ridicule to a woman of sensitive mind, is a powerful weapon . . . but there is not an emotion equal to fear and the threat of personal chastisement. . . . They will listen to the voice of authority." The more women became hysterical, the more doctors became punitive toward the disease; and at the same time, they began to see the disease everywhere themselves until they were diagnosing every independent act by a woman, especially a women's rights action, as "hysterical."

With hysteria, the cult of female invalidism was carried to its logical conclusion. Society had assigned affluent women to a life of confinement and inactivity, and medicine had justified this assignment by describing women as innately sick. In the epidemic of hysteria, women were both accepting their inherent "sickness" *and* finding a way to rebel against an intolerable social role. Sickness, having become a way of life, became a way of rebellion, and medical treatment, which had always had strong overtones of coercion, revealed itself as frankly and brutally repressive.

But hysteria is more than a bizarre twist of medical history. The nineteenth-century epidemic of hysteria had lasting significance because it ushered in a totally new "scientific" approach to the medical management of women.

While the conflict between women and their doctors in America was escalating on the issue of hysteria, Sigmund Freud, in Vienna, was beginning to work on a treatment that would remove the disease altogether from the arena of gynecology. In one stroke, he solved the problem of hysteria and marked out a new medical specialty. "Psychoanalysis," as Carroll Smith-Rosenberg has said, "is the child of the hysterical woman." Freud's cure was based on changing the rules of the game: in the first place, by eliminating the issue of whether or not the woman was faking. Psychoanalysis, as Thomas Szasz has pointed out, insists that "malingering *is* an illness—in fact, an illness 'more serious' than hysteria." Secondly, Freud established that hysteria was a mental disorder. He banished the traumatic "cures" and legitimized a doctor-patient relationship based solely on talking. His therapy urged the patient to confess her resentments and rebelliousness, and then at last to accept her role as a woman.

Under Freud's influence, the scalpel for the dissection of female nature eventually passed from the gynecologist to the psychiatrist. In some ways, psychoanalysis represented a sharp break with the past and a genuine advance for women: it was not physically injurious, and it did permit women to have sexual feelings (although only vaginal sensations were believed to be normal for adult women; clitoral sensation was "immature" and "masculine"). But in important ways, the Freudian theory of female nature was in direct contrast with the gynecological view which it replaced. It held that the female personality was inherently defective, this time due to the absence of a penis, rather than to the presence of the domineering uterus. Women were still "sick," and their sickness was still totally predestined by their anatomy.

Jean Sharpe, M.D.

THE BIRTH CONTROLLERS

There is a widespread misconception that before the advent of the condom and later, more sophisticated devices, men and women were completely unable to control the number of children they produced. While birth control has become a subject of public debate only in recent years, contraception is certainly nothing new. As early as 1850 B.C. Egyptian medical experts described mixtures to be rubbed on, swallowed, or inserted to prevent pregnancy. Interest in the subject has never waned.

In the early 1800s a new discussion evolved in Europe concerning economic and social justifications for contraception. Robert Thomas Malthus, clergyman and son of an English country gentleman, became well known for his dire predictions about the population "explosion." Malthus directed his population concerns toward the poor, claiming that their production of too many children caused poverty. Efforts to provide relief to the poor were fruitless or even harmful since making their lives better would encourage them to have still more children. The early birth-control movement in Europe and later in the United States was deeply influenced by Malthus, and most early European groups were called Neo-Malthusian Leagues.

In these years the selection of contraceptives was quite limited. Before the development of rubber condoms provided another widely available contraceptive in the 1800s, most people depended on techniques which had been known for centuries: withdrawal (by far the most widely used), douching with a wide variety of chemical mixtures, intravaginal sponges or cloths (supposedly offering a mechanical barrier to the sperm). Unsophisticated as these methods may seem, people *were* able to control their own reproduction; when economic pressures made the limitation of family size critical to survival, such as during national depressions, men and women did, in fact, have fewer children.

Until the late nineteenth century, contraception in the United States remained a private affair; there was little public discussion of birth control or mention of the subject in state or federal laws. That period in U.S. history was one of great social unrest and change. In 1873, in an upsurge of Victorian moralism, a self-righteous Anthony Comstock and his Society for the Suppression of Vice joined forces with an equally self-righteous Congress and enacted federal legislation (the "Comstock Laws") prohibiting the mailing, transport, or importing of "obscene, lewd, or lascivious" materials. The laws were passed with little discussion; most of those who voted were not even aware that "all information and devices pertaining to preventing conception" were included in the ban. Thus, contraception came under public control, and open discussion and exchange of information about birth control were stifled. Even physicians for a long time could not legally give contraceptives to their private patients. However, many continued to do so privately in their offices, usually without interference.

The late nineteenth and early twentieth centuries, influenced by industrialization and urbanization, were periods of radically changing ideas. There were new ways of thinking about the family, about sexuality, about standards of living. A discussion in the *New American Republic* at the turn of the century frankly stated that "the modern family" limited its size in order to enjoy a certain "style of living" and "social position" they felt would be threatened by more children. Indeed, the shrinking size of the American family at this period was a matter of great concern to many people. President Theodore Roosevelt, representing one faction of the upper class, insisted that the American people were committing "race suicide." He felt that the family should be the "servant of the state" and should provide children to build national strength. Furthermore, he considered the "worst evil" to be that the "old native American stock" was less fertile than the immigrant population. "Race suicide," more explicitly by the upper and middle classes, formed a basis for struggles against birth control by some individuals interested in maintaining the power of the upper class.

The influences of this period also produced new ways of thinking about the status of women. Feminist reformers had long been struggling for property ownership and the vote. By the early 1900s a few more militant feminists had begun to ask broader questions about women's roles.

One of these was a nurse, Margaret Sanger. In New York's Greenwich Village she became closely associated with some of the outstanding socialists, labor organizers and feminists of the period. Margaret Sanger was very much drawn to the new ideas she encountered, and soon joined the Socialist party. At the same time she also met well-known anarchist and feminist Emma Goldman, a long-time advocate of the right of women to contraception.

Margaret Sanger kept up her nursing career. In the course of her work as a visiting nurse, she was called to a Lower East Side tenement to treat a young woman who had tried to abort herself. The physician told the woman not to "get caught" again, that another pregnancy might be fatal for her. His only reply to her pleas for advice about contraception was that her husband should "sleep on the roof." Three months later, Margaret Sanger was called to see the same woman, but this time the abortion attempt proved fatal. As a nurse, she had witnessed similar tragedies time and time again, but that night was a turning point for her. She renounced nursing—"I will not go back to merely keeping people alive . . . I was finished with palliatives and superficial cures; I was resolved to do something to change the destiny of mothers whose miseries were as vast as the sky." Margaret Sanger's answer was to teach women about birth control.

Shortly thereafter, Margaret Sanger traveled to France, where she felt she could learn more about contraception. There, she learned about methods of birth control and exchanged ideas with French radicals involved in the birth-control movement. Returning to the United States, she wrote and printed a newsletter, *The Woman Rebel,* which damned the Rockefellers (she blasted John D. as a "blackhearted plutocrat whose soft flabby hands carry no standard but that of greed"), religion (with which, she stated, the upper class was trying to "drug" the labor force), and marriage (which she described as a "form of property regulation in which wives are sex-chattel"). She also published a controversial and illegal pamphlet discussing various contraceptive techniques and urging women to learn to use them and teach them to each other. Much of Margaret Sanger's early work was directed toward the emancipation of women. She wrote and lectured passionately of the right of women to be free from compulsory family life and child-bearing, free to find other means of fulfilling their lives.

A few of her Greenwich Village friends joined Margaret Sanger touring the United States, lecturing on birth control. Although this was a period of great upheaval and activity in the American social-ist-labor movement, most individuals involved in it did not see birth control or women's issues in general as being of great importance to their cause at that time.

In 1914 postal authorities declared *The Woman Rebel* illegal under the Comstock Laws and brought charges against Margaret Sanger. After months of frustrated legal maneuvering, she decided to leave the country to avoid imprisonment. Her year of exile in London was the most critical period in the development of her ideas about the struggle for birth control.

Margaret Sanger's closest associates in England were the prominent English Malthusians, the Drysdales, and Havelock Ellis, the internationally recognized sexual psychologist. These friends became her tutors and under them she studied not only contraceptive techniques but population economics and eugenics. Her mentors instilled in her the value of prudence, and insisted that to be successful in the United States she must concentrate on only one issue—birth control—and leave aside denunciations of capitalism, oppression of women and religion. She also traveled to Holland to visit Europe's first birth-control clinic. There she met with birth-control specialists who taught her the use of the diaphragm. They also insisted that contraception was strictly a medical matter, not something women could "learn and teach others."

While Margaret Sanger was traveling and studying in Europe in 1915, the birth control movement in the United States began to assume organizational form and direction. No doubt influenced by Margaret Sanger's dramatic exile, supporters of birth control formed groups for public advocacy of contraception. Emma Goldman began to speak more explicitly on birth control and lectured all over the United States. Most of the organizing was among upper-middle-class women, generally quite conservative, who shunned association with Emma Goldman and other radicals. In 1915 they organized the National Birth Control League, the first American birth-control organization. The League worked to change state and federal laws prohibiting birth control.

In 1916 Margaret Sanger returned to the United States and went on a national speaking tour to generate public interest in birth control. Back in New York City, she opened the first American birth-control clinic in the Brownsville area of Brooklyn. Clinic workers expected police interference and it came soon after the clinic opened. Both Margaret Sanger and her sister, Ethel Byrne, the clinic's co-founder, were arrested, tried, convicted and jailed; the clinic was closed. Their trials and imprisonment, Ethel Byrne's hunger strike and the resultant forced feedings by authorities generated tremendous public sympathy for them and for the birth-control movement. As women became aware of the existence of better contraceptives, they became more and more vocal in their demands for these services.

Public interest in birth control increased and the League grew. Margaret Sanger gradually came to the conclusion that to lead an effective struggle to make contraceptives accessible to all women, she would need more support than could be supplied by the handful of political radicals who had taken up the fight. Thus, she joined forces with the women of the League and became leader of that organization. (The League later became known as the American Birth Control League—ABCL.)

By the 1920s the nature of the birth-control movement was set:

the ABCL then boasted more than 37,000 members, mostly white, middle-class, native-born Protestant women. Birth control was touted as a way to protect American society from the immigrant masses and the unfit, rather than a step toward better health and the emancipation of women. The propaganda of the birth-control movement reflected the eugenics concern of the upper-middle class and underscored the conversion of the movement from a radical program of social change to a conservative program of social control.

While Margaret Sanger and upper-middle-class women were building a base of support, the reactions of the medical profession to birth control were mixed. Doctors felt that the birth-control movement was a propaganda struggle waged by "hysterical women," and associated it with the proliferation of over-the-counter contraceptive devices—"quackery"—and not a subject for legitimate medical interest. However, internationally birth control was coming to be a subject for serious medical investigation, and it was a potentially profitable part of medical practice. The attitudes of most physicians probably represented a mixture of these ideas. As a result, most physicians, even those who gave contraceptives to their private patients, felt that association with the ABCL and Margaret Sanger was professionally damaging. Medical acceptance of birth control was also seriously limited by the fact that, with the exceptions of condoms and the diaphragm with spermicidal jelly, there were no effective, medically safe contraceptives that could be easily used by large numbers of men or women.

During this period, the laws were undergoing changes that allowed licensed physicians more space to prescribe contraceptives legally. New York state law had for several years allowed physicians "lawfully practicing" to give out birth-control information "for the cure or prevention of disease"; but most physicians had regarded this as applying only to venereal disease. In 1918, a U.S. Supreme Court opinion (regarding an appeal of the case of Margaret Sanger's clinic) specifically allowed a very broad definition of the word "disease," giving M.D.'s a wider latitude by which to judge the legal conditions warranting contraception.

In 1923, Margaret Sanger opened another clinic, the Clinical Research Bureau (CRB), across the hall from the ABCL offices. For legal purposes it was operated as the private office of Dr. Dorothy Bocker, clinic physician. The functions of the CRB included provision of services, but it was to be "above all, a first-class center for medically supervised study of contraceptive techniques." In 1924, Dr. Bocker published a report on over a thousand cases from the CRB. The clinic's wide experience with birth control began to command the interest of physicians.

One of the physicians most interested in the medical study of birth control was Robert L. Dickenson, New York gynecologist and 1920 president of the American Gynecologic Association. At the same time the CRB was established, Dickenson was drawing together a group of New York gynecologists and obstetricians as the Committee on Maternal Health (CMH) for the purpose of carrying on ". . . a series of impartial, well-staged clinical tests" of contraception. Their reasons for getting involved with such clinical studies were clearly stated by Dickenson, ". . . we as a profession should take hold of this matter [contraception] and not let it go to the radicals and not let it receive harm by being pushed in any undignified or improper manner . . ." As the CRB stood, neither the CMH nor any other "responsible medical organization" would go near it. Dickenson visited the clinic and commented that "to the medical profession in general . . . the activity of Mrs. Sanger and her organization are an anathema . . . However careful the professional part of the work may be, many feel that the sale of the *Birth Control Review* on the streets and the agitation for repeal of the law make their movement a dangerous one." Even the ladies of the ABCL were considered "radical" by the cautious and conservative medical profession.

Dr. Dickenson and the CMH attempted to conduct a study of contraceptive techniques by setting up an office to refer women wanting contraceptives to one of seven hospitals in the city that had agreed to cooperate. The program failed; the hospitals were reluctant to give such information and the patients were shy; they wanted a "special clinic."

As the '20's passed into the '30's, medical interest in clinical contraception grew. Margaret Sanger, the ABCL and the CRB remained officially isolated from the organized medical profession, but physicians in New York and all over the country were coming to see birth control as a part of medical practice. Elsewhere in the world, researchers were investigating various new contraceptive methods. The first intra-uterine device (IUD) was developed in Germany and rejected as being unsafe. Japanese and Austrian scientists published new studies on the "safe period" and this became increasingly popular. Public interest in and discussion of birth control was increasing and the movement continued to gain momentum. ABCL members continued lobbying efforts directed toward organized medicine and state and federal legislators.

At this time, the only medically permissible (thus only legal) indications for birth control were quite similar to those used in the case of most abortions today: a large family, endangerment of a woman's health or cases in which pregnancy could mean maternal death. A woman's own wish not to be pregnant was not considered. Physicians gave out information to "deserving" women—those who had done their duty to society by bearing a minimum number of children.

Finally in 1930, a federal court decision allowed "advertisement and shipment of contraceptive devices intended for legal use . . . for the prevention of disease." This court decision essentially released the supply of contraceptives from the strict control of the physicians. This growing demand for contraceptives, along with the liberalized law, resulted in a booming business in non-prescription methods of birth control. *Fortune* magazine reported that in the 1930s, American women spent over $219 million annually for contraceptive materials. They further added that "the medically approved segment of this business is pitifully small and as a result, many women are being duped and physically harmed." One critical review stated that "neither the government, the American Medical Association, nor any other organization will give a woman any advice as to the merits of these products."

The liberalized laws, increased public acceptance, growing demands for birth-control services by women, demands for medical leadership, and not least of all, the yearly $210 million going to nonmedical birth-control services—all had their influence on the organized medical profession. In 1937, the AMA issued a cautious statement endorsing birth control in clinics under strict medical supervision. Shortly thereafter, physicians of the CMH won a long struggle with the ABCL and essentially gained control of the Clinical Research Bureau. In the late 1930s, the ABCL merged with the now doctor-dominated CRB to form the Planned Parenthood Federation of America (PPFA). The new board was, not surprisingly, controlled by male physicians. Slowly but steadily, PPFA began organizing local chapters all over the country, often on the base of already existing birth control groups. Wherever local chapters were organized birth control clinics soon opened.

PPFA was administered and controlled by professional men from the top down. On a local level, the actual work of establishing chapters and clinics was generally carried out by upper-middle-class women. While most propaganda of the movement discussed provision of birth control for working-class women, patients who used the clinics were also middle and upper class.

Early in the 1930s, federal government agencies were quietly involved in supporting birth-control services for certain ethnic groups. Indirectly, federal money went to provide contraceptives to migrant workers in the Southwest and to Indians on reservations. Through state Maternal and Child Health programs, federal funds supported birth control in eight Southern states (none in any other parts of the country) where "child-spacing" was a part of public health programs for poor, mostly black women.

Economic pressures of wartime provided an impetus for further federal involvement with family planning. In the early 1940s, proponents of birth control were hailing it as "an effective weapon in creating a strong people . . . to defend our way of life." Even more importantly, the war industries demanded workers and with the men overseas, women were needed. It was obviously not efficient to have women workers away from the job having babies. The U.S. Public Health Service pushed states to provide birth control for women in war industries. Women had to be kept on the job line and off the maternity ward.

As the war came to an end and the United States became the political and economic leader of much of the world, federal government and private businessmen with interests overseas broadened their interest from the "population problem" at home to that abroad.

Awareness of the world "population problem" was not completely new. The stage had been set years before by Malthus and in the United States historian Will Durant had warned that to "offset the yellow peril," America should "spread birth-control knowledge abroad so as to decrease the quantity of peoples whose unchecked reproduction threatens international peace." A *New York Herald Tribune* cartoon of 1946 showed, under the title "Freedom from Want," a figure of kindly Uncle Sam with a basket of food confronting the starving slant-eyed masses with outstretched bowls. Uncle Sam says, "Birth control, maybe you'd better come along."

The '40's and '50's saw a tremendous increase in concern over population. One after another private organization sprang up, dedicated to the proposition that overpopulation of the world is the central menace of our age: the Hugh Moore Fund, The Population Reference Bureau, the Committee to Check the Population Explosion, and, most powerful and respected of all, the Population Council, established, funded and administered by the Rockefellers. The overlapping rosters of these groups read like *Who's Who* in high finance and business in the United States—Rockefellers, Du-Ponts, Fords, Mellons. All have worked tirelessly and contributed heavily to publicizing the population menace, birth-controlling Third World peoples abroad, and influencing the U.S. government to step up its involvement in birth control both at home and abroad.

Many government officials, fearful of domestic controversy (especially among the staunchly anti-birth-control Roman Catholic hierarchy) held to a publicly conservative position on birth control. In 1958 a presidential commission suggested that ". . . foreign development aid be extended to local maternal and child welfare programs for the formulation of national policy plans on population and to further research on population control." President Eisenhower's reply was, "I cannot imagine anything more emphatically a subject that is not a proper political or governmental activity . . . This government . . . will not . . . as long as I am here have a positive policy . . . that has to do with the problem of birth control . . . That's not our business." Eisenhower held to that stand, but he was the last president to take a position against federal government involvement in birth control.

Until the late '50's birth-control programs in the United States and overseas were seriously hindered by the fact that there were no highly effective contraceptives suitable for mass distribution. In 1959, Oppenheimer reported on his use of an intrauterine coil that effectively prevented conception with few side effects. Numerous varieties of IUDs followed which could be manufactured cheaply and distributed by the hundreds of thousands. At the same time, clinical trials of the first oral contraceptive were carried out, primarily among poor Puerto Rican and Haitian women. In 1960, "The Pill" (Enovid) was introduced to the U.S. market.

These technological advances radically influenced the birth-control scene in the United States. There were now available at least two highly effective methods of birth control which were suitable for mass distribution. The ever profit-oriented drug companies enjoyed an economic boom unlike anything since the antibiotic era. Not surprisingly, the industry jumped aboard the birth-control bandwagon.

In the early '60's, the major private birth-control organization, PPFA, joined forces with the populationists. Until then, PPFA's primary public thrust had been to stress the relationship of family planning to maternal and child health. In 1962, the Federation merged with the World Population Emergency Fund, a citizens' group created two years earlier to foster support for birth-control overseas. The merger was explicitly ". . . to create a strong U.S. organization for action on domestic and international population problems." The new organization was Planned Parenthood–World Population (PP-WP).

In 1963, private populationists and PP-WP began a major public push for significant federal involvement in birth-control programs, foreign and domestic. Influential, long-time members of those population groups already mentioned established The Population Crisis Committee to be ". . . the political arm of the population control movement," to publish ads, lobby government officials and promote public support for government aid to family planning.

At that time the primary thrust of the populationists was still toward the "teeming masses" of Asia and Latin America. The U.S. government joined the Fords and Rockefellers, who had long taken an active interest in controlling the birth rate of the foreign poor. The U.S. Agency for International Development quietly supported birth control abroad for nearly a decade before the United States did so openly at home. In the mid-60's, Congress approved amendments to the Foreign Assistance Act and the Food for Freedom Act, authorizing use of US funds in these programs for birth control. President Johnson firmly established his position in his 1965 State of the Union Address saying, "I will seek new ways to use our knowledge to help deal with the explosion in world population . . ." And further, in his "Birth Control Bargain Speech," he stated that ". . . less than $5 invested in population control is worth $100 invested in economic growth."

While efforts to spread birth control overseas continued, developments in the United States demanded the attention of populationists and the federal government. The decades of the '40's and '50's brought huge waves of rural Southern Blacks and later, of Puerto Ricans, to settle in urban centers of the Northeast. Unrest in the ghettos and rising welfare and unemployment rolls made the poor all too visible; state and federal governments found it easier to "control" these populations than deal with their problems. This approach was reinforced by sociologists, who asserted that the poor's fecundity contributed to poverty.

The "discovery" of poverty in the 1960s resulted in a proliferation of government agencies to wage the "war on poverty." The Office of Economic Opportunity was one of the first of these. In 1965, it was the first federal agency to make a direct grant for birth-control services. Not surprisingly, this initial program was developed in a low-income community in the South.

Along with the "discovery of poverty," the federal government also "rediscovered" mental retardation and entered into this war with a similar battle plan. Government-sponsored studies determined that premature births were associated with a higher incidence of mental retardation, and that prematurity was more common among young, poor women having children close together without adequate prenatal care. So, in the '60's, Congress passed the Maternal and Child Health and Mental Retardation Amendments to the Social Security Act, providing funds, at first just for prenatal care, later with more and more emphasis on birth control.

The interest of the federal government in the profitable domestic effects of birth control was growing rapidly. With that "$5 investment" in birth control, the government could hope to decrease "illegitimacy," cut down the welfare rolls, and lower the number of mental retardates who burden the society. No wonder J. Mayone Stycos, population expert in residence at Cornell University, called birth control "the bargain of the decade."

Up to now, Congress had had little to say directly about birth control. In the mid-60's Senator Ernest Gruening, with an impressive list of Senate co-sponsors, introduced the first significant domestic family planning legislation to the Congress, calling for establishment of an Office of Population Affairs and for a White House Conference on Population. Its significance lay in the fact that it prompted extensive public hearings which stretched over two years and involved more than one hundred witnesses—leading spokesmen of the populationists, churches, welfare agencies and medicine. The hearings, in the words of supporting legislators, for the first time publicly "documented the existence of a critical family-planning problem in the U.S.," "established the utter inadequacy of the government's response to the problem" and "demonstrated to the Congress the breadth of religious and political support for government action."

By the late '60's Congress was ready to act. Although they still had lingering fears about the reaction of anti-birth-control forces, legislators were becoming even more disturbed by rising discontent among the poor in the United States, particularly in the inner cities. In 1967, Congress enacted legislation requiring the states to provide family-planning services in their public health programs and to women on welfare. Federal funds were allocated to finance the "social services" necessary for the "prevention of illegitimacy and the strengthening of family life" among welfare recipients. OEO made family planning a "National Emphasis" program and Congress, in a most un-Comstockian gesture, rescinded previous restrictions against use of federal funds for birth-control services to unmarried women. The "War on Poverty" may have been grinding to a halt, but the "War on Human Reproduction" was escalating.

Under the Nixon administration, the birth-control offensive expanded. Until now, the government had not, except in small measure, provided contraceptive services directly. Early in 1968, Senator Joseph Tydings, long-time proponent of family-planning legislation, started pushing for passage of a major bill committing large amounts of government personnel and funds to domestic birth control programs; discussions of the bill stretched over the next three years. In July, 1969, in the first presidential address ever directed solely to the "problem of population growth," President Nixon proposed the adoption of a national goal to provide, in the next five years, birth-control services to all U.S. women who want them.

In the fall of 1969, HEW Secretary Finch established the National Center for Family Planning Services. The Center's impact was not apparent, however, until Congress in 1970 passed the Tydings-sponsored Family Planning Services and Population Research Act. This act was the first legislation dealing solely with family planning and sought eventually to provide such services to all poor women. The law also gave the National Center power to coordinate all federally funded domestic birth-control programs. Some of the Center's administrators are primarily concerned with family planning as a health service to women. However, they seem overwhelmed by those with a heavy population-control orientation.

It is clear that President Nixon is [was] committed to population control. But the private populationists are still marching several paces ahead. The President still opposes abortion. His Commission on Population Growth and the American Future (chaired by John D. Rockefeller III) has called for the liberalization of abortion laws. The Commission also recommends expansion of day-care facilities, liberalized laws concerning voluntary sterilization and increased efforts to provide contraceptives to teen-agers.

PP-WP still occupies the unique position of being the leading provider of family-planning information, education and services. As repository of expertise in the country in birth control, it has significantly helped shape legislation and public policy. PP-WP today is a loose conglomeration of local affiliates with a central office and administration in New York City. General policies are set by the national office, but each affiliate is generally free to pursue its own priorities, provide what services it wishes to whom it wishes depending upon the inclinations of the local staff. Nationally, PP-WP now stresses family planning as a right for the health and welfare of mothers and children; local affiliates may choose other emphases. For example, in Chicago the PP-WP affiliate passed a resolution adopting the two-child family as an ideal, one expression of its heavy population-control orientation.

The past ten years have seen significant changes in PP-WP, particularly in regard to its relation to the government. Nationwide, many affiliates are already essentially dependent on federal funding. Others, such as the New York City affiliate, have tried to maintain their independence. But recently, PPNYC has had both internal and external pressure to accept more government money. For example, in the past six years, Medicaid cutbacks in New York City have thrown huge numbers of "medically indigent" women into the lap of PPNYC for contraceptive care. Last year PPNYC felt they could no longer operate without federal funds. They are now seeking federal money for training, information and education, venereal disease screening and treatment, and direct subsidy of patient services.

The history of the birth-control movement in the United States reveals at least two groups with differing motives for their involvement: those who want to make birth-control services available to all who want them as a right and matter of health; and those who are using birth control as a way to further their own institutional and class interests. At present, the latter are clearly in control.

Their primary objectives are to:

(1) decrease the welfare rolls by decreasing the birth rate of the poor rather than by attacking the roots of poverty;

(2) obscure fundamental problems such as poverty and racism, implying that the poor can climb the economic ladder simply by using birth control and having smaller families;

(3) control population growth, both at home and abroad, helping to control growing unrest among the poor and maintain the political and economic status quo.

Most efforts of the birth controllers have been directed toward women. Women looking for total health care often find that while birth-control services are easily accessible and free, other services are not. Contraceptive care is offered in a specialized clinic that pays little attention to other aspects of health, even closely related ones such as venereal disease or gynecologic problems.

The Women's Movement has been deeply involved in fighting for the right of women to birth control and abortion services. Now they find that the federal government, wealthy businessmen, and almost everyone else seems interested in it as well. As stated by one women's group, ". . . we find that a portion of our fight [for birth control and abortion] has a reactionary as well as a progressive potential. We have been trying to open up laws around birth control and abortion without moving to effectively control its use . . . Although we have gained much in momentum and awareness in the last years, we are perhaps further from real female control of reproduction than we were when we started." Women have long been the consumers of birth-control services. They are now beginning to realize that they must control the policies, direction and administration of these programs.

PART TWO

THE MEANS OF REPRODUCTION

Barbara Seaman

THE DANGERS OF ORAL CONTRACEPTION

In 1967 a delegation of Western journalists was granted an interview with Boris Petrovski, the Soviet Minister of Health. Asked why the Pill was not being used in Russia, Dr. Petrovski replied, "We do not want our children born with deformed hands and feet."

The journalists were confused. Had Dr. Petrovski mixed the Pill up with thalidomide? There was then no hint, in the annals of Western medicine, that the Pill might be associated with any such birth defects.

Six years later, in 1973 and '74, U.S. researchers such as Audrey and James Nora at the University of Colorado, and Dwight Janerich of the New York State Health Department, confirmed that a thalidomide-like syndrome, involving limb defects, does occur in a small number of the offspring, especially males, of mothers exposed to hormones during the early weeks of pregnancy. In some cases this exposure is due to hormonal "pregnancy tests" while in others it is associated with "breakthrough" pregnancies that occur on the Pill. (These are less rare than we think. While the Pill is near-perfect in theory, in practice, six percent of Pill users get pregnant each year, and most continue taking these hormones until the pregnancy is diagnosed—which may not be for months.)

If the Russians knew so long ago that the Pill causes birth defects, why weren't we informed? Why, whenever we uncover a new and alarming side effect do some doctors and population controllers rush to minimize its importance? It's bad to frighten women, according to this doctrine, but all right to kill and maim us. Many of the doctors who won't hear a word said against the Pill have personal or professional ties with drug companies. For example, Dr. Robert Kistner, author of a book and many articles defending the Pill, has performed research for the following companies: William Merrell, Mead Johnson, Cutter, Squibb, Searle, Parke-Davis, Upjohn, Wyeth, Lilly and Orgenan. In his writings he is identified merely as a Harvard professor, not by his other connections.

In 1975 we were notified, as if out of the blue, that the Pill is associated with a much-increased risk of heart attacks. Users in their thirties are three times more likely to have heart attacks than non-users. In their forties, users are five or six times more likely. A woman in her early forties who does not take the Pill stands an annual risk of one in 5,000 of suffering a heart attack. If she is a Pill user, her risk increases to one in 1,000.

These studies were performed in England. Upon learning of them, our FDA Commissioner urged American doctors to stop prescribing the Pill to women past forty. The FDA appears to be on its toes, and yet. . . . In 1969, when I was preparing a book called *The Doctors' Case Against the Pill,* I called on Dr. John J. Schrogie, who was then the FDA's principal expert on the subject. Dr. Schrogie admitted he was extremely worried about heart attacks in Pill users. "There is a confluence of factors which seem to be coming together at the same time," he told me. "We have a situation where the changes in lipid (fat) metabolism are going in the same direction, in essence, as the changes in carbohydrate metabolism. If you add changes in coagulation (blood clotting) activity on top of this, what can be created here is a fairly high risk of premature cardiovascular disease."

Did the FDA warn American women that, theoretically, the Pill was apt to be dangerous to their hearts? No. Did the FDA order that the pertinent studies be done in this country? No. Instead it was left to the British, who have fewer Pill users than we and a lower budget for this type of research, to clarify the issue many years later. In the meantime, women have died, women who might have chosen not to take the Pill *if* they understood the risks.

The Pill was a brainchild of Margaret Sanger, founder of Planned Parenthood, popularizer of the diaphragm, and an indomitable fighter for women's rights. Surviving jail, ridicule and peltings with rotten fruit, she, more than anyone, made birth control respectable. In 1950, at the age of 68, Ms. Sanger was introduced to Gregory Pincus, a reproductive scientist from Massachusetts. She raised some $150,000—mainly from her friend Katharine McCormack, heiress to a farm-machinery fortune, to get Pincus started on research toward a "universal" contraceptive.

Animal researchers had known for a generation or more that steroid hormones could prevent ovulation. They were reluctant to try such experiments on humans for at least three reasons: a) Some hormones, especially those in the estrogenic group, were believed to be cancer-producing. By 1940, numerous studies had been published with titles such as "Estrogens in Carcinogenesis" and "The Significance of Hormones in the Origin of Cancer"; b) The physiology of female reproduction depends on a delicate, imperfectly understood "feedback" system. If you introduce extra ovarian hormones (such as those used in the Pill) you interrupt the normal, oscillating "stop" and "go" signals that trigger pituitary hormones which, in turn, seem to mediate most of our metabolic functions; c) The whole idea was financially impractical, as low-cost progestational products, strong enough to be effective by mouth, were not available.

Problem (c) was solved by dramatic advances in chemistry. In 1951 Dr. Carl Djerassi, now a Professor at Stanford as well as an officer of the Syntex drug corporation, perfected norethisterone, a progesterone-like substance. Similar formulations were to follow from the Searle Company and other manufacturers. The Pill, combining artificial progestins and estrogens, became economically feasible.

By 1955 Pincus's experiments, performed in collaboration with Dr. Min-Chueh Chang, and Dr. John Rock, were bearing fruit. Early versions of the Pill were tried out on mental hospital inmates. Pincus gave a progress report at an International Planned Parenthood Meeting in Japan, but according to Paul Vaughan, author of *The Pill on Trial,* the other scientists attending the conference were more alarmed than impressed. Sir Solly Zuckerman, a pioneering British anatomist, said, "The fact that you could suppress an ovary by means of estrogen or progesterone—well, you could do it with almost any steroid hormone—that had been known for years and years. We need better evidence about the occurrence of side-effects in human beings; there is an urgent need for prolonged observation before we draw any firm conclusions."

More than twenty years have passed, but the debate continues, unabated among scientists, and unrevealed to most Pill users. For example, last January, the *New England Journal of Medicine* reported that the bile of Pill users is considerably more saturated with cholesterol than the bile of other women. This is a nearly universal side-effect, which may and sometimes does produce gall bladder disease. An editorial accompanying this report was entitled "Hormone Use to Change Normal Physiology—Is the Risk Worth It?" The author, Dr. Donald M. Small, didn't think so, for, in his words, "The Pill abolishes the normal cycle, distorts metabolism, and causes serious disorders in some users. . . . The whole question of the use of drugs to alter normal metabolism must be raised."

When the Pill was approved as a contraceptive in 1960, we were led to believe it had been tested on thousands of women in the hills of Puerto Rico. In truth, as a Senate investigation revealed in 1963, the FDA's decision to approve Enovid was based on clinical studies of only 132 women who had taken it continuously for a year or longer. Most of the other subjects drifted in and out of the program, and were lost to follow-up. Three young women died but were not even autopsied.

Privately, many reproductive scientists were as happy with these developments as, say, Dr. Einstein was with the nuclear weapons race. For example, Sir Charles Dodds, the creator of synthetic estrogen, said this to his colleagues in 1961: "The women who have continuous treatment with the contraceptive pill have an entirely different hormonal background due to the pituitary inhibition. One cannot help to wonder what will happen if this state of affairs is allowed to continue."

Publically, though, the Pill was accepted because favoring it there were two mighty arguments. After the word *no,* it is the most effective and convenient reversible contraceptive ever devised. No wonder Margaret Sanger lusted for it, and no wonder other liberated women, such as Claire Booth Luce, have been moved to comment that with the Pill, "Modern woman is at last free, as a man is free, to dispose of her own body, to earn her living, to pursue the improvement of her mind, to try a successful career."

In addition, menstrual distress plagues many women, and in perhaps one case in twenty (especially during adolescence and menopause) this is so severe as to be incapacitating for days at a time. The Pill can cure such problems for, in point of fact, it eliminates menstruation. Women who take Pills with estrogen in them neither ovulate nor menstruate but, due to the artificial manipulation of hormones, they have something called "withdrawal bleeding," which resembles menstruation. (A few Pill users experience an increase in "menstrual distress," especially irregularity, but improvement is more the rule.)

Weighed against these benefits, a thoughtful woman may want to consider the risks she is taking, before she decides in favor of the Pill.

By 1969 and '70 the evidence against the Pill had grown so weighty that two successive FDA Commissioners, Dr. Herbert Ley and Dr. Charles Edwards, as well as the HEW Secretary, Robert Finch, all affirmed that every Pill-using woman had the right to be informed what she was getting into. Detailed consumer labeling was devised by the FDA and it was announced that this labeling would be included in every Pill package. The American Medical Association objected on the grounds that it could needlessly frighten many women, as well as interfere with the doctor-patient relationship. A compromise was reached. Only the briefest labeling was included in the packages, but a pamphlet called "What You Should Know About the Pill" was printed up and sent to doctors for them to give their patients.

Few women have had the opportunity to read "What You Should Know About the Pill." The AMA has distributed only six million copies (and most of these have apparently gone into doctors' wastebaskets) even though one hundred million Pill prescriptions have been written in the United States since 1970.

There are three basic types of Pill available, the *combined,* which provides progestins and estrogens simultaneously, the *sequential,* said to provide these ingredients in a sequence more reflective of the normal menstrual cycle, and the newer, *progestin-only* varieties. Brand names in the first category (combined) include: Norlestrin, Ortho-Novum, Ovral. Sequential brands include Ortho-Novum SQ and Norquen. Progestin only contraceptives include Nor Q-D, Micronor and Ovrette. [As this goes to press in February 1976, three major drug companies have announced that they will stop marketing sequential Pills. The Pills being withdrawn are Oracon made by Mead-Johnson, Ortho-Novum SQ made by Ortho and Norquen made by Syntex. However, supplies currently on the market will not be recalled and women taking these Pills are being advised to continue them through their present menstrual cycle while they ask their doctors for an alternative.]

The combined Pills are the most reliable. Taken according to directions, with no skipped Pills, they are said to be 99 percent effective. As noted, however, their actual "use" effectiveness is 94 percent. In some populations it is even lower, for one must be motivated to make the Pills work, one must *take* them.

The sequential Pills, which comprise about 10 percent of the U.S. market, are less reliable and possibly more dangerous than the combined. There is some indication that sequential users might have a risk of clotting disease which is higher than that found in users of the combined formulations. There has also been a suggestion in two recent studies that sequential pills, containing what is called "unopposed estrogen," may be associated with cancer of the endometrium. The FDA Commissioner says he may remove the sequential brands from the market.

The progestin-only Pills are the least reliable, quite possibly less reliable than, say, a good brand of fresh condom. They also produce frequent bleeding irregularities, leading to a high drop-out rate. On the other hand, they may be less apt to produce clotting disorders or high blood pressure than the Pills containing estrogen.

As this is written, the FDA is in the process of revising its labeling on the Pill. Cancer is a particularly thorny issue, for one study suggests a tentative association between the Pill and breast cancer, while others do not. As mentioned, the sequential Pill may be associated with endometrial cancer, and there is also new evidence linking the Pill with cancer of the liver. Pill users have also been shown in some studies to have higher rates of early-stage cancer of the cervix, but this evidence is still considered tentative.

The FDA has announced, once again, that it plans to make the labeling on the Pill available to consumers. We shall see. There is apt to be industry and medical lobbying against such a move, for a great many women refuse to take the Pill when they see all that is involved. Here is a summary of the contraindications and side effects, presently acknowledged by the FDA.

• You should not take the Pill if you have *ever had* clotting disorders, cerebral vascular disease or coronary occlusion. You should not take it if you presently have impaired liver function (as in hepatitis), tumors, known or suspected breast cancer, or undiagnosed vaginal bleeding. You should not take the Pill if there is any chance you might be pregnant.

• Pill use increases your risk of developing blood clots four- to elevenfold. It doubles your risk of stroke.

• If you are aged twenty to 44, and do not use oral contraceptives, your annual risk of being hospitalized with a blood clotting disorder is five in 100,000. If you use oral contraceptives, your risk increases ninefold—to 45 in 100,000. There is some evidence that products containing 100 mcg. or more of estrogen bear a higher risk of clotting disorders than those containing lower amounts.

• If you are going to have surgery, you should discontinue the Pill at least two weeks before, and not resume until at least two weeks afterwards. Pill use increases your risk of post-surgical clotting disorders.

• Stop taking the Pill and call your doctor immediately if you develop severe leg or chest pains, cough up blood, experience sudden and severe headaches, or cannot see clearly.

• The Pill may cause liver tumors, involving serious or fatal hemorrhage, and may also be linked to cancer of the liver.

• The Pill should be avoided for a period of time (up to three months) before deliberate conception.

• The Pill doubles the risk of gall bladder disease, decreases glucose tolerance, and increases certain blood fats.

• Small but significant numbers of women develop high blood pressure on the Pill. It is usually reversible. Women who had high blood pressure during pregnancy may be more likely to have this effect.

• Breakthrough bleeding, spotting, and absence of menstruation are frequent side effects. A check-up should be performed. Doubling of pills or changing to brands with a higher estrogen content may increase the risk of blood clots.

• Women with a history of irregular or scanty menstruation may not regain their ovulation or periods after stopping the Pill. Women with such a menstrual history should be encouraged to use other contraceptives.

• Oral contraceptives are more effective in preventing intrauterine than ectopic pregnancies. Hence the ratio of ectopic to intrauterine pregnancies is higher in Pill users. Every patient who becomes pregnant while using the Pill should be evaluated carefully to determine whether the pregnancy is ectopic.

• A small fraction of the hormones in the Pill has been identified in the milk of nursing mothers. The long-range effects to the infant have not been determined.

• A complete medical and family history should be taken before the Pill is prescribed. The Pill should not be taken for more than one year without further examination.

• Endocrine and liver function tests may be affected by the Pill. Fibroid tumors may increase in size. Conditions influenced by fluid retention, such as epilepsy, migraine, asthma or kidney dysfunction may be affected by the Pill. Patients with a history of depression should be carefully observed, and the drug discontinued if serious depression recurs. If jaundice develops, the Pill should be discontinued. The Pill may cause a deficiency of certain vitamins, such as pyridoxine (B6) and serum folate.

The following adverse reactions are known to occur in patients receiving oral contraceptives: nausea, vomiting, abdominal cramps and bloating, breakthrough bleeding, spotting, change in menstrual flow, cessation of menstruation during and after use, fluid retention, skin discoloration (possibly permanent), breast tenderness, enlargement and secretion, weight increase or decrease, change in cervical erosion and secretion, reduction in breast milk when used after childbirth, jaundice, growth of uterine fibroid tumors, rash, mental depression, reduced tolerance to carbohydrates.

The following adverse reactions have been reported in users of oral contraceptives, but research is incomplete: temporary infertility after discontinuance of treatment, premenstrual-like syndrome, intolerance to contact lenses, change in corneal curvature, cataracts, changes in sex drive, occurrence of involuntary jerking movements, changes in appetite, cystitis-like syndrome, headache, nervousness, dizziness, fatigue, backache, hirsutism, loss of scalp hair, skin disease, hemorrhagic eruption, itching, vaginitis, and metabolic disease.

The following laboratory results may be altered by the use of oral contraceptives: liver function, blood clotting, thyroid function, metyrapone test, pregnanediol determination, glucose tolerance test, serum lipid values, serum folate values.

These can add up to a lot of trouble, but some women think that their choice is take the Pill or get pregnant. Nothing could be further from the truth. Many other methods are extremely reliable, if they are used conscientiously. (And conversely, the Pill doesn't work if it's not used carefully either.)

For the impulsive person, the IUD and (after one has finished one's family) sterilization may be attractive, for they do not require any further effort. However, both of these methods may have painful side effects.

For the disciplined person, the so-called "barrier methods" (the "greasy kid stuff" it was called in the sixties, when hopes for the Pill were still running high) are making a strong comeback. If you wish a diaphragm, get it from a doctor who fits you properly and instructs you in it exactly. Doctors who take pride in accurate diaphragm-fitting claim that their patients can achieve a 98 percent success rate with it. Truly disciplined persons may also be successful with the temperature method or rhythm. Other improvements in the rhythm method are presently being researched.

The combination of condom and spermicidal foam, while not necessarily aesthetic, is almost foolproof. These can be purchased in a drugstore without a prescription, and offer the further advantage of protection against VD.

New versions of the foam come in tampon-size dispensers you can carry in your purse.

While we are on the subject of VD, here is a final, little-known fact about the Pill. It changes the hormone balance of the vagina, making it more susceptible to VD, as well as to other annoying infections. The women who, using *no* method of birth control, has sex relations with a VD infected man, is thought to have a one-third chance of contracting his infection. If she uses condoms and/or foam, her chances are considerably lower. If however, she is on the Pill, her chances of contracting VD from one exposure jump to more than 90 percent.

But what about the health of *former* Pill users? Although, as we have noted, some ten million United States women may take the Pill at any given time, this is an ever-changing population. Two users out of three stop within five years because of side-effects. Some of these return to the Pill later.

Apparently, most of the problems associated with the Pill are reversible, although some, such as skin discolorations, are usually not. Some women undergo a "period of adjustment" after stopping the Pill, while waiting for their own pituitary and ovarian hormones to reassert themselves. During this interim, women may notice temporary undesirable changes in their skin, hair and figure, as well as the absence of menstruation and ovulation. (One woman

I know, a dancer, failed to menstruate for two years after stopping the Pill but then her period came back normally.) In *Lunaception*, a recent book by Louise Lacy, the author records how, at the suggestion of a nutritionist friend, she got her "in-house" glandular system working again by priming it with extra doses of vitamins B and E.

Mark Dowie and Tracy Johnston

A CASE OF CORPORATE MALPRACTICE AND THE DALKON SHIELD

In 1971, Dr. Hugh J. Davis, associate professor of gynecology at Johns Hopkins, decided to write up his experiments with a new intrauterine device he had been using at the university's family-planning clinic. He heads the clinic, which is part of one of the country's most prestigious medical schools. The clinic, like the Johns Hopkins Medical School, is in the middle of one of the worst ghettos in Baltimore, and Davis spends a lot of his time prescribing pills, inserting IUDs and advising poor black and Latin American women how to prevent unwanted children. One of the many lawyers who do the talking for him now says Davis thinks of pregnancy as "a social evil—contributing to poverty, unhappiness and unrest."

Although Davis's book, a slim volume sprinkled with charts and graphs and called *The Intrauterine Device for Contraception,* was not stacked up alongside the cash registers of bookstores across the country, many doctors read it eagerly. The results of research performed under the auspices of Johns Hopkins could certainly be trusted, and doctors everywhere were anxious for information about the various plastic loops and squiggles and paper-clip-like things they had inserted in over three million women in America. They still know almost nothing about intrauterine devices, except that somehow a foreign object in the uterus usually prevents pregnancy.

At that time, the entire subject of contraception was especially controversial. Pill men and IUD men were known to exchange bitter comments at conventions and engage in primitive avoidance rituals if they discovered each other at the same party. The Davis book, since it came from Hopkins, was discussed by most everyone in the field and widely reported on in women's magazines.

In his book, Davis gives evidence that the IUD is a better birth-control device than the Pill—almost as efficient and much safer. More important, he indicates that a certain new IUD recently put on the market works better than any of the old ones.

To be sure, Davis doesn't directly recommend the Dalkon Shield over the Lippes Loop, the Saf-T-Coil, the Copper-7 or its other competitors; such recommendations in medical texts are considered highly unprofessional. The Shield's experimental results just look a lot better. The comparisons appear to be thorough, scientific and convincing. On every graph, on every chart and in every analysis, the Dalkon Shield is first.

The only thing the book does not say about the Dalkon Shield —and the full story has not been told before—is that Davis had not only tested it, he had invented it, along with his good friend Irwin Lerner, and he was making money on every new Shield sold. At the time the book was published, Davis had already made $250,000 on the sale of the Shield to the A. H. Robins Company, one of the largest pharmaceutical houses in the United States. In five years' time, before the Shield would be removed from the market amid increasing publicity about deaths and injuries to women who used it, Davis would earn well over $300,000 more in royalties and consultants' fees.

·   ·   ·

No one knows exactly how many women have been killed by the Dalkon Shield. As of last January, 17 American women had died. There have been a number of deaths since, but the government totals and releases such figures only once a year. Statistics from the dozens of other countries where the Shield has been in use—mostly in the Third World—are fragmentary or nonexistent. In other ways, too, the full story of the device that has left untold hundreds of women sterile, and that is still in use by more than a million women around the world, has been hard to get. Doctors do not easily reveal secrets about each other. Also, all the principal characters in this story are under orders from their lawyers not to speak, for the Dalkon Shield has become one of the most litigated products in pharmaceutical history.

Since Davis would not talk to us, it was difficult to get a full picture of this paradoxical man, who teaches at a leading university and runs a clinic for the poor, yet who succumbed to the temptation of making big money by the most unethical means. We could assemble only a fragmentary picture of him from others' reports. Thomas Kemp, a lawyer handling many of the cases for Robins, describes Davis as "tall," "neat" and a man of "overwhelming heart." Davis's wife says she hopes the true story about her husband will get out, but she doesn't know what it is. "Work is work and home is home," she says on the phone over the sounds of children giggling, and Davis doesn't mix the two. Still another picture of him comes from a woman who once worked in his clinic, who described him as "the most efficient man I ever met." She said he once used a vacation to have his appendix taken out, just so that he would lose no work time if he ever got appendicitis.

Luckily for our story, though, there are sworn depositions in the Dalkon case, and although Davis is cagey and doesn't reveal a thing when he talks to lawyers, Irwin Lerner is a garrulous guy and tells the story of the Dalkon Shield with relish.

"Win" Lerner is an inventor, really. He started off in 1948 as an electrical engineer in oil development. He went on to computers and then typewriters, where, he claims, he developed the Selectric. In 1960 he got interested in the medical supplies field and started working for a company making polyethylene tubing, bloodtest equipment, automatic pipettes and all sorts of things a burgeoning medical market could use. He met Hugh Davis in 1964, while trying to push one of his inventions, and the two men liked each other right away. Also, they realized, according to Lerner, how they "could use each other's expertise."

The Davis-Lerner association started out as business (they worked on several products together from 1964 to 1967) but it soon turned into friendship. In fact, it was on Christmas Day 1967, while the two families were opening presents and sitting around Davis's home in Baltimore, that the idea for inventing a new IUD came to them.

Each man claims it was the other who first came up with the idea, but whatever the case, both were very excited about it. The two men would call each other up at midnight and three o'clock in the morning to discuss the project. Davis would tell Lerner the little that was known about IUDs and the failures of the ones already on the market: they caused pain, cramps and bleeding; they didn't work; they came out. And Lerner would discuss ways of solving each problem. For the expulsion problem, they had a unique solution: a disk-like IUD with stubby tentacles whose barb effect would hold the device in the uterus. Within a few months Lerner had his first model of the Dalkon Shield, and in August, Davis took a few of them fresh from the Pee Wee Plastic Company, where they had been manufactured, and inserted them into some patients at his clinic. Patients had heard about dangers from the Pill and were quite willing to try a different contraceptive. Initial results looked good, and one month later Lerner applied for a patent.

Instead of donating the device to a medical institution for study, Lerner and Davis decided to market it themselves and to get private physicians across the country to test it for them. Lerner says Davis had some money from Hopkins, which he used to buy Dalkon Shields, and over a one-year period, Davis inserted 640 of them into women (558 clinic patients, 82 private patients) and carefully noted down the "results." He wrote them up and published them in February 1970 in the *American Journal of Obstetrics and Gynecology*, the leading journal in the field. They were remarkable to say the least, especially the pregnancy rate—the lowest among all IUDs (1.1 per cent). The article concluded, "Taken all together, the superior performance of the Shield intrauterine device makes the technique a first choice method of contraception control."

Meanwhile, other doctors across the nation were beginning to hear about the device that had impressive Johns Hopkins statistics behind it, and many were sending for it to try out on their own patients.

One of the people who read of Dr. Davis's exciting discovery was Mary Bolint. She was a junior at the University of Arizona in Tucson at the time and was engaged to Ned Ripple. She planned to go to law school after college, so she wanted to wait to have children until after she finished four more years of school. Contraception was an important factor in her life, and so she informed herself about such things. "What makes me angriest now," she says today, "is that I didn't just go to my doctor and let him put whatever he wanted in my body, I studied all the statistics carefully." She read glowing reports of the Dalkon Shield in a feminist health book and asked her doctor if she should have one. Since he too had heard favorable reports, and since a model had been specially designed for women who had never had children, he inserted a Dalkon Shield into Mary's uterus. Carefully following the instructions that accompanied the product, he warned her that she might experience some minor discomfort and slightly heavier bleeding with her period. The pain, however, was immediate and acute. Mary returned to her doctor, who told her it would subside. It did, but her first period was profuse and painful. Again, her doctor promised that once her system grew used to the device all would be well.

After a few months the pain during her period became tolerable. Mary and Ned were married, and she was accepted into law school during her senior year. She continued to study hard and became an avid modern dancer.

The rise of the Dalkon Shield really began with Davis's research at Hopkins, and the more closely you look back on it, the less scientific it appears. For one thing, the women tested didn't sign any consent forms, so no one knows what Davis told them about the fresh-off-the-drawing-board gadgets he was putting into their uteri. Also, many people claim that Davis regularly told his IUD patients to use spermicidal foam during the tenth to seventeenth days of their cycle, which would leave it unclear whether his study reported the contraceptive effects of the Dalkon Shield or of the foam. Davis said the people who came to his clinic wouldn't use foam even if they were told to, but that is questionable. In any case, Davis admits that at least some of the 82 private patients in his study might have taken his suggestion to use foam, and that makes his research findings dubious. It is as if, in studying a new headache remedy, he had told patients to take aspirin as well. Also, the study sounds less impressive when you realize there was an average of only 5.5 months testing per woman—not much time to get a reliable pregnancy figure.

Hindsight aside, however, after the *Journal of Obstetrics and Gynecology* article was published, the Dalkon Shield began to take off. Additional help had come to Lerner and Davis on New Year's Eve 1969, in the form of Dr. Thad Earl. He was a small-town practitioner from Defiance, Ohio, and had inserted the Shield into some of his own patients and thought it was a great idea. He offered Lerner, Davis and their lawyer, Robert Cohn, $50,000, and got a 7.5 per cent interest in what became "The Dalkon Corporation." (The name was probably an amalgam of Davis, Lerner, and Cohn.)

Lerner had been the inventor, Davis the scientist whose research at a famous institution had validated the invention, Cohn the lawyer who had put together a corporate framework that would allow everyone to get rich, and now, finally The Dalkon Corporation had what it needed to get off the ground: Thad Earl, the enthusiastic salesman willing to go on the road drumming up publicity. If you don't have a large marketing organization or the capital to advertise, about the only effective way to sell a new medical product is to set up demonstration booths at medical conventions. Earl proved to be an energetic salesman. IUDs were not, at the time, classified as drugs, so Dalkon Shields could be hawked just like new office furniture to doctors browsing in convention hallways. Earl passed out the Shields from his booth and showed everyone the impressive testing results of Dr. Hugh Davis of Johns Hopkins.

One warm spring day toward the end of her senior year in college, while Mary Bolint was shopping for dinner, she began to feel uneasy. Suddenly an enormous wave of nausea swept over her. She left her groceries and walked as fast as she could to her car, where she lay down in the back seat. She had been dancing all afternoon, preparing for a summer arts festival, and hoped that she was simply overtired. She remained dizzy and confused, however, and had to ask a friend to drive her home. Her main worry was appendicitis. That would have spoiled her summer of dancing and working. She worked as a nurses' aide in the local hospital and was saving her money for law school.

She made it home, cooked a small dinner and went to bed early—tired and sore. The pain grew worse through the night and at six A.M. she woke her husband Ned. She barely had enough strength left to ask him to take her to the hospital, and he rushed her to the emergency ward, where her condition was quickly diagnosed as appendicitis. When the doctors opened her up, however, they found a healthy appendix, but large abscesses on her ovaries. They drained the abscesses, took out her appendix and sewed her up. When she awoke she told her doctor she was using a Dalkon Shield and asked him if he thought it should be taken out. He said he didn't think it was necessary since he had never heard of IUDs causing infection, but that he would remove it if she wanted. She decided to leave it in and was released from the hospital in a few days. She returned home satisfied that she had made the right decision. The infection was gone and, even if the Dalkon Shield was uncomfortable, it couldn't be as dangerous as the Pill.

It was 1970, and the scene was a medical convention in Ohio. Thad Earl was there selling Dalkon Shields and found himself set up in a booth next to one run by John McClure, a salesman for A. H. Robins Company. The two men began talking; their chit-chat quickly turned to business talk, and suddenly the promoters of the Dalkon Shield had a big break beyond their greatest dreams.

Robins is headquartered in Richmond, Virginia, and has assets of $186 million and subsidiaries in more than a dozen foreign countries. Tranquilizers and appetite suppressants are among the best-selling products of its large line of drugs; it also makes cosmetics, Robitussin cough syrup, Chapstick and Sergeant's Flea Collar, which *Forbes* business magazine accused of killing pets.

At the time Thad Earl and John McClure got to talking outside their convention booths, Robins was looking for an entry into the growing contraceptive market. Its rivals Schmidt and Ortho had captured the Pill business and were beginning to reap enormous profits from their own IUDs. When McClure started chatting with Earl, he didn't waste time. Within a few days after their meeting, Robins acquisition manager flew to Defiance, Ohio, to watch Earl make a few insertions of the Dalkon Shield and to talk medicine and markets. A week later the company's medical director, Dr. Fred Clark, flew to Baltimore to meet Hugh Davis.

Davis told him, by Clark's account, "that the company that takes the Dalkon Shield must move fast and distribute much merchandise and really make an inroad 'in the next eight months.' " Several other people Davis knew were working on similar devices. The courtship quickly intensified; both sides were eager to consummate.

Within a few days Lerner and Cohn, Dalkon's lawyer, flew to Richmond to work out a deal. After three days of negotiating, everyone returned home richer. Robins paid The Dalkon Corporation $750,000 for the patent, which was split among Lerner, Davis, Earl and Cohn according to their interests in the Corporation. Also, an agreement was made (and this is where the big money comes in) that the four men would split ten per cent royalties on all gross sales of the Shield by Robins in the U.S. and Canada. Finally, Earl was retained by Robins as a $30,000-a-year consultant for three years; Davis consulted at $20,000 a year for five years; and Lerner consulted for one year at $12,500 and two more at $2,500.

As the deal was being made, however, something was discovered that proved to be a portent of troubles ahead. Dr. Fred Clark, the Robins official who had flown up to Baltimore to meet Hugh Davis, dictated a three-page memorandum to the files on his return to Richmond. In it he said that of the 832 patients Davis had tested so far, 26 had become pregnant. This would raise the pregnancy rate from the previously published 1.1 per cent to close to three per cent. The dates on the Clark memo show that Hugh Davis was aware of this new, less impressive result back in February when his *Journal* article was published.

(Robins lawyers claim that Fred Clark's memo about a higher pregnancy rate is merely a typo. They say Clark never read the typed version of the notes he dictated and that he meant to say "an additional six" rather than "26." But their claim sounds weak, for there is other material in the subpoenaed files that indicates Clark did not believe Davis's figures were as impressive as he had first heard.)

Although not quite the corporate equivalent of a smoking gun, the memo has become an important document in the Dalkon affair. It indicates that both Davis and Robins are guilty of promoting the Dalkon Shield with false statistics. The crucial importance of the pregnancy rate becomes clear when you imagine a fetus having to share a uterus with a small crab-shaped piece of plastic. Most of those 17 deaths were due to blood poisoning caused by infection and spontaneous abortion among women who got pregnant while wearing the Dalkon Shield.

Readers of five national medical journals in December 1970 found themselves looking at a remarkable two-page advertisement. It became known in Robins' ad department as the "flying uterus" ad, and it was Robins' way of beginning the vigorous promotion of the Dalkon Shield it had bought only six months earlier. The ad's art page is a painting by a prominent medical artist, Arthur Lidov. It shows a cross-sectioned uterus floating through the sky toward the reader with a Dalkon Shield nestled in it. The Shield looks like some sort of space bug out of the pages of Ray Bradbury —it's about the size of a small fingernail, is made of white plastic and its most notable feature is the little spines or legs surrounding it to keep it from slipping out of the womb. It also has a "tail" or piece of string attached to facilitate medical removal.

It turns out that the string is more important than it would seem. In fact, technically speaking, it is the culprit of the Dalkon affair. According to most researchers (although not Robins) who have since studied it, its construction (which is multifilament, meaning several threads wound together) acts like the wick of a kerosene lamp and allows bacteria from the vagina to creep up and enter the uterus, where massive infections leading to blood poisoning, and eventually death, can result.

The copy on the companion page of the advertisement, with the "scientific" findings from Dr. Hugh Davis's earliest research, boasts of the 1.1 per cent pregnancy rate, and says nothing about the women in the study also using foam or being tested for an average of less than six months. Davis is impressively footnoted as a research physician with citations from the articles he published. He is not cited as a businessman who had just collected $250,000 from his share of the sale of the Shield to Robins.

For the next few years, everything went wonderfully for Robins. The Dalkon Shield was inserted into 3.3 million women in the U.S. and overseas. Robins reaped huge profits from it (each device had only a few cents' worth of plastic in it, but sold for $4.35 retail). The Shield was hailed as the latest thing in IUDs, particularly good for women who had not yet had children. E. Claiborne Robins, Sr., chief executive officer of the company started by his grandfather in 1878, was proud of his officers and was looking forward to the day when the Dalkon Shield would be as familiar a product as Chapstick.

Not long after her "appendectomy," when the abscesses on her ovaries had been discovered and drained, Mary Bolint again began feeling pain and nausea. She went directly to the gynecologist in the hospital where she was working for the summer. He tried in his office to remove her Dalkon Shield but was unable to do it, and so she was put in an operating room where it was removed surgically. For two days after the operation Mary remained in the hospital, running a temperature of 104 degrees and experiencing almost constant dreamlike hallucinations. When her temperature returned to normal several days later, she was sent home with antibiotics. She was still too weak to work or dance, so she stayed home to cook for Ned, who was working. She grew weaker day by day, and finally her parents convinced her to come home to Louisiana, where they could take care of her. Her mother flew to meet her and took Mary to the plane. When they arrived in New Orleans, a flight attendant had to carry Mary off. After she had been home for a few days the fever returned and again she was rushed to the hospital, where she was found to have septicemia, or blood poisoning. For ten days she was kept in intensive care, receiving intravenous antibiotics. During that time, her appendectomy scar burst open from new abscesses on her ovaries, which were again drained. When she finally regained her strength after a month, she flew to San Francisco to join Ned and begin law school. She hoped at last that she could put the painful memories behind her and look ahead to law school, a career, a good marriage and, someday, children.

Up to this time all the characters on the corporate side of the Dalkon history have been men. (One wonders how different this story might be had the subjects of their experiments and sales been men also: would it have taken 17 deaths and hundreds of painful operations on male genitalia before a new variety of condom, say, was taken off the market?) But one woman played a role in the discovery of the Dalkon Shield's dangers, although, unfortunately, her warnings were ignored by higher-ups.

She is Dr. Ellen (Kitty) Preston, a Southern woman who got her M.D. in 1950. She had worked as a physician in private practice and for the State of Virginia Health Department before coming to Robins to be chief of the Antibacterial and Miscellaneous Division (the Shield came under Miscellaneous). In 1971, Preston wrote a memo to medical director Fred Clark (the same Robins official who had flown to Baltimore to meet Hugh Davis and had discovered Davis had been using inflated statistics). In her memo, Preston said that she and Daniel French, president of Robins' Chapstick Division, were concerned that the Dalkon's multifilament tail might display "wicking qualities." She was predicting the source of the very problem that was to lead to so many injuries and deaths among women who used the Shield. On August 20, 1971, Clark replied with a curt letter saying that it was not up to Drs. Preston and French to test the Shield. He indicated in the letter that he was passing the problem to Dr. Oscar Klioze, the company microbiologist. But did he ever do so? In a sworn deposition four years later, Dr. Klioze said he had never heard of the Preston and French memos, and when he was shown them he swore he had never seen them.

It was one of Dr. Ellen Preston's duties to answer medical inquiries from doctors regarding the Shield. After her rebuff by Clark, she responded to at least one doctor who wrote asking about the possibility of "wicking," saying that as far as Robins knew, such a problem did not exist.

Robins must have been having some second thoughts about the Shield's safety, for around this time it did its own testing, came up with a pregnancy rate of 2 per cent, somewhat higher than Davis's, and cited the new figure as well in its ads. However, some other studies done at the same time that showed vastly greater pregnancy rates—one by Dr. Johanna Perlmutter at Beth Israel Hospital in Boston (10.1 per cent) and one by the Kaiser Medical Center in Sacramento (5.6 per cent)—Robins simply chose to ignore.

Two weeks after she had arrived in California to enter law school, Mary Bolint again began experiencing fever and nausea. She went to a doctor and told him her history. He examined her and said she had a new large abscess on her left ovary and that if it burst she might die. Very scared and sick, Mary decided to fly back to Lancaster, Pennsylvania, where her father-in-law, a doctor, could supervise her medical care. On the plane east she began to wonder if it would ever end. She was going in for her fourth operation in four months.

While she was under anesthesia, the surgeon made a six-inch incision from her navel down to the top of her pubic bone and two 1½-inch incisions on either side of her abdomen to drain the infection. The doctors were working to save her reproductive organs, but cautious not to give her too many pain-killing drugs because her nervous system was by now so weak. Mary lay in bed for two weeks with tubes and needles running in and out of her body and was in constant excruciating pain.

When she recovered and again flew home to Louisiana to recuperate, she was badly scarred all over her abdomen, emotionally drained but dimly grateful that she would still be able to have children.

Let us backtrack in time a little to take up another strand of the Dalkon story. It is an important one, for it involves a slip for which —in the unlikely event that the law is enforced justly—one of the principals could go to jail.

In January 1970 the controversy over the damaging side effects of oral contraceptives was at its height, and a Senate Subcommittee headed by Senator Gaylord Nelson was holding hearings on the subject. One of the experts on contraception they called in to testify was Dr. Hugh Davis. Davis took a stand against birth-control pills with high estrogen content and for IUDs, especially "the new ones" that have been developed. He disapproved of the collection of information regarding the side effects of the Pill, saying that they were vastly "underreported." He said information regarding contraception supplied to women is not adequate, and that gynecologists aren't all that informed about it either. "They are busy," he said. "They read the brochures and information that the drug houses tend to pump into them, I am sorry to say."

It is true that IUDs are generally safer than the Pill, but, sensing that Davis might have some special stake in his strong case for the IUDs, one of the committee members asked if he had a patent on any intrauterine device. Davis mentioned an IUD (not the Dalkon Shield) he had co-invented ten years earlier that was never marketed. The time to tell it straight came, however, when the question was put more bluntly.

"Then you have no particular commercial interest in any of the intrauterine devices?"

"That is correct," replied Dr. Davis.

For the first time in the whole murky history of the Dalkon Shield, someone had clearly and indisputably broken the law: Davis had committed perjury. In flatly lying under oath to the

Senate Subcommittee, Davis had committed a felony—one that carries a prison sentence of up to five years and one for which a whole host of people, from Alger Hiss to one or two of the lesser Watergate defendants, have done time in prison. To date, Davis has not been indicted or charged.

The first hint of trouble for Robins in the Dalkon matter came in 1973, and it came, surprisingly, from a man in an Army uniform. He was a witness at a federal hearing called to discuss whether or not medical devices should be subject to the same kind of controls as regular drugs. The hearings dealt with every device imaginable, from pacemakers to artificial kidneys, but on May 30 Army Major Russel Thomsen stole the show by recounting his experiences with the Dalkon Shield. Like so many doctors, he said, he had trusted his medical journals and assumed their editors made sure their authors and advertisers were responsible. On the strength of Robins' advertisements and Davis's article, he had convinced his patients to switch to the Dalkon Shield, only to see them go through a great deal of suffering because of it. Thomsen described cases of septic abortion, pelvic inflammatory disease, massive bleeding, incessant cramps. Some of his patients had almost died. He said he was "revolted" by the gap between the glossy advertising claims and the occurrence of serious and even fatal complications. His testimony about the gruesome effects of the Dalkon Shield was in most major American newspapers the following morning.

After the Dalkon Shield became a public issue, a flood of reports like Thomsen's began coming in from throughout the country. After a year of such information-gathering, Robins got word, finally, of a death in Arizona due to the Shield. From this point on, Robins at last began to act responsibly. The company went to the Food and Drug Administration with the information, and when four more deaths were reported soon after, Robins decided to send out a strongly worded "Dear Doctor" letter to every physician in the country. The letter warned doctors about possible septic abortion and death from the Dalkon Shield and recommended that women who got pregnant with the Shield be given therapeutic abortions. Similar warnings were printed on the packages of new

Shields being manufactured. All this seems reminiscent of the Surgeon General's warning on cigarette packs, with one difference: as with prescription drugs, the ultimate recipient never gets to see the label.

Things began looking bad for Dalkon sales. Within weeks of the Dear Doctor letter, the Planned Parenthood Federation sent a memorandum to its 700 membership clinics. It suggested that they immediately cease prescribing the Shield and recommended that they call in all patients then wearing it, advise them of the dangers and offer a substitute contraceptive. They also said the 26.4 per cent of the women in their clinics fitted with the Dalkon Shield experienced severe cramps and bleeding.

Davis was interviewed by the press around this time. He was known as the Shield's co-inventor, but not as someone who still owned a piece of the action. "The whole thing has been blown out of proportion by a certain amount of deliberate design," he reportedly said. "There are large commercial forces that are quite interested in selling new IUDs."

While all the fuss was going on, the Food and Drug Administration began hearings on the Dalkon Shield. Robins executives were frightened, and the highway from its headquarters near Richmond to Washington was soon filled with scouts and lobbyists it was sending to the hearing. According to Dr. Richard Dickey, a member of the FDA's Ob/Gyn Committee, which conducted the hearing, "throughout the entire proceedings the halls and offices of the FDA were crawling with the Robins men. It was disgusting."

Finally, though, before the FDA committee made its recommendations, Robins itself suspended sale of the Shield. It was a difficult decision for the company, as Dalkon had recently moved into the lead in national IUD sales. But in 30 short days, the deaths reported to the FDA had risen from four to seven and the septic abortions from 36 to 110. By this time, also, many people were pointing to the possibility of "wicking," which was the subject of the Preston/Clark memos written back in 1971. Now, in 1975, Robins knew its product was commercially dead, and wanted to forget it. Only, as things turned out, it couldn't.

The day Mary Bolint was scheduled to leave Louisiana to fly back to California for another try at law school and a normal life with her husband, she came down with a high fever. Despairingly, she checked into the hospital again. When doctors opened up her abdomen this time, they found that the infection was everywhere. To save her life they performed a complete hysterectomy and rinsed her peritoneal cavity with antibiotic fluid. During recovery, the intern told Mary that for a while he couldn't get a blood pressure on her and her pulse measured 150.

"I knew from working as a nurses' aide," she says, *"that it meant death, but you know, I didn't care. In fact I was relieved. My skin was gray, my hair was falling out and I weighed about 100 pounds."*

Throughout the rise and fall of the Dalkon Shield, one irony is how seldom anyone actually broke the law. Hugh Davis did, when he perjured himself by telling senators he had no commercial interest in any IUD. But his having that interest in the first place in a harmful device he and the Robins Company were vigorously promoting by questionable means was not really illegal.

Most doctors we talked to either avoided comment on the Dalkon controversy or seemed to genuinely consider it business as usual. Even Dr. John Brewer, editor of the *American Journal of Obstetrics and Gynecology,* sidestepped the issue. We asked him if he considered it unethical for Davis to have published an article in his journal praising the IUD Davis co-owned, without revealing his financial stake.

"I don't know what you're talking about and I consider it no business of mine."

"But we know lawyers have been taking depositions from you," we persisted.

"I just answer their questions," Brewer replied. "Until you told me this minute, I had no idea of what it was all about, and I don't want to know."

Others in the medical profession say this kind of conflict of interest is fairly common. Many medical researchers are paid by drug companies to test new products and don't mention that fact in their statistical write-ups. Aside from his distortion of statistics, the main thing medical people consider unusual about what Davis did is that he developed the Dalkon Shield while using the clinic and the prestige of Johns Hopkins. Doctors who are out to make big money in the medical market are usually not at medical schools.

A 1976 law (passed largely because of the Dalkon controversy) will make it somewhat harder for anyone to profiteer from a new medical device in precisely the same manner Davis and the Robins Company did. Medical devices are now subject to many of the same kinds of government monitoring and approval as drugs have been.

Nonetheless, we can still expect drug companies to rush new drugs and devices onto the market as fast as whatever the current law allows. Not because the companies mean harm, but because they have no choice. If a drug or device is tested more cautiously or for a longer time than the law requires, or advertised with less distortion or oversell than the law permits, someone else will corner the market with a competing product. That's why Hugh Davis warned Robins the company had to "move fast and distribute much merchandise."

As long as there is a free market for medical products, that's the way business will be done. Indeed, though there have been civil lawsuits aplenty as a result of the Dalkon Shield, the whole affair has been considered so normal a way of conducting free-enterprise medicine that Johns Hopkins took no action against Davis, state medical authorities censured neither Davis nor Earl and the government left the A. H. Robins Company and The Dalkon Corporation alone.

A product that has been heavily promoted and advertised gathers a certain kind of momentum, a momentum that can carry it right over obstacles like bad publicity, studies of its dangers and the like. In the case of the Dalkon Shield, this momentum brought a curious coda to its story: throughout the entire controversy over the Shield, long past the time Major Thomsen had testified before the Senate committee, past the time Robins sent out its "Dear

Doctor" letter, past the time Planned Parenthood and HEW clinics stopped using them and right up to the moment Robins took the Shield off the market, the U.S. foreign aid program was busily sending huge quantities of the device to more than 40 countries throughout the world.

The Agency for International Development's population control program is in the hands of Dr. R. D. Ravenholt, a man whose enthusiasm for birth control as a solution to the world's problems borders on the fanatical. When one of us visited his office several years ago she found it filled with charts of female reproductive organs, packages of condoms, and models of a small vacuum cleaner-like device Ravenholt was promoting at the time as the latest in birth-control techniques. When she got up to leave, he said "Here, take these," reaching into a small box overflowing with little packets of Pills.

"But I don't use Pills," she replied.

"That's all right," he said. "Give them to your friends."

Only when the FDA ruled the Shield unsafe (which was some time *after* Robins had stopped selling it) did Ravenholt and AID try to recall any Shields. They managed to get back fewer than half of the 769,000 Shields they had given away.

Today Mary Bolint has regained her health, but her entire abdomen is a mass of scar tissue. She can never have children. For a long time, she says, she could not think about the Dalkon Shield. Now she is one of many women engaged in lawsuits against the A. H. Robins Company and Hugh Davis, Irwin Lerner, Thad Earl and Robert Cohn.

Robins spent $5 million in litigation costs over the Shield last year, and more suits are yet to come. The company is setting aside a reserve from its profits to cover future lawsuits, and its stock value has dropped sharply. All told, though, Robins' corporate health is not bad: profits were up 26 percent in the first half of 1976.

Hugh Davis still teaches at Johns Hopkins and still heads the university's Family Planning Clinic. He does not return phone calls from the press. Thad Earl is still in private practice, although he has moved to Arizona. "Win" Lerner is still an engineer, working for himself at "Lerner Labs." Like the others, he had been told by his lawyers to say nothing, but he is the only one who sounds frustrated with this prohibition. Lerner would like to tell the whole story, he says, but he can't. The Dalkon Corporation still exists, he adds, and maybe someday it will come up with a new product.

Dr. Ellen Preston, the woman whose memo about "wicking" first pinpointed the danger of the Dalkon Shield, still works for A. H. Robins in Virginia. She has been forbidden by company lawyers to talk about the case with anyone.

Some 800,000 women in the United States and an estimated 500,000 in other countries are still wearing the Dalkon Shield as a birth-control device. Planned Parenthood and several similar groups have considered recommending that all women wearing Shields have them removed immediately. But these organizations have decided not to do so, for recently it has been discovered that removal of the Shield frequently causes lesions of the cervix, followed by serious infection.

Claudia Dreifus

STERILIZING THE POOR

They sit quietly on her lap as she weeps: the two living children of Guadalupe Acosta, two little girls with coffee-tone skin and classic Indian faces. Clean and pretty in their starched dresses, the girls are with their mother as we meet in the East Los Angeles offices of her attorney, Antonia Hernandez of the Model Cities Law Center.

Mrs. Acosta, a large, somber-looking woman of thirty-five, has taken the morning off to talk with me. The children have been brought because, well . . . baby sitters are expensive. And also because Lupe Acosta finds it hard to be away from them for any sustained period of time. Though Mrs. Acosta has given birth to four infants, it is only these two children—the middle ones—that she has been able to nurture and raise. There was a first baby, born out of wedlock in Mexico, who was taken from her and given to a relative for adoption. The fourth child died shortly after birth at L. A. County General Hospital on August 21, 1973. And it was after that delivery that doctors at L. A. County sterilized her. Without her knowledge. Without her informed consent. And it is because of this sterilization that Lupe Acosta's common-law husband abandoned her. The operation is the reason she cries throughout our interview, the reason she holds her two daughters to her body *so tightly*.

"I didn't want to go to L. A. County Hospital," she begins. "I heard they didn't treat you right there and that they made the women suffer. I had a private doctor. When I was nine months pregnant, he told me that the baby's head was too big and I would have to go to the County Hospital because they had better equipment."

The child's head was more than just too big; it was severely malformed—anencephalic, it had no brain. Because of the abnormality, the pregnancy lasted eleven months. For the last month of term, Mrs. Acosta attended weekly prenatal clinic sessions at County—where, not once, was she counseled about sterilization.

However, on August 20, 1973, eleven months and eleven days pregnant, Lupe Acosta entered L. A. County in the final stages of labor. "When I was being examined, they pushed very hard on the stomach," she recalls. "Very, very hard. With their hands. One doctor would have one leg open. The other doctor would have the other leg open. And then, there were two doctors just pushing down on my stomach and I couldn't . . . I couldn't stand it. I pushed one doctor because I couldn't stand the pain. When he came back, he hit me in the stomach and said, 'Now lady, let us do what we have to.' I felt very sick. I was sweat all over, *sweat.* I kept telling them to do something to bring the baby. . . . They kept me in that condition from six o'clock in the evening till three o'clock in the morning. That was the last time I saw the clock— the last time I remember anything."

A question to Mrs. Acosta from her lawyer: "Do you remember signing a consent form?"

"No," she answers. "I don't remember signing anything. Only when I left the hospital—perhaps an exit paper?"

The day after Mrs. Acosta's caesarean delivery, her common-law husband came to her bedside. "He told me the baby was alive and in an incubator," she says, weeping at the mere recollection. "Seven days later the doctor came round to take out the stitches and I asked him how my baby was. 'What baby?' he asked. 'Your baby died when it was born.' " That's how Acosta learned the fate of her fourth child.

But more was to come. A month after delivery, she arrived at

County for the standard postnatal check-up. "My common-law husband, he told me to get the Pill at the hospital," she recounts. "When I asked the woman doctor, she asked me if I knew what had happened to me. I said, 'No.' And then the doctor told me, 'Well, you won't need the Pill because they tied your tubes.' I said that I didn't sign anything. She said, 'Your husband did.' And then I told them he wasn't my husband."

When Lupe Acosta got home that night, she was alternating between fury and hysteria. "I became very angry," she says, "and I asked him why he had done that—he had no right. He told me that he didn't sign anything except for a paper for a caesarean. He said, 'If I had signed the paper, would I have sent you for the Pill?' "

The relationship between Guadalupe Acosta and her common-law husband of eight years quickly deteriorated. Built into Mexican culture is the idea of *machismo,* a value that says a man's masculinity is measured by the number of children his wife produces. Given the reality of *machismo,* a sterile woman is considered worthless—useless. On a smoggy day last autumn, Lupe Acosta's man abandoned her and the two children. She was, as a result, forced on welfare. Then the tubal ligation hemorrhaged and she was hospitalized. Nothing has gone right in her life since August 1973. Sometimes she gets pains from the tubal ligation. "And my nerves and my head are in great pain," she complains. "Ever since the operation, I am very inattentive. Not forgetful, inattentive. People sometimes have to tell me things twice. It's not that I don't understand them, it's that I'm not there."

It was a different story for Maria Diaz (not her real name). In 1972, Mrs. Diaz, pregnant with a third child, was living with her family in Hermosillo, Mexico. Because Mrs. Diaz, then thirty-two years old, was a legally immigrated resident of the United States and because her husband had not yet attained that status, it was decided she should journey to Los Angeles alone for the infant's birth. "My brother-in-law told me it would be better for the baby to be born in the United States," she recalls.

Mrs. Diaz explains all this as she pours coffee for me and her lawyer, Antonia Hernandez. It is a warm July afternoon. The three of us are sitting in the living room of her spotlessly clean cottage in Glendale, California. On the walls hang dimestore prints of John F. Kennedy and Emiliano Zapata—as well as lovingly mounted crayon scribblings by the children. "Yes, I went there because I thought it would be better," explains Mrs. Diaz who, like her husband, works as a baker. "I could cross the border freely and my husband could not—so I went alone."

On April 6, 1972, Maria Diaz and her brother-in-law arrived at L. A. County Women's Hospital; she was in labor. For three-and-a-half hours they sat in the waiting room until the hospital would admit her. Then, after several more hours of labor, she was informed that the child would be born by caesarean section. "I told them I could not accept the caesarean operation because my husband was not there and I could not do as I pleased. . . . When they were talking about the caesarean, I heard the doctors use the word 'tubes.' The doctors said they were going to tie my tubes because it would be dangerous for me to have more children. I told them I could not accept that. I kept saying no and the doctors kept telling me that this was for my own good."

Maria Diaz was approached repeatedly during the final stages of her labor. A tube was pushed into her vagina. She was crying with pain. Nevertheless, the attending staff continued pressing her for sterilization. She was drugged and "they had already given me anesthesia when I signed the consent form for the caesarean and they were still insisting that I would accept the tubal operation and I was still saying, 'No, no, no.' "

Finally, Mrs. Diaz broke down. "I was in great pain," she tells us. "I thought I was going to die. The two other children, the pain was nothing like this. I got angry and I cried, 'If you're going to do *anything,* do it, but let me have my baby now because I feel I am going to die.' I remember very little after that because it was like a dream and I was in great pain."

"Did you sign a paper for the caesarean?" I ask.

"For the caesarean, yes," Maria Diaz answers, "but for the tubal —no."

"Is it possible that you told them verbally to go ahead?" I inquire.

"I *know* that I didn't because there was a nurse or a receptionist at the hospital who showed me the chart and there was no indication that I approved. The chart said I rejected all their efforts for sterilization, but I don't remember everything. It's possible in the pain . . . but I don't remember doing that."

Mrs. Diaz discovered she was sterile some weeks later during her postnatal clinic visit. "When I heard that, I started to cry," she recalls. "The doctor said, 'Don't cry. It's best for you that you not have any more children. In Mexico, the people are very, very poor and it's best that you not have more children. At that moment, I thought—but I didn't say it, 'What is it to you? You're not my husband.' "

When Mrs. Diaz wrote her spouse of the operation, he sent back a letter saying he didn't understand what she was talking about. "To this day," she says—speaking in a low voice, so that her husband, who sits outside, will not hear, "he is very angry. There are constant problems. Fighting. He says, 'Surely we will part. You never lacked home. You never lacked food. Why did you let them do this to you?' "

Since the operation, Maria Diaz says, she has become nervous, *rare.* That's the word she uses: *rare.* "Now the child is three years old and I think I should be pregnant now, according to the pattern I'd established, but I can't. I go to the doctor every month for the nerves. For a year, I was sick with the wound—the scar that did not close. . . . I feel very bad and I want more people to know this so it won't happen to someone else."

"She's a brave woman," Antonia Herandez tells me later. "It's dangerous for her to speak up with her husband not yet fully immigrated. We could have had many, many more plaintiffs on the lawsuit, but the women were afraid of the Immigration and Naturalization Service. . . ."

About the lawsuit: Mrs. Diaz, Mrs. Acosta, and nine other Los Angeles area Chicanos are suing USC-L.A. County Medical Center, certain John Doe doctors (the women do not know the names of their sterilizers), the State of California, and the U. S. Department of Health, Education and Welfare. These women, with one exception, were all sterilized at County; they claim the practice of pushing these operations on the poor is a part of national sterilization epidemic they want stopped. The plaintiffs demand a new set of self-enforcing federal guidelines that will make coercion more difficult; consent forms in English and Spanish; consent forms written on a reading-level comprehensible to all women; conformity by California with the 1974 federal ban on sterilization of women under the age of twenty-one—the California limit is eighteen. What's more, the women are suing for financial damages. "We are asking for money," explains Antonia Hernandez, "because money is the only thing that doctors understand."

To prove her point, Hernandez hands me the legal documents of *Dolores Madrigal et al.* v. *E. J. Quilligan, Director of Obstetrics at USC-L.A. County et al.* These documents are so filled with pain that even the cold, objective tone of legalese cannot blunt the suffering that has obviously occurred:

Maria Hustado: "I do not remember the doctor telling me anything about tubalization. All that I remember is after the doctor injected my dorsal, spinal cord, he told me, 'Mama sign here. No more babies. Sign here.' "

Maria E. Figueroa: ". . . A doctor asked me if I wanted to have a tubal ligation. . . . I told the doctor that I did not want to be sterilized since my husband and I planned to have another child. . . . I was groggy from the drugs, exhausted from the labor, as well as from the doctor's constant pressuring. Finally, I told the doctor, 'Okay, if it's a boy, go ahead and do it. . . . My daughter Elizabeth was born by caesarean operation. While my husband was visiting me in the medical center, the doctor came to my bed and informed me that he had performed a tubal ligation on me."

Reading through the papers, one begins to perceive a pattern. Few of the plaintiffs spoke more than minimal English; they were Mexican and poor. The women were pressured into the procedure during the stress and agony of childbirth—a time when they could not possibly make an informed decision about an irreversible operation. *Even* if they had spoken the language. *Even* if they had been given all the facts.

A few unadvertised, unpleasant bits of information about tubal ligation: the death rate is significantly higher than for long term use of the IUD or the Pill. According to the Health Research Group study on "Surgical Sterilization: Present Abuses and Proper Regulation," the death rate on hysterectomy (often improperly used for sterilization) is 1,000 deaths per million; for tubal ligation, 1,000 per million; for laparoscopic tubals, the mortality rate goes down to 300 per million. According to that same study, the death rate for IUD is nine per million women; for pills, it is thirty-one per million. It should be said, however, that we still do not know all the long-term effects of use of the birth-control pill. There has yet to be a full generation of women who have used oral contraception for their full fertility-life. It is possible that ten or twenty years from now we may see a cancer epidemic among Pill users; the evidence still isn't in. But the point is this: based on what we *now* know, as dangerous as the Pill is, it seems to be safer than sterilization.

Once a woman has had a tubal, she must consider herself permanently, irrevocably sterile. Legal remedies for coercion are rare, expensive, and generally unavailable to the poor. Besides—no judicial award can ever compensate a woman for her stolen fertility; a woman involuntarily sterilized suffers many of the permanent psychological impairments of a rape victim. Between 10 and 30 percent of all women who voluntarily agree to it later regret the operation. Though a costly operation for reversal exists, it is successful in only 10 to 20 percent of all cases.

But the doctors told the women little of this. Consent forms were pushed at women in the throes of labor—women who were drugged, women who were under anesthesia. Sometimes, the physicians even disposed of the minimum legal nicety of a signed consent form; they simply cut without permission. And, if one is to believe the sworn affidavits of eleven women, the L. A. County obstetrics staff, in its zeal to sterilize, was dispensing medical misinformation as if it were aspirin. Though tubal ligation is one of the few operations that is 99 percent elective, an unusual number of Chicanas were told that they would die if they did not submit. Some patients were misled into thinking their tubes could be "untied" at some time in the future. Others were told that there were legal or medical limits on the number of caesareans that patients were permitted—an untruth to say the least. As the late Dr. Alan F. Guttmacher, a leading American authority on contraception, explained: "By tradition the American obstetrician is prepared to sterilize any patient who desires it at the time of the third caesarean section. How magic number three was derived is unknown to me."

"It would be a mistake to think of the situation at L.A. County as an isolated fluke. This is happening all over the country," asserts Dr. Bernard "Buddy" Rosenfeld, the thirty-three-year-old co-author of the Ralph Nader-sponsored Health Research Group study on forced sterilization. To prove his point, the two of us sneak our way past security at USC—L.A. County's dormitory for house staff. Rosenfeld wears his medical whites—he is an MD; I wear a most unjournalistic pair of dungarees. We knock on doors, introduce ourselves as researchers doing a "rough study" on informed consent practices, and ask interns and residents to tell us what they have witnessed at *other* institutions where they have trained. None of the physicians we speak with know that I am a reporter, that I am making careful notes after each interview, that their comments will see print.

Rosenfeld and I are looking for two things: we want to know whether the L. A. County house staff, recent arrivals from some of the ranking medical schools around the country, have seen abuses similar to those that have occurred here. We also want to know whether the 1974 federal guidelines against coercive sterilization are being enforced. Those regulations specifically ban sterilizations on women under twenty-one; prohibit operations on women less than seventy-two hours after they have signed consent forms; require a careful counseling procedure so that patients truly learn that the operation is permanent and that there are other birth-control choices.

For Buddy Rosenfeld, our visit to County is an odd kind of homecoming. In 1973, he was an obstetrics resident here. Then, when he began to raise the issue of forced sterilization with the house staff; when he began speaking with newspaper reporters; when he signed his name to the Health Research Group study;

when he made all the noise that led to The Big Scandal—well, *then,* Rosenfeld was "not renewed" for his second year of training. Dr. Rosenfeld's training remains incomplete. He supports his family by working the midnight shift at half a dozen private hospital emergency rooms around Los Angeles. E. J. Quilligan, Chairman of the L.A. County department of obstetrics and gynecology, says, "Rosenfeld was evaluated and found to be an unsatisfactory doctor."

"Nonsense," says Dr. Rosenfeld in reply. "My evaluations were above average. Besides, I think what I did was in the best tradition of medicine. I mean, I helped curb some terrible suffering. Yeah, maybe I did ruin a promising career, but L. A. County is now one of the cleanest institutions in the country."

Apparently. But that is hardly saying much. Judging from our "rough study" interviews, forced sterilization is a part of academic training at more than a few major teaching hospitals around the nation. The doctors we interview seem to accept coercion as an everyday fact of medical life—few of them are even aware of the moral significance of what they have witnessed. For instance, a friendly intern who has just completed studies at Wayne State Medical School in Detroit, recounts the most remarkable things in perfect innocence:

"Most of our patient population was black, inner city," he explains. "We had a lot of young girls come in . . . thirteen and sixteen and they'd have two or three children. In those cases, we'd ask 'em, often when they were in labor, if they wanted tubal ligations. There were *so many* young girls and most of them had a real low mentality. We'd tell them about birth control and they wouldn't take it. It would get some of the residents really mad.

"With sixteen year olds, you needed the parents' permission. *That* usually wasn't hard to get. The parents weren't in labor. Some of the parents said, 'No.' They liked having the babies around. Sterilization was offered to women in labor no matter what their age. Those over eighteen you didn't need the parents' permission. . . ."

"You mean you sterilized *sixteen year olds?*" asks an incredulous intern from Milwaukee, who has been sitting on the side, taking the discussion in.

"Well, yeah . . . if they had two kids. But we didn't do many abortions, though. The residents didn't like to do them. You know, you look at a fetus and you see it is a formed human being, so we didn't do many. There was beginning to be a whole lot of trouble. Detroit's blacks, they're really very anti-white. They were having all these meetings about 'genocide.' "

A similarly pleasant doctor up the hallway claimed his training institution, Jefferson Davis Hospital—Baylor Medical School in Houston, Texas, was a good deal less discriminating:

"Our patient population was 80 percent black, 15 percent Chicano and 5 percent what you'd call poor white trash," he twangs in a voice of pure honey. "There wasn't any racism there. No more than here. If a resident wanted to practice doing a laparoscopic [tubal ligation], he'd push it, sure. There was a basic social pressure that three children were enough. If a woman came in with two children and wanted a tubal, we would try to talk her out of it. But if a woman came in with five children, we'd sell the operation—sure. Women were approached in clinic and sometimes during labor, sure. We'd ask a woman in labor, if her chart wasn't available. . . ."

An intern who had done his medical school rounds at UCLA—Cedars of Lebanon Hospital in Los Angeles: "I did see instances of women in labor being asked. I didn't see any prejudice against Mexicans or blacks *per se,* but the ward patients weren't given as much information on sterilization as the private patients. Often an intern would say, 'I want to do a tubal.' That was a big influence in prompting them to do it—they wanted to get another tubal under their belt."

"Why are women approached about sterilization during labor?" I inquire. "It seems so unfair."

"It's expedient," the intern explains. "Although it's like asking a drowning person, do they want to get out of the water."

A female intern in a nearby room had recently completed obstetrics rounds at Riverside General Hospital in nearby Orange

County. The patients there were also Mexican. "I didn't see any *real* pushing but it was often suggested after labor," she commented dryly. "The doctors would say, 'Do you want to go through this again?' Mostly, the doctor's individual philosophy towards sterilization had a lot to do with whether or not a patient was approached."

"You don't consider asking a woman about the procedure after labor, pushing?" Rosenfeld asks.

"Not really," she replies. "Now when I was down in Nicaragua, *there* we pushed. People would come in with nine children and they didn't have food and we pushed them."

A pediatric intern, formerly at New York's Bellevue Hospital: "There was a large Puerto Rican population and I think a lot of women didn't know the full consequences of what was happening to them. There was a language problem. Many of the women thought their tubes could be untied."

A former medical student from the University of Chicago, where the patient population is primarily black: "No one ever said to a woman, 'We don't trust you with taking the Pill,' it would be presented very *positively.* 'This is the best thing for you. This will be the easiest thing for us.' Mostly, we'd approach women with large families and we'd tell them this was the best solution. We would explain the world population problem."

An intern previously at Barnes Hospital, St. Louis: "Whether or not a patient was approached positively about sterilization depended on the doctor's own approach. A woman on welfare with a large family was more likely to be approached earlier than a woman not on welfare. No one was pushed, though."

Another intern, formerly at UCSF–San Francisco General Hospital: "It was always explained—*if* the patient asked, yes, she'd be told it was permanent. If there was a big rush, the staff wouldn't bother. There was concern by some of the students that minority groups were getting pushed, so the hospital became very careful. They're slick now. Although official policy has changed, the attitudes of the doctors didn't. They became slicker at talking patients into tubals. Tubals are way up and the birthrate is way down."

For three nights, Rosenfeld and I wandered through the bleak hallways of the house staff dorm—a building which one intern jocularly described as "decorated in a style of early hysterectomy." We spoke with twenty-three doctors. Nine of them had either witnessed coercion or worked under conditions that could easily lead to it: hard-selling, dispensing of misinformation, approaching women during labor, offering sterilization at a time of stress, on-the-job racism. At L. A. County, we found four doctors who had worked at institutions where the operation was softly, slickly sold. Only four physicians could honestly and unequivocally state that they had trained at hospitals that were clean. Six doctors gave us answers that amounted to "no opinion." Of those six, three had trained at Catholic institutions where sterilization is strictly prohibited; the other three were USC–L. A. County trained. "I didn't see anything," said one L. A. County doctor defensively. Another L. A. County man provided us with the most bone-chilling statement of all: "I guess the problem we have here is a problem of philosophies. Most of the patients are Mexican and they have a different philosophy from *us.*"

"At one major teaching hospital, the Women's Hospital Los Angeles County Medical Center, the following increase in the number of sterilization procedures occurred in the two-year interval between July 1968 and July 1970: Elective hysterectomy—742 percent increase; elective tubal ligation—470 percent; tubal ligation after delivery—151 percent."

—*Health Research Group Report on Surgical Sterilization, October 1973*

"In 1968, my own mother went into County to give birth to my baby sister. The doctors told her that she would have to get her tubes tied because if she had another baby, she would die. For the longest time, we were very worried. But then, we went to our own family doctor and he told us there was nothing wrong with her."

—*Antonia Hernandez, Attorney, Model Cities Law Center*

* * *

There is a wounded innocence to Dr. Edward James Quilligan's manner as he shifts about restlessly during an interview in his textbook-lined office at L. A. County Women's Hospital. Before this sterilization exposé broke, his was one of the great medical success stories: a distinguished career; more than sixty professional publications; membership on nearly every important policy-setting council within his specialty; the chairmanship of the Obstetrics and Gynocology Department at USC–L. A. County Medical Center, one of the three top obstetrics residencies in the country. And now he must face lawsuits and accusations and suspicious journalists.

"We have tried in every instance to comply with what we thought was good medical practice," Dr. Quilligan says. He is a fiftyish man; bald and heavy. "In my opinion, there is no physician on staff here who wants to sterilize people for welfare reason or other reasons. I *know* these doctors and I've worked with them and I feel they're solely interested in the patient's interest."

As for the Health Research Group's study on sterilization he grimaces at the mere mention of it. "Yes, certainly, their statistics are correct," he says. "I don't have the figures in front of me, but I don't think the total ever got above 5 or 6 percent of all who came in. This was not a high sterilization rate compared to the rest of the country. You would get the feeling from the article that we sterilized everyone who walked in, when that just isn't the case. We *turn down* a lot of patients for sterilization!"

"How do you manage that?" I inquire.

"Well, let's just say we counsel them so that they don't want it," he replies.

That's a candid admission; It means that Dr. Quilligan understands that the type of counseling a patient receives will determine her ultimate decision. And at L. A. County, until most recently, counseling was a haphazard business, dependent on circumstance and the whim of the attending doctor.

Dr. Quilligan is asked about Bernard Rosenfeld, who has been conducting "informal studies" of physicians' attitudes for some year now; Rosenfeld's interviews have shown that the L. A. house staff has witnessed a good deal of coercion during training. "Most of the patients that are sterilized are seen by these residents here," asserts Quilligan, "and *they* don't tell *me* that there's a lot of coercive sterilization going on. And they object strongly to Dr. Rosenfeld going around saying that they have."

"So if there is very little forcible sterilization going on," I interject, "then why are so many women suing—here and elsewhere? What's their motive?"

Quilligan looks at me coldly. "It's very difficult to understand a patient's motives when she's changed her mind," he explains. "Personally, I'm just anxious to see the patient get what she wants. Now, *that* can get you into trouble because some patients will say, 'I don't ever want to have another baby!' And the sympathetic doctor, feeling he's done his best, sterilizes her. She may go home and change her mind. Or she may find her husband is angry. Suddenly, the doctor is the bad guy."

Bad guy or good guy? Something unfortunate was happening at L. A. County because on February 22, 1974, Dr. Quilligan was compelled to issue a memo to his impeccable staff: "Effective immediately, patients will *not* be approached for the first time concerning sterilization when they are in labor."

Nevertheless, Dr. Quilligan wants me to know about all the fine improvements that have been made on his service: "In early 1974, the HEW guidelines came out stating that certain criteria had to be followed if federally funded hospitals were to maintain their grants. There should be a waiting period and the minimum age should be twenty-one. We abstracted those guidelines and put them out as law, here."

Not quite. In December 1974, Robert Kistler, an investigative reporter for the *Los Angeles Times,* telephoned Quilligan to ask him if he was complying with the then seven-month-old HEW orders. The doctor answered that he could not recall seeing them. So Kistler read the rules to Dr. Quilligan, who according to the December 3, 1974, *Los Angeles Times* commented: "Well, I would have to agree with that; in some areas we're probably not following them at the present time."

Eventually, County did move into full compliance with federal regulations. There is now a special sterilization counseling clinic, one of few in the country. "What we're doing," Dr. Quilligan explains, "is making sure that every patient goes through the counseling clinic; they have to take a test at the end of it to make sure they know what's happening." A group of specially trained female counselors has been hired. "They can have little rap sessions with the girls and ask questions," he says.

Finally, Dr. Quilligan wants us to know what a trial this has been for the hospital. "The thing that's bothered me most," he complains, "is how the adverse publicity has affected our patients. . . . They come here in great fear, feeling that we're going to grab them and sterilize them—which is the furthest thing from our mind."

It can't happen here. That is the defensive response most people have when I tell them the L. A. county story. Interestingly, USC–L. A. County Medical Center seems now to be one of the few institutions in the United States actually conforming to law. According to a study made by Elissa Krauss for the American Civil Liberties Union, few major teaching hospitals are following the 1974 HEW orders. In November 1974, when the guidelines were nearly half a year old, Krauss sent questionnaires to the heads of OB-GYN departments of 154 ranking teaching hospitals. Less than a third of the queried chairmen granted the ACLU the courtesy of a reply. And of the fifty-one respondents who did answer the poll, one in three gave replies that showed conformity with the letter and spirit of the Federal guidelines. "Thirty-six major teaching hospitals are in non-compliance with Federal regulations on sterilization," said the ACLU report. "These institutions—plus another twelve hospitals responding to this questionnaire—should be subject to immediate withdrawal of funding because they are in complete non-compliance. . . ." But will those hospitals lose their federal monies? Not likely. The Department of Health, Education, and Welfare has yet to move against a single institution named by the ACLU.

It can't happen to me. That is the response of educated middle-class women when they hear about forced sterilization. Not true. Doctors who learn to push sterilization on indigent patients during training will do the same in private practice. There is profit in it. A gynecologist earns nothing for dispensing condoms or the birth-control pill. The bill for an IUD insertion is rarely more than $100. However, average fees for a tubal ligation begin at $300. Elective hysterectomy is $600—plus. I remember that honey-voiced gynecologist-to-be from Houston whom we spoke with one summer evening in the L. A. County dorm. His eyes gleamed when he spoke of hysterectomy: "In Houston, a lot of well-to-do women would come in and they'd want hysterectomies because their friends had them. Maybe the indications weren't so strong, but why shouldn't we take her womb if it makes her feel better?" Several of my friends have recently submitted to tubal ligations; the doctors call it "Band-Aid surgery." Yet, one study showed 1,594 serious complications and nineteen deaths out of 63,845 operations surveyed.* My friends are middle-class and well educated. Nevertheless, the same medical practice that sells tubals to the poor under the stress of labor, sells my affluent friends the lie of Band-Aid simplicity for a dangerous operation.

Ultimately, we are all, as Guadalupe Acosta understood, helpless in the face of a medical system that has little accountability. It was Mrs. Acosta, of all the protagonists, who had the sharpest focus on what had happened. I once asked her if she thought the physicians at L. A. County were racist. "I don't know about things like that," she replied, clutching at her two babies. "You go to the hospital so sick, so dependent, one doesn't ask questions."

Few of us do.

---

*As more laparoscopic tubals are done by doctors, the safer they'll become. The danger is in going to a physician who has little experience with the procedure. But even when safety isn't a factor, there are many harmful side-effects to this "Band-Aid" operation.

Rita Arditti

HAVE YOU EVER WONDERED ABOUT THE MALE PILL?

How will men feel about receiving a capsule? Will they give up this one stronghold of male ego, even if temporarily? Will they voluntarily agree to sterilize themselves, as nine million women Pill users in this country are doing every day? Or will they balk?

—*From Now to Zero: Fertility, Contraception and Abortion in America,* by Leslie and Charles Westoff, 1971

One of the fallacies that has permeated our minds on the topic of reproduction is the belief, conscious and unconscious, that women are the reproductive units of the species. The fertility of the male is rarely taken into consideration, as if women reproduced by themselves. We forget that we are fertile only during a limited period of our lives, between adolescence and menopause, while males are fertile all through their lives. Moreover, women are fertile only during a certain portion of the menstrual cycle. If we think in terms of male fertility and focus on the male as the target for birth control, we begin to get a feeling of the exploitative framework on which birth-control ideology has been based. The language used in the contraceptive literature gives us a clue to the frame of mind of the scientists involved: "executive hormones" is a common term used to refer to male hormones; an important gland like the pituitary is called the "master" gland. The concern for females regards their appearance and not their health: ". . . females, in the absence of their sex hormones, lose their soft smoothness and become wrinkled."[1]

As I've pointed out in another article,[2] "scientific" rationalizations are offered for the fact that many more contraceptive agents are being developed for use by females than for males. *Contraceptive Technology* lists 29 potential methods to regulate fertility in the female, 9 for the male and 6 for use by either male or female. The argument is put forward that females have many more steps in their reproductive system which are amenable to manipulation: the maturation of the egg, ovulation itself, the transport of the egg, fertilization, transport of the fertilized egg, etc. According to the established viewpoint, the male reproductive system offers much less with which to work. Only four steps can be interfered with: the production of sperm cells, the storing of sperm, its transport and the chemical constitution of the seminal fluid. However, this argument does not tell the whole story, and it is easy to construct a case for males being the ideal target for contraception if one cared to do so. . . . The fact is that their reproductive system is less complex and a concentrated research effort aimed at understanding one or two areas could conceivably bring more results. Males do not have a cycle, and complications arising from changing levels of hormones would be avoided. Their sex glands, placed outside the body, are more accessible and easier to work on than women's organs.[3] In statistical terms, male birth control is an ideal method because males can produce as many children as the number of women they have intercourse with, while women are restricted to about 1.4 pregnancies per year. (And so on.)

The condom, the only method of reversible contraception available for males, is definitely underplayed in the United States. It is the number 1 method of contraception in England, Japan and Sweden. In Japan, the condom industry has taken care in presenting the condom as a device that will enhance sexual pleasure: condoms are made in a variety of shapes and colors: light blue, violet, pink, forms ranging from plain to "reservoir tipped," "two-stage pagoda nipple end," "sponge pattern with narrow neck," etc. Research is done on ways of perfuming it, adding hormones for the female in the exterior and perfecting the packaging to make it practically noiseless.[4] Some of these extras may be harmful for women (adding hormones), others are plainly absurd. In this country it is hardly promoted by physicians, compared to the Pill and the IUDs, and in fact, its use dropped considerably in the sixties with the advent of the Pill.[5] It has an image associated with prostitution and secretive sexual relations and 22 states have laws which restrict its sale, distribution, advertising and display.[6] The condom is a highly efficient method (used in combination with a foam it is as effective as the Pill) and it offers the best available protection against veneral disease. It is unique in that it is totally free of side effects, its use is easy to understand and it offers visible proof of effectiveness immediately after use. It is still one of the better available methods.

"Loss of libido" is one of the main concerns expressed by researchers in the area of male contraception. Very few meaningful studies have been done on this issue, and it is hard to understand what the concern is exactly about. Observations on rats, hamsters and rabbits are difficult to extrapolate to human males and the issue is approached in a vague and inconclusive fashion. "Loss of libido" is almost never taken into consideration when dealing with female contraception, the obvious bias being that women do not have anything to lose since the "active" force in sexual intercourse stems from the male. "Loss of libido" might very well express psychological resistance and depression arising from the fact of being the target of birth control, a role that most men are not socialized into. A recent study suggests that this might indeed be the case: in an experiment where males were taking a contraceptive pill, two of the males reported "loss of libido" during a period in which they were taking a placebo pill containing a sugar (they thought they were receiving a birth-control agent). After an initial period of 8 weeks (3 weeks taking the placebo and 5 weeks taking the contraceptive pill), their libido returned to normalcy. In the same experiment, other males reported increased libido, which may have been connected to general relief and less anxiety in the area of sexual intercourse, because of the diminished probability of pregnancy for their partners.[7]

Regarding "loss of libido," vasectomies, a surgical procedure in which the two vas deferens are cut and tied off, are invariably presented with the accompanying theme that "masculinity" will not be affected and sexual relations will actually improve. "The atmosphere in our house has become a relaxed and happy one. Our own children, our pupils and our careers have benefited too. As for our sex life, we both can only say—WOW," writes a couple to the surgeon who performed a vasectomy on the husband.[8] Although vasectomies have increased from a few thousand in the fifties to a peak of 850,000 in 1971,[9] this is not a method that is going to appeal to the majority of males, and the term "vasectomy revolution" flamboyantly used by the "experts" in the field is hardly justified. The men most likely to seek a vasectomy are married ("vasectomy couples" is a common term in the literature), have 2 or 3 children and are in their middle thirties. It is certainly not a method that is appropriate for single people who are not interested in having children during a certain phase of their lives.[10]

Even though a particular vasectomy may be successfully reversed, vasectomies should be considered a permanent sterilization procedure. Research on clips, valves and plugs that will allow for a "turn-on, turn-off" situation is being carried on,[11] but there is *no* way to know in advance how effective they will be for each individual case. For one thing, vasectomies may have a permanent sterilization effect even if the vas deferens is recanalized and anatomical integrity has been achieved. This is because antibodies against the sperm may have been produced as a result of the occlusion of the ducts, and the immune system of the male will now continue producing these antibodies which will render the male sterile. There are also speculations that the anti-sperm antibodies might not be absolutely specific to the sperm. If that were the case "side effects" could arise in vasectomized males.[12]

Feeding on the male's fear of loss of fertility, commercial sperm banks have sprung up in the last few years in different parts of the country. Sperm banks were forcefully proposed in the sixties by Herman Muller, an American scientist who won the Nobel Prize in 1947 for his work on radiation and genetic material. Muller envisioned the banks to be a solution to the problems of humanity; he truly believed that out of conscious selection of germinal material, a society will arise where only the highest human qualities would exist. He spoke of "worthy genetic material," "superior lot of children," and very appropriately "germinal capital." His hope was that "normal" people would be happy to raise children of "truly outstanding and eminently worthy personalities" so that those distinguished citizens (i.e., men) would be free of the dilemma of having to raise their families or devoting their energies to other causes: ". . . their germinal material would tend to be sought by others, if not in their own generation, then later, and to a degree more or less in proportion to their achievements. Thus they would be free to give their best services in whatever directions they elected."[13]

For $80 to open an account and an annual fee of $18, a customer is directed to a small room with a comfortable armchair and pornographic magazines. His ejaculate is examined, diluted with a glycerol preservative and stored at $-196°C$ in liquid nitrogen. He is now a depositor at the bank which is also interested in buying sperm at $20 per ejaculate to sell to couples in which the male is sterile. Idant Company first opened a branch in suburban Baltimore, followed by a New York one in December 1971. It envisions banks in 20 major cities and plans to expand internationally (Japan, England). Genetic Laboratories, Inc. of Minnesota, opened in 1970 and has banks in 5 major cities. Although not enough data exist to indicate that frozen sperm can retain its fertilizing power after 16 months, the banks anticipate indefinite preservation of the sperm. No regulations in any state govern their operations.[14]

Who is going to use the banks? Obviously men who regard their semen as truly special. For example: a member from a prominent family from Minnesota deposited sperm in the bank to make sure that his family line will be continued in case his only son turns out to be sterile. The bank advocates are, not surprisingly, concerned to show that high-quality offspring will result for their depositors and are explicit about the results: "I shall show you a photograph of one of our older children born of frozen semen. He is a 16-year-old boy, 6 feet tall, in excellent health and an A student."[15]

The mere idea of a sperm bank tells clearly what, in our culture, seems worth preserving. But not all sperms are equally precious. It is very unlikely that the banks will open accounts in Kerala or Gujarat, where "festivals" and "vasectomy camps" have been held and tens of thousands of poor Indian males have been sterilized in a few months attracted by small amounts of money, some food or clothes for them or their families.[16] In my view, sperm banks have eugenic connotations and reinforce individualistic and competitive attitudes connected with parenting and family issues.

§ Research for Male Contraceptives

In 1970, when the Ford Foundation awarded Alan Jones at the University of Manchester, England a grant for research on male anti-fertility chemicals, Jones commented that this type of research had to be done at universities because the drug companies have a "repugnance" toward the idea of tampering with male fertility.[17] Although a variety of compounds have been tried on male animals, very few chemicals have been tested on human males.

A fact that is easily overlooked is that the testes (like the ovaries) depend upon the pituitary in order to produce sperm cells and sex hormones. The pituitary produces FSH* and LH** both in men and women. In men, FSH stimulates sperm production and LH stimulates the production of testosterone (sex hormone). It follows that sperm production can be stopped by stopping the production of FSH. Hormonal contraceptives could be as effective in males as they are in females. Testosterone has been tried as a male contra-

---

*FSH = follicle stimulating hormone.
**LH = luteinizing hormone.

ceptive and it does suppress sperm production. But there are indications that increasing the level of testosterone might stimulate cell growth in the prostate and increase the chance of blood clotting.[18] In fact, the use of hormones in males will probably give rise to side effects similar to those suffered daily by women who are taking the Pill. In 1973, a brief report in an English medical journal presented a case of pulmonary embolism in a man who had been taking an oral contraceptive. The patient, a 47-year-old transvestite had been taking on his own initiative one tablet of "Gynovlar 21" daily for 25 days before being admitted to the hospital.[19]

A combination of hormones, an *estrogen* to inhibit sperm production supplemented with an *androgen* that will deal with the eventual "loss of libido," is the current approach to male hormonal contraception. Also, instead of trying hormones that are relatively unknown and for which human testing will have to be delayed until toxicological testing is carried out on animals, it makes sense to try hormonal compounds that have already been approved for sale to treat a variety of conditions. For instance, a group of compounds containing a combination of an androgen with an estrogen is currently used in the treatment of osteoporosis in men (a condition in which the bone tissue decreases in density and there is great susceptivity to fractures). Initial studies on men with osteoporosis receiving the hormones had shown that these men had stopped producing sperm. The hormones were then tried on healthy male volunteers who took a capsule twice a day with their meals. By the 63rd day of hormone treatment, the number of sperms produced was significantly decreased and so was the motility of the sperm (100 million sperms or more per ejaculate is considered normal). After the treatment was stopped the sperm number became normal and as motile as before the treatment. It was during the course of this experiment that two of the men reported "loss of libido" while they were taking a placebo pill, *before* the hormones were administered![20] The idea of testing for contraceptive effects compounds that have already been on the market for a long time, and for which no extensive animal testing would be necessary, is a good one and it might give impetus to hormonal research.

Of the nonhormonal compounds tried, the most promising were

the *diamines,* a series of compounds that totally inhibited sperm production without interfering with the sex hormones. Work with these compounds was abandoned after the discovery that when the subjects ingested alcohol, side effects appeared. There was also concern about a higher occurrence of hepatitis. It now seems that these experiments will be re-evaluated and that further work to establish an effective dose that will minimize toxicity will be undertaken.[21]

A new chemical has attracted attention in the last couple of years: *5-thio-D-glucose,* which interferes successfully with tumors and spermatogenesis in mice. It is not clear why interference with the utilization of sugar would inhibit spermatogenesis, but diabetic men have been reported to have a decreased sperm count and their sperm is less motile. This compound is not scheduled for clinical trials in the near future since the scientist working with it (Roy L. Whistler at Purdue University, Indiana) is currently reported to be "out of funds."[22] But this compound does look interesting and it might provide some hope.*

Reports have appeared linking high temperature to intrascrotal infertility. In some cases a two-week regime of 30° cold baths has caused an increase in sperm count and motility of the sperm, but clinical trials have not yet been carried out and the state of this research is quite preliminary.[23]

Other chemicals have been tried in the last few years, but though they are effective in stopping sperm production, they all seem to have toxic effects and may cause genetic damage. It is important to keep in mind that many substances effective as anti-fertility agents have proved to be mutagens. This can cause genetic damage to the cells that survive the treatment, and the damage could be transmitted to the progeny when fertility is restored. In other words, damaged sperms could still fertilize an egg and as a result an abnormal embryo could develop. This might lead to a miscarriage or to the birth of an infant with a genetic defect.

*Being an analog of sugar, it could be less toxic than other chemicals. Also, this is the first time that a chemical other than a hormone or an alkylating agent has been shown to interfere reversibly with spermatogenesis.

§ Other Considerations

The issues involved in male contraception go well beyond biological problems and technological matters. On the one hand, there is the reluctance of the pharmaceutical companies to invest in areas that might turn out to be unprofitable. In 1962, the introduction of the Kefauver-Harris Amendment to the Food and Drug Act (under which the FDA derives its authority) caused the number of new drugs to drop dramatically. Research expenditures in the area of contraception have been greatly reduced and it is likely that there will not be many new birth-control agents in the next decade. The government regulatory requirements have been singled out as the chief reason why so many drug companies have completely ceased all research toward new contraceptives. It costs about $10 million to develop an agent with a new mechanism of action over a span of 10 to 14 years. If the results from the tests in animals are controversial, a complete loss of the investment can result. This is the reason why drug companies are stopping this type of research and for the next few years we will get only new formulations or different delivery systems for already existing contraceptives.[24]

On the other hand, the mere mention of male contraception is anxiety-producing for many people since it reminds them of the fact that males and females are biologically equally responsible for reproduction. Sexual programming in our culture demands from the male suppression of feelings and extreme emphasis on "achievement." Male contraception raises fears of "loss of libido" and castration. Emphasis on "manliness" and performance do not allow for rational and caring communication to take place around the issues of sexual intercourse and birth control. It is obvious that the re-education of men around this topic is crucial, both for the development and acceptance of new agents and for the better use of existing ones. For instance, most sex education and health courses dealing with birth control are directed toward the female. Teenage birth control means birth-control methods for young girls. Among those teenage boys who receive no education about their bodies and contraception are the future doctors and researchers who will continue to ignore men's responsibility in contraceptive affairs. Also, it is easier to experiment on women than on men, since Planned Parenthood clinics and individual obstetricians can reach vast numbers of females, who, in need of contraception, will be "appropriate material" for clinical trials. Thus the cycle continues.

The attitudes of women toward male contraception are themselves varied and give an indication of the tensions to which most women's sexual lives are subject. Many females feel that even if male birth-control methods were available, they would not welcome their partners using them since errors or lapses of responsibility would result in their becoming pregnant. They do not feel relaxed or comfortable with the idea of being dependent on somebody else for their contraceptive needs. It is clear that lack of trust between the sexes can render the best contraceptive totally ineffective.

Effective contraception can exist in a very oppressive context. As pointed out before, a typical male-dominated society like Japan relies on the condom as the number 1 method of birth control and that does not guarantee any improvement in the position of women. Dehumanized sexual intercourse can coexist with any technical breakthrough and the most violent rape can be performed with the ideal contraceptive. Consciousness raising around the issues of sexuality, birth control and male participation have to go hand in hand with the scientific and technological work to develop contraceptive methods for the male. Men must share the responsibilities and risks that up to now have been born by women alone.

For the next few years, though, the sexual politics of the research establishment plus the profit motive of the drug industry makes it very unlikely that we will be presented with a safe, simple and effective contraceptive for *either* sex.

Claudia Dreifus

ABORTION: THIS PIECE IS FOR REMEMBRANCE

January, 1977. The human memory is painfully short. I sit here in my New York living room watching television news. On my color screen is Joseph Califano, the man Jimmy Carter has designated as Secretary of Health, Education and Welfare.*Mr. Califano is before the Senate Finance Committee presenting his views on policy matters. How does Califano feel about abortion? Well, he's opposed to it personally, but the law's the law and the Supreme Court has spoken. So, how does Califano, who will be administering the Medi-

*August 10, 1977. Since this was first written, the Right-to-Life movement has scored new victories. Califano, backed by President Carter, succeeded in obtaining congressional passage of a second Hyde Amendment to the 1977 HEW appropriations banning Medicaid funds for abortion; the Supreme Court, going back on its earlier proabortion decision, has ruled that states do not have to pay for abortions for the indigent unless they choose to; U. S. Federal Judge Francis Dooling has lifted the preliminary restraining order on enforcement of the Hyde Amendment, in effect since last year. As this book goes to press, Medicaid abortions are now nonreimbursable in most states, "except where the lives of mothers are endangered." Califano has even ruled out abortion in cases of rape and incest. In New York, however, Governor Hugh Carey, a Catholic, has resisted the pressure of antiabortionists by continuing state payments for the procedure. Since Carter's ascendency to the presidency, all three branches of the federal government have become activists in their opposition to abortion. The Right-to-Lifers' next goal is to eliminate abortion for all women, rich and poor.

caid program, feel about the use of public funds to finance the abortions of the indigent? Well . . . um . . . he's against using federal money to pay for the abortions of anyone, rich or poor, he mumbles.

I listen with astonishment. Certainly the Honorable Secretary knows that only poor women can use Medicaid. Certainly he knows that the attempt to cut the indigent off from abortion is the first step in making it unavailable to all. I keep thinking about how in 1976 Congress passed the Hyde Amendment, ordering the end of Medicaid payments for abortion. For a week or so—before a federal court ruled this new statute discriminatory, inner-city hospitals were flooded with emergencies of a kind they had not seen since the days before the 1973 Supreme Court decision: perforated uteruses, uterine hemorrhaging, self-induced death. Someone should tell Mr. Califano a few facts of life: women always have, always will, abort pregnancies they cannot afford to bring to term. The question is safety and sanity. The question is a woman's right to live her own life.

As I watch Mr. Califano doing his political footwork, I keep wondering about how we've forgotten what times were like before the Supreme Court ruled that the right to terminate pregnancy is the right to privacy. Memory is so short. If it were not, there would be a mass movement to oppose the cruelties of the Right-to-Life movement. I wonder why the hundreds of thousands of women who've benefited from liberalized abortion haven't spoken out in their own self-defense? I wonder too, about Catholic women who've availed themselves of legal abortion by the tens of thousands—why haven't they moved to counter their coreligionists on crusade. Yes, there's an amnesia on this question: no one wants to think back to the time, ten, seven, six years ago when a wandering IUD or a leaky condom meant a woman would confront danger and possible death. But I remember. In my files is a piece I wrote years ago, on an early lawsuit: Three hundred New York females sued New York State to get rid of what was, in 1970, a highly restrictive abortion law. What follows is for remembrance.

Winter, 1970. The sign outside the Washington Square Methodist Church in Manhattan's Greenwich Village read: "Women of the

world unite, you have nothing to lose but your coat hangers!"
Inside the century-old church a hundred spectators and reporters
had assembled to hear the first day of depositions in the Great
Abortion Suit.

About the lawsuit: Three hundred women and a group of feminist lawyers, Florynce Kennedy, Diane Schulder, Carol Lefcourt
and Nancy Stearns, had sued the State of New York, New York
County and Bronx County for the abolition of all restrictions on
abortion. The women complained that prohibitive laws were a
violation of privacy, freedom of religion, equal protection under
the law, and the right to life and liberty. At first the lawsuit was
thought of as nothing more than a legal ploy to focus attention on
a grave problem; no one thought it had a chance to make it through
the mire of the judicial system. But it turned out that the papers
had been well drawn, and word was around town that this lawsuit
might just make constitutional history. Justice Edward Weinfield
of the U. S. District Court for the Southern District of New York
thought the feminist arguments were interesting and he gave the
women their (our) first victory by convening a three-judge panel
to hear the case. Because of Judge Weinfield, there would be a trial
and *Abramowicz v. Lefkowitz* would eventually go to the Supreme
Court; the constitutionality of all abortion laws would, finally, be
questioned.

Things were quite difficult in that winter of 1970. In New York,
only the certain mortality of the mother was enough to provide a
reason for legal termination of a pregnancy. Doctors' committee's
ruled on all applications for abortions, rarely granting them. Only
in Washington, D.C. were abortions slightly more available. In
most of the United States the rich aborted by going abroad; the
poor went to backroom butchers; everyone constantly searched for
the name of a bona-fide doctor who performed the operation illegally.

What made the *Abramowicz* case unique was the fact that
women, for the first time, were deemed to have a special interest
in the legality of abortion laws. But if Judge Weinfield had given
women's rights a victory by hearing the case, he'd given it only a
half-hearted one. When a group of male Catholic physicians de-

manded to be treated as *interveners* in the action, the justice agreed.
(An intervener is a person or group who by virtue of his or her
special interest in a case, can get equal status before the court if he
or she feels the contending parties will not fairly represent his or
her interests.) What's more, Justice Weinfield set the women back
one step further by refusing to hear their testimony in open court.
He was busy, he said, and he preferred both sides to take depositions which he would duly consider. This was a disappointment.
The feminists wanted the judge to hear firsthand the voices of
female victims. And that was why everyone was in the Washington
Square Methodist Church that cold morning, the cameras, the
plantiff-women, the reporters: depositions would be presented publicly. *We, the victims of abortion laws, are here this morning to speak
our bitterness.*

First on the rostrum was Florynce Kennedy, a black attorney
with a fast mind and sharp wit. Ms. Kennedy was about to introduce the plaintiffs to the press when an unidentified ruddy-faced
man burst into the room; standing with him were three prosecutors, defendants in this case: Assistant New York County D. A.
Burton Lipshe, Assistant Bronx County D. A. Marian Belenky,
and Assistant New York State Attorney General Joel Lewittes.
And this red-faced man was screaming: "This is a circus, an absolute circus!"

"And just who are *you,* anyway?" Flo Kennedy demanded.

He was Thomas Ford, father of seven and lawyer for the intervening Catholic physicians, and he was furious: "This is *incredible.*
There are *newspaper* people here. Depositions cannot be taken
under these circumstances." As Ford muttered that he would not
be party to a travesty of justice, the various prosecutors shook their
heads in agreement. Manhattan Assistant D. A. Lipshe stalked
over to the court reporter and demanded his objections be recorded: "To hear these ladies would be nothing more than a waste
of time. They have nothing factually relevant to present to this
case. Besides, anything a woman who's had an abortion would say
should be stricken from the record because of its inflammatory
nature." With that, the D.A.s, the court reporter and the press
exited and headed downtown to the federal courthouse for a talk

with Justice Weinfield. The D.A.s wanted female testimony excluded from the record. Failing in that, they sought a ban on reporters from deposition hearings. I stood in the church lobby somewhat stunned. I was one of the women who was to testify about my illegal abortion and I couldn't believe that my experience was irrelevant.

Downtown at the courthouse, Judge Weinfield offered Solomon-like compromises: the women would be permitted to present whatever witnesses they pleased; the hearings, however, would take place inside the courthouse and thus cameras were banned, but not the press. As a final measure, Justice Weinfield admonished Flo Kennedy to stop calling Thomas Ford unspeakable names.

Testimony began in the federal courthouse with Mr. Ford absent from the proceedings. The plaintiff-women observed this and speculated that Flo Kennedy, who'd called him everything from a "puppet" to a "no-good son-of-a-bitch," had frightened him off the case. No such luck. Mr. Ford, it turned out, had other legal obligations to tend to, and in his place he sent William McHill, another lawyer, who looked and sounded like his twin. "So you're the new lackey for the Friends of the Fetus," Flo Kennedy hissed at McHill. He was speechless.

First to the stand for the feminists was Rabbi David Feldman, bald and fiftyish, the author of *Birth Control and Jewish Law*. It was the rabbi's view that Jewish women were inhibited in the practice of their religion by restrictive abortion laws. "In the Jewish religion," Feldman explained, "we do not consider abortion to be murder. Rather, we are always governed by the needs of the mother."

One of the D.A.s was curious as to why a Jewish woman's freedom of religion was inhibited by the abortion law? "Very often members of my congregation come to me with problems concerning unwanted pregnancy," the rabbi replied. "There's nothing I can do to help them—not legally. I cannot tell them to become criminals."

"Have you ever thought of sending the women to a lawyer?" inquires the same district attorney.

Rabbi Feldman looks at the prosecutor incredulously. "Now what good would *that* do?"

"Well, um . . . uh . . . the lady could get advice on the law."

For three days a parade of feminist demographers, social workers and physicians told what they knew about the human effects of abortion laws. Then, on the fourth day, the real experts were brought in: women who've known the butcher block, women who've known what it meant to be a prisoner of one's body.

Lucy Wilcox* a thirty-seven-year-old free-lance writer, was among the first to speak out. Wilcox was nineteen when she became pregnant; she was a strict Catholic and frightened to death of the idea of abortion. Of course, the father of the child did not want to marry, and so Wilcox went to a religious welfare agency for help. They sent her to Chicago, where she was placed in the home of a wealthy Catholic couple as a housemaid. There she worked six and a half days a week. Twenty-five dollars weekly wage—room and board included. Twelve hours a day of hard, backbreaking labor. Because this "charitable" family provided her with a minimal amount of food, Wilcox spent most of her wages on meals. "I was afraid the child wouldn't be born healthy otherwise." Two weeks before giving birth, Lucy went to the Misericordia Home for Unwed Mothers where she toiled in the laundry before going into a thirty-hour labor.

"The nun who interviewed me intensively after the baby was born informed me that there was a long waiting line to adopt babies like mine—that is, babies whose parents are both Anglo-Saxon and educated, and where at least one parent is Catholic," Lucy Wilcox recalled. "She also intimated that these couples contributed large sums to the Church in return for the babies. The rumor in the hospital was that for babies like mine a couple might contribute as much as a thousand dollars. Having paid $250 to them to deliver this saleable product, I was somewhat annoyed. Ten days later I left the hospital. This was the most painful part of the entire

---

*Not her real name. "Wilcox" is the pseudonym this witness used in Florynce Kennedy and Diane Schulder's book about the lawsuit, *Abortion Rap*.

experience—leaving the baby behind. Like most mothers, I felt it was the most beautiful baby I'd ever seen." When Ms. Wilcox finished her story, even the Friends of the Fetus seemed misty-eyed. The defendant District Attorney remained unmoved. Assistant State Attorney General Joel Lewittes demanded Wilcox's remarks be struck as "irrelevant."

Testimony continued for all that week and on into the next. Grace Paley, the prizewinning author, told of a personal experience that showed how restrictive abortion statutes prevented all women from getting decent medical care. She'd been pregnant and was bleeding heavily. Paley went to her family doctor who accused her, falsely, of trying to self-abort. He refused her medical treatment and caused a life-threatening crisis that resulted in miscarriage.

Another writer, Susan Brownmiller, went to the stand and gave moving testimony of her abortion experience. The first time Brownmiller had gotten pregnant was in 1960. She'd gone to Cuba then, when Havana was still an abortion-mill for North Americans. It was all fairly easy. But when Brownmiller became accidently pregnant in 1963, Cuba was closed to visitors and Ms. Brownmiller had nowhere to turn. She told the court, "I went to my own gynecologist and told him I had no intention of having the baby since I wasn't married," Brownmiller recalled. "He said he couldn't help me at all, but that I would be able to find something because I was a 'resourceful young girl.' When it was over, he promised to put me on the Pill. From there, I called the famous Pennsylvania abortionist Dr. Robert Spencer, who said he wasn't practicing anymore. He gave me, however, the name of a doctor in Baltimore. Spencer said he didn't know much about the guy—just that he might perform an abortion.

"I went to Baltimore and handed the doctor $350. He gave me three blank pieces of paper for my signature. To sign those papers was a fearsome thing, for it seemed that he wanted to absolve himself of any guilt if anything happened to me. He then said he was not going to perform the usual operation on me . . . he was experimenting with a new method . . . and that he would inject needles into my stomach." Brownmiller panicked at the thought of needles in the belly and experimentation; the panic caused the doctor to refund her money and tell her to get lost. "I learned later he was probably experimenting with the saline injection method," she said, "which is only good for women who are five or more months pregnant. I was barely three."

After Baltimore, Ms. Brownmiller flew to Puerto Rico. She'd been told of a clinic there. However, upon arrival, she discovered her clinic had gone out of business. Desparately she hunted throughout San Juan for another doctor. Somehow she found an abortionist and went immediately to his office. "How much money do you have?" the physician asked after he'd examined Brownmiller.

"I have what I was told to bring. Three hundred dollars."

"Not enough," shouted the doctor. "Not enough! Get out of here! I don't just take people off the streets. Do you think I run a charity or something?"

With that, Susan Brownmiller began to cry. It was all too much for her, the strain, the anxiety, the expense, the fear. From some place of deep internal strength she found the courage to be bold. "Listen, mister," she told the doctor, "I'm not leaving here till I get an abortion. If you don't take care of me, I'm going to the police." She got her abortion.

When Brownmiller finished her story, it was my turn to go to the stand.

Abortion. It's a hard thing to talk about. Not because abortion is murder, as the Friends of the Fetus had suggested, but because admitting to an illegal operation was admitting to being a criminal. In 1970 there were penalties for what I'd done. But aside from all that, there was an even more important reason—illegal abortion can be one of the most painful experiences in a woman's life. An unwanted pregnancy forces one into an underground existence. Careless home remedies. Foolish attempts to self-abort. Endless searches for one humane doctor who might be cooperative. No doctor? Well then, a nurse? Or a woman with some experience? Anybody! My three-month pregnancy was a period of my life I've worked hard to forget. It was a time of incredible self-mutilation and butchery, all of which I did willingly because I had no other choice. Recalling that very bad time was excruciating for me.

"Was there ever a time when you had an abortion?" began Nancy Stearns, one of the feminist lawyers.

"Yes . . . when I was nineteen," I answered.

"And would you tell us about that?" asked Stearns, in a voice that encouraged.

So, nervously, I told the court how I became pregnant despite careful use of contraceptives, how I thought my life was over because responsibility for this child rested with me. In 1964 I was unmarried, a student, a very unwilling candidate for motherhood. To me the idea of an unwanted child was a curse; I could envision only a terrible life for it. Besides, I had a certain kind of future planned for myself, one that would be destroyed by early motherhood. I asked for help. None of my schoolmates knew of an abortionist. Friends told me folk remedies and I tried them all—massive doses of gin, nutmeg, mustard baths, moving heavy furniture. When my attempts at home medicine failed, someone brought me a carton of large blue pills usually used for migraine headaches. It was said that if I took an overdose of this medicine I might miscarry. I didn't. I did, however, go deaf for twelve hours.

In the end, someone, I don't even remember who, located that angel of mercy, Dr. Robert Spencer.* Spencer (he died some years ago) was a real doctor, who ran an illegal clinic in Ashland, Pennsylvania; a humanitarian who never charged more than a hundred dollars for a procedure. Spencer's D and C was performed in less than an hour—with anesthesia, a miracle in those days of illegal operations—and once it was over, I was free. I was again a human being with a future. "Spencer's clean and safe D and C made all the difference to my life," I concluded. "Yet when I think about that whole experience what makes me most angry is that my pain and suffering were all needless."

Thomas Ford, who'd returned to the case after his initial ab-

---

*Obtaining Dr. Spencer's fine services was always a matter of luck. Periodically, the law would come down on him, or his health would fail. Then, the doctor would explain to callers that he was unavailable. I was more fortunate in my timing than Susan Brownmiller, who tried to reach Spencer a year earlier and found his practice temporarily suspended.

sence, had a question for me at the end of my testimony. I wondered if he'd ask something personal, something sharp, something angry. I had, after all, offended his most basic beliefs.

"Miss Dreifus . . . Miss Dreifus," he queried in pure Brooklynese.

"Yes, Mr. Ford?"

"Miss Dreifus . . . are you married?"

Flo Kennedy was on the floor with laughter.

It was easy enough for Flo Kennedy to poke fun at Attorney Ford and his clients; the Friends of the Fetus had, after all, such distorted views about the glories of motherhood and the basic functions of womenkind that they were often unconsciously funny in their testimony. But in 1970 the Fetus-Friends had the weight of the law on their side, and this was not humorous. Later, the Supreme Court would turn the tables and many of the interveners would go on to form the Right-to-Life-Movement. As I sat in the courtroom my guts churned. I realized that these men, particularly the doctors, had power over my life. One witness for the interveners, Dr. Joseph Ricotta, an obstetrician-gynecologist from Buffalo, was an attending physician at three major Erie County hospitals. He had a booming practice and to hear him speak he knew all there was to know about the foolish creatures who were his patients. One thought kept flashing through my mind during Ricotta's testimony: Do women *really* trust their bodies to this man?

Ricotta was a chubby fellow who sat uncomfortably in his chair and who used the kind of imperious tones that teachers reserve for inferior pupils. For the most part he wanted the court to know that women weren't quite rational as a group, not quite mature. He *knew*. He'd delivered thousands of babies in his time and he'd done "a great deal of work restoring fertility to sterile women." Most women were best off as mothers, Ricotta maintained; pregnancy was a calming influence. "I am opposed to legalized abortion," he testified. "It would encourage women to have an operation they wouldn't otherwise think of having. I wouldn't perform such an operation even if the mother threatened to commit suicide . . . The danger in repealing the law is that women tend to follow fads. You know . . . miniskirt, maxiskirt, midiskirt. Well, there's nothing uglier than a four-hundred-pound woman in a miniskirt. I ask you, is *that* responsible?"

Yet another Friend of the Fetus proved even more disturbing than the all-knowing Dr. Ricotta. He was André Hellegers, a most distinguished professor of obstetrics and gynecology at Georgetown University Medical Center, an advisor to the Pope (no less) on birth control. His was a highly technical testimony; he wanted to show that the fetus had an independent life from its mother and thus a separate right to legal status. To prove this, Hellegers spoke enthusiastically of experiments where impregnated cow uteruses were transplanted into rabbits, and then retransplanted back to cows. Eventually, these bovines gave birth to perfectly normal calves—proof positive, to Dr. Hellegers, that fetuses are independently viable. What didn't seem to enter the professor's consciousness were a few small considerations. Namely, that human beings aren't cows. Or that he'd hardly proved viability—after all, the scientists did have to remove the uterus as well as the fetus, too, and the uterus is part of the female, so the embryo is *not* independently viable. Nor did Hellegers consider the possibility that human females might not like having their uteruses removed—should he be thinking of extending the experiment. For him, women seemed invisible. A woman, her body, her wishes, were quite secondary to his conception of Woman as Breeder. "To what extent should a woman's own feelings be considered in granting an abortion?" he was asked during testimony.

"No more weight than you'd give a child," he answered with a smile.

Dr. Armand DiFrancesco, a ranking Buffalo psychiatrist with a résumé a mile long, agreed with Professor Hellegers completely. Dr. DiFrancesco was, among other things, connected with three hospitals, a director of psychiatric care at a home for unwed mothers, and a consultant to the Erie County District Attorney's office. "In my twenty years as a psychiatrist, I have never seen a case where abortion provided an acceptable solution to the problems of a pregnant woman," he told the court. "Requests for abortion are based on fear—fear of responsibility, fear of health, economic fears, and social fears. The role of a psychiatrist is to foster the development of mature and responsible attitudes to enable patients to cope with fear. A psychiatrist does not aid his [sic] patient when he permits self-indulgence or diminished responsibility." Despite the scientific tone of DiFrancesco's presentation, he concluded his observation on why abortion should be illegal with the words: "Man is suggestible, but woman is twenty percent more so."

The taking of depositions went on for much of the winter of 1970—with all sides presenting witnesses. In the spring, just as Judge Weinfield was to begin considering the case, something unexpected happened: New York's legislature repealed its repressive law. Suddenly, New Yorkers had the most liberal abortion law in the country. Responding to the new legal situation, Judge Weinfield dismissed *Abramowicz v. Lefkowitz* as moot. Though abortion was still illegal in most American localities, the feminist challenge would not go to the Supreme Court. "It was upsetting—the dismissal," Flo Kennedy recalled. "We wanted to eliminate killer-laws everywhere in the United States. We really wanted a test case."

That big test came, however, in *Rowe v. Wade* and *Doe v. Bolton*, decided in January of 1973 by the Supreme Court. With some limitations, the high court stated that a woman's right to privacy was her right to terminate pregnancy. Theoretically, abortion was legal.

Theory, however, was not practice. From the moment of the Supreme Court's pronouncement, two complementary forces worked to limit the operation's availability. On one hand, there were the Right-to-Lifers, who saw abortion as the Antichrist; on the other, there were the traditional factors of medical greed and power that make all health care subject to the caprice of individual physicians. The second factor worked quickly to make abortion too expensive for the non-Medicaid poor. Though new cost-saving technologies were quickly introduced into a network of doctor-financed abortion clinics, the price of a legal operation was often not much lower than it had been during the covert backroom days. (A friend of mine paid $600 for a perfectly legal suction aspiration out-patient abortion; the going rate for the more complicated D and C in prelegalization times was rarely that amount.) Legal or not, poor women, young women, rural women, small-town women, still had grave difficulty in terminating pregnancy. Long after the court ruled, the Alan Guttmacher Institute estimated that 30 percent of all American women who wanted abortion could not obtain it.*

And of course, there was The Backlash—which wasn't a backlash at all, but a well-organized campaign by one religion's hierarchy to inflict its dogma on a whole nation. While Catholic clergy and laity were confronting the bishops on true issues of conscience, the hierarchy responded by turning abortion into The New Crusade. From the pulpit abortion was called murder, and though Catholic women, in large numbers, availed themselves of legal abortion, the Church threw its resources into an effective national campaign to nullify the Supreme Court's decision. In a Pittsburgh diocese, Joanne Evans Gardner of NOW found that the Church had contributed "over $400,000 from 1971 to 1974 either directly or indirectly to finance anti-abortion programs."**

Well financed, using the Church as an organizational backbone, the Right-to-Lifers were and are everywhere, with their self-righteous lectures and their magnified photos of dead fetuses and their biased facts. In Boston in 1975, they managed to initiate the trial and manslaughter conviction of Dr. Kenneth Edelin, a physician who'd done nothing more than perform a legal abortion on a woman who wanted one. During the last presidential campaign, they made abortion such a negative issue that no major candidate

*For an excellent description of how the Supreme Court decision has been aborted, see Cisler and Clapp's, "Abortion Ruling—Some Good News . . . Some Bad News." *Majority Report,* October, 1975.

**See "Confronting The Enemy," a pamphlet on the Right-to-Life Movement edited by Joanne Evans Gardner. 80¢ from KNOW, Box 86031, Pittsburgh, Penn. 15221.

would endorse the Supreme Court decision. More ominously, the mandatory motherhood lobby succeeded in 1976 in gaining the passage through congress of the Hyde Amendment, which cut off federal funding for Medicaid abortions. As of this writing, the constitutionality of the Hyde Amendment is going through the courts and its validity is still undecided. However, as a new tactic, the Pro-Lifers are calling a Constitutional Convention to draft an amendment that would completely nullify *Rowe v. Wade*. In this, they have much official support. Ellen Lietzer, Coordinator of the American Civil Liberties Union's Reproductive Freedom Project issued a recent warning: "It is clear that we are losing the battle to keep abortion safe and legal for all women . . . Don't say it will never happen, that's how we lost the Hyde Amendment. Indeed, if the Supreme Court rules favorably on the public hospital and Medicaid abortion cases now pending, the only realistic legislative avenue for restricting abortion will be a constitutional amendment."

Somehow, it all came together with Mr. Joseph Califano and his anti-abortion prattle on my television screen. He seemed a handsome man, Mr. Califano—and around Washington, it was said, he was a fine civil liberties lawyer; but as he spoke, all I could feel was pure, cold terror. Here I was in 1977 hearing pre-Neanderthal talk from a man who would be making health policy for a whole nation. After a decade of feminist activism, I had naively assumed that a woman's right to her body had been firmly established, that no politician would dare use the airwaves for Mandatory Motherhood propaganda. But Mr. Califano was, and is, a politician, and an astute one, and that was part of what disturbed me: if the social atmosphere didn't permit it, he would have to have hidden his private views. The truth is that on this issue feminists had grown complacent and smug. It was as if no one remembered that nine men had given us the right to our bodies; it was as if no one wanted to think that another group of men could seize that right from us. Reflecting on all of this, I went to my files and pulled out a photograph the National Abortion Rights Action League distributes. Numbly, I put the picture in an envelope and addressed it to Mr. Joseph Califano, Washington, D.C. It was a photograph of a woman who lay dead on her bathroom floor— that's where her husband found her. Spreadeagled. She was the mother of three and she had tried to self-abort by flushing lye into her uterus. At the bottom of the picture was a photo credit: Hennepin County Minnesota Coroner's Office.

Adrienne Rich

THE THEFT
OF CHILDBIRTH

Childbirth has nowhere been regarded merely as one possible event in a woman's life. The Hebrews saw in women's travail the working of "Eve's curse" for tempting Adam to the Fall. The Romans called it *poena magna*—the great pain. But *poena* also means punishment, penalty. Whether as a "peak event" or as a torture rack, childbirth has been a charged, discrete happening, mysterious, polluted, often magical; in our current idolatry, a triumph of technology. Thirty years ago, in *Male and Female,* Margaret Mead noted the violence done by American hospital obstetrics to both infant and mother in the first hours of life.[1] Within the last few years, partly within and partly outside the women's movement, criticism of technologized childbirth has been growing, notably in California, where an important case is under appeal by a group of midwives in Santa Cruz who are charged with practicing medicine without a license.

Two recent books, with differing tones and perspectives, criticize the depersonalizing of hospital birth (American-style, though increasingly faddish in Europe) and recommend alternatives. Frederick Leboyer, a French obstetrician, is Americanized in the sense that he assumes that the mother's problems have been solved by hospital delivery; for him the radical issue is the handling of the newborn in the delivery room immediately after birth. Suzanne Arms, an American photographic journalist and a mother, is concerned with the warping of childbirth in modern obstetrical practice, its transformation into a "medical event" with consequent physical and psychic damage to both mother and child.

The technology of childbirth began with the forceps, first used in the seventeenth century by surgeons as a means of hastening slow labors, but forbidden to—and criticized by—midwives. The forceps and its monopoly by male practitioners were decisive in annexing childbirth—previously a woman's event often taboo to men —to the new medical establishment, from which women were barred. The annulment of pain by ether-inhalation was discovered by a Georgia doctor in 1842; both ether and nitrous oxide were shortly after used in dentistry by Horace Wells and W. T. Morton, and the term "anesthesia," suggested by Oliver Wendell Holmes, soon became accepted. In 1847, using ether in a case of childbirth, James Simpson in Scotland showed that contractions of the uterus would continue even if the woman was unconscious, and proceeded to experiment with and use chloroform to relieve the pains of labor.

A fierce theological opposition was mounted; the clergy attacked anesthesia as a "decoy of Satan, apparently offering itself to bless women; but in the end it will harden society and rob God of the deep earnest cries which arise in time of trouble for help."[2] The lifting of Eve's curse seemed to threaten the foundations of patriarchal religion; the pain of labor was for the glory of God the Father. Alleviation of female suffering would "harden" society, as if the sole alternative to the *mater dolorosa*—the suffering and suppliant mother, epitomized by the Virgin—was the fanged blood-goddess, devourer of her children.

This view still finds expression in anti-abortion rhetoric, and has extended beyond any single issue to feminism in general. After the horrible and lingering death of Mary Wollstonecraft from septicemia, the Rev. Richard Polwhele complacently observed that "she had died a death that strongly marked the distinction of the sexes, by pointing out the destiny of women, and the diseases to which they were peculiarly liable."[3]

In the nineteenth century the educated woman was seen as a

threat to the survival of the species. "Deflecting blood to the brain from the 'generative organs' . . ., she had lost touch with the sacred primitive rhythms that bound her to the deepest law of the cosmos."[4] (This was a view later shared by D. H. Lawrence and Hitler.) Patriarchal society would seem to require not only that women shall assume the major burden of pain and self-denial for the continuation of the species, but that a majority of that species —women—shall remain essentially uninformed and unquestioning.

The identification of womanhood with suffering—by women as well as men—has been tied to the concept of woman-as-mother. The idea that a woman's passive suffering is inevitable has worn many guises in history; not only those of Eve or the Virgin Mary but later masks such as Helene Deutsch's equation of passivity and masochism with femininity. If the medieval woman saw herself as paying by each childbirth for Eve's transgression, the nineteenth-century middleclass woman could play the Angel in the House, the martyr, her womanhood affirmed by her agonies in travail. Oliver Wendell Holmes supplies one version of the rhetoric:

> The woman about to become a mother, or with her newborn infant upon her bosom, should be the object of trembling care and sympathy wherever she bears her tender burden or stretches her aching limbs. The very outcast of the streets has pity upon her sister in degradation when the seal of promised maternity is impressed upon her. The remorseless vengeance of the law . . . is arrested in its fall at a word which reveals her transient claim for mercy.[5]

The value of a woman's life would appear to be contingent on her being pregnant or newly delivered. Women who refuse to become mothers are not merely emotionally suspect, they are dangerous. Not only do they refuse to continue the species, they also deprive society of its emotional leaven: the suffering of the mother.

It was therefore a radical act—*the* truly radical act of her entire reign—when Queen Victoria accepted anesthesia by chloroform for the birth of her seventh child in 1853. In so doing, she opposed clerical and patriarchal tradition and its entire view of women; but her influence and prestige were strong enough to open the way for anesthesia as an accepted obstetrical practice.

It was also under Victoria that the female body became more taboo, more mysterious, more suspected of "complaints and disorders," and the focus of more ignorant speculation, than ever before. Female sexual responsiveness was deemed pathological, and the "myth of female frailty" dominated the existence of middle and upper-class women. Childbirth and gynecology were now increasingly in male hands, and the developing medical profession had no more interest in female self-determination than any other institution. If education was supposed to atrophy the reproductive organs, women's suffrage was seen as creating "insane asylums in every county, and . . . a divorce court in every town."

Clitorectomies and ovariotomies were performed on thousands of women as a form of behavior modification for "troublesomeness," "attempted suicide," and "erotic tendencies." The professed "reverence" for (upper-class) women in Victorian England and America consisted largely in an exaggerated prudery.[6] At the onset of labor, the woman was placed in the lithotomy (supine) position, chloroformed, and became the completely passive body on which the obstetrician could perform as on a mannequin. The labor room became an operating theater, childbirth a medical drama, the physician its hero.

In the early twentieth century various forms of anesthesia were developed specifically for labor. "Twilight Sleep," a compound of morphine and scopolamine, was widely used until it was discovered to have a highly toxic effect on the infant. Sodium amytal and nembutal were found to produce after-amnesia (while only partly blunting pain), and of nembutal Sylvia Plath's heroine in *The Bell Jar* bitterly remarks, "I thought it sounded just like the kind of drug a man would invent."[7] The development of caudal or saddle-block anesthesia meant that a woman could remain conscious and see her baby born, though she was paralyzed from the waist down. Speert and Guttmacher, in their textbook *Obstetric Practice,* admit that the use of caudal or saddle-block anesthesia can prolong the second stage of labor, by producing "uterine inertia . . . (and) the absence of voluntary expulsive efforts by the mother," thus rendering a forceps delivery "necessary" where the child might have been born more swiftly and without instruments.

There are certain valid reasons for the prevention of exertion by the mother—such as heart disease, tuberculosis, or a previous Caesarean,[8] but women are now asking what psychic effect a state of semihelplessness has on a healthy mother, awake during the birth yet unable to participate actively, her legs in stirrups, her wrists strapped down, her physical engagement with the birth process minimized by drugs and by her supine position. This "freedom" from pain, like sexual "liberation," places a woman physically at the disposal of men though still estranged from her body. While in no way altering her subjection, it can be advertised as a progressive development.

In the 1940s, the English obstetrician Grantly Dick-Read related pain sensation to fear and tension and began to train prospective mothers to relax, to breathe correctly, to understand the stages of labor, and to develop muscular control through exercise. Dick-Read placed great emphasis on the role of calm, supportive birth attendants throughout labor, especially the obstetrician, who was to act as a source of confidence and security rather than as a surgeon needlessly interfering with or accelerating the birth process. He held that anesthesia should always be available but never involuntarily imposed on the woman or administered routinely.

Dick-Read's work was of considerable importance and many of his observations are still interesting. However, his attitude to women is essentially patriarchal. While in genuine awe of the female capacity to give birth, he writes of "the inborn dependence of woman" finding its natural outlet in her dependence on the doctor. "Biologically, motherhood is her desire," he remarks, and *"Varium et mutabile semper femina,* but never more so than in childbirth."[9] For him, childbirth is a woman's peak experience and purpose in life. Remove fear, reinforce ecstasy, and childbirth can be "natural"—that is, virtually without pain. But the male obstetrician remains in control of the situation.

• • •

During the Thirties and Forties, Soviet doctors began applying Pavlov's theories of the conditioned reflex to childbirth. There had been, earlier, successful deliveries in Russia under hypnosis and in post-hypnotic states. This led to increased emphasis on "suggestion," which was the basis for the first prenatal training: the creation, during pregnancy, of "complex chains of conditioned reflexes which will be applicable at the confinement. The pregnant woman learns to give birth as the child learns to read or swim." The conditioning toward pain was to be altered and new reflexes set up; the method is described as "verbal analgesia," using speech as a conditioning stimulus.[10]

In 1951, Fernand Lamaze, a French doctor, visited maternity clinics in the USSR which used the "psychoprophylactic method," and introduced the method at the French maternity hospital he directed, one serving the families of the Metallurgists' Union. Lamaze, far more than Dick-Read, emphasized the active participation of the mother in every stage of labor, and developed a precise and controlled breathing drill to be used during each stage. Where Dick-Read favors a level of "dulled consciousness" in the second stage, Lamaze would have the mother aware and conscious, responding to a series of verbal cues by panting, pushing, and blowing. However, as Suzanne Arms points out, the Lamaze method "has the unfortunate side-effect of greatly altering a woman's natural experience of birth from one of deep involvement inside her body to a controlled distraction." In her "militant control over her body," she is "separate and detached from the sensations, smells, and sights of her body giving birth. She is too involved in . . . control."[11]

The work of Sheila Kitzinger in England moves beyond that of Dick-Read and Lamaze to a much broader concept of childbearing as part of the context of a woman's entire existence. Her "psychosexual" method stresses the woman's learning to "trust her body and her instincts" and to understand the complex emotional network in which she comes to parturition. She insists on both physical and psychic education for childbirth if the mother is to retain "the power of self-direction, of self-control, of choice, of voluntary decision and active cooperation with doctor and nurse." She strongly favors giving birth at home, usually with a midwife.

The mother of five children herself, she is obviously in a better position to evaluate the sensations of labor than is a male physician; and she unequivocally states that "pain in labour is real enough." But she also describes the sensuous experience of the vagina opening during expulsion—not as painless, but as powerfully exhilarating. Her grasp of female reality is far broader than that of Dick-Read or Lamaze, but like other writers on "prepared" childbirth, she assumes that babies are born only to married women, and that the husband—present and emotionally dependable—will be an active figure in the birth chamber; and she unhesitatingly states that "the experience of bearing a child is central to a woman's life."[12]

Recently, in the United States, there has been widespread interest in various combinations of the Dick-Read, Lamaze, and Kitzinger approaches. The move toward midwife-deliveries and away from the depersonalizing hospital and obstetrician has been a crucial aspect of the women's health-care movement. There is, however, much to question in the idealized photographs of young and lovely pregnant women, naked or in flowered dresses, in rural communes, romanticized as hippie earth-mothers. The conditions affecting the majority of mothers—poverty, malnutrition, desertion by the father, inadequate prenatal care—are ignored in these accounts.

"Prepared" or "natural" childbirth has been a middle-class phenomenon in this country: but even its crusaders acknowledge with Pierre Vellay that "under good physical and psychological conditions" "the woman can expect childbirth without any pain, provided that no family, money or social worries upset her just before the birth,"[13] and with Lamaze that "it is natural for a mother to feel depressed about her child's future when her own is overcast." Shulamith Firestone, as an early feminist theorist, was understandably skeptical of "natural" childbirth as part of a reactionary "counterculture" having little to do with the liberation of women in general.

Firestone sees childbearing, however, as purely and simply the victimizing experience it has often been in patriarchal society. "Pregnancy is barbaric," she declares, and "childbirth *hurts.*" She discards biological procreation from this shallow and unexamined point of view, without taking account of what biological pregnancy and birth might be in a wholly different political and emotional setting. Finally, Firestone is so eager to move on to artificial reproduction that she fails to examine the important relationship between maternity and sensuality, pain and female alienation.[14]

Ideally, of course, women would choose not only whether, when, and where to bear children, and the circumstances of labor, but also between biological and artificial reproduction. But I do not think we can project any such idea onto the future—and hope to realize it—without examining the shadow-images we carry in us, the magical thinking of Eve's curse, the social victimization of women-as-mothers. To do so is to deny aspects of ourselves that will rise up sooner or later to claim recognition.

In 1955, 1957, and 1959, I gave birth to my three children—all but the first normal births—under general anesthesia. In the case of my first labor an allergic reaction to pregnancy, which was presumed to be measles, might have justified medical intervention. But in each subsequent pregnancy I used the same obstetrician, and was "put out" as completely as I had been for the first. Labor seemed to me something to be gotten through; the child—and the state of motherhood—being the mysterious and desired goal.

During those years I often felt apologetic in talking with women who had had a baby by some variant of the Dick-Read method, or had attempted it. I was told: "It hurt like hell, but it was worth it"; or, "It was the most painful, ecstatic experience of my life." Some women asserted that they had ended crying for anesthesia; others were on the delivery table, anesthetized against their will. At that time, even more than now, the "choice" a woman made of the mode of delivery was likely to be her obstetrician's choice. But, among those who were awake at delivery, a premium seemed to be placed on the *pain endured* rather than on an active physical experience. Sometimes I felt that my three unconscious deliveries were yet another sign of my half-suspected inadequacy as a woman: the "real" mothers were those who had "been awake through it all."

I think now that my refusal of consciousness (approved and implemented by my physician) and my friends' exhilaration at having experienced and surmounted pain (approved and implemented by their physicians) had a common source: we were trying in our several ways to contain the expected female fate of passive suffering. None of us, I think, had much sense of being in any real command of the experience. Ignorant of our bodies, we were essentially nineteenth-century women where childbirth (and much else) was concerned. (But, unlike our European sisters, none of us dreamed of having a baby at home, with a midwife. In the United States that was a fate reserved for the rural poor.)

We were above all in the hands of male medical technology. The hierarchal structure of the hospital, the definition of childbirth as medical emergency, the fragmentation of body from mind were the environment in which we gave birth, with or without analgesia. The only female presences were nurses, whose training and schedules precluded much female tenderness. (With gratitude and amazement, I woke in the recovery room after my third delivery to find a young student nurse holding my hand.) To lie half-awake in a barred crib, in a room with other women moaning and tossing under drugs, where "no one comes" except to do a pelvic examination or give an injection, is a classic experience of modern childbirth. The loneliness, the sense of being in prison, powerless and forgotten, is the chief collective experience of women who have given birth in American hospitals.[15]

Brigitte Jordan, an anthropologist studying childbirth in different cultures, describes routine hospital delivery in the United States as:

a complex of practices . . . justified, on medical grounds, as being in the best interests of mother and child . . . induction and stimulation of labor with drugs, the routine administration of sedatives and of medication for pain relief, the separation of the laboring woman from any sources of psychological support, surgical rupturing of the membranes, routine episiotomy, routine forceps delivery, and the lithotomy position for delivery, to name just a few.[16]

Her point is not that medical interference should never occur, but that childbirth here is a "culturally produced event," pursued with the same relentless consistency of method without regard to individual aspects of labor. Episiotomies are justified as preventing tearing in the perineum, but tearing is much more likely when a woman gives birth in the lithotomy position than when squatting, on a birthstool, or (as in the Yucatan) supported in a hammock. Forceps deliveries are also more often required in the lithotomy position, where the full force of gravity cannot aid in the expulsion of the child.

Jordan stresses that in cultures as different as Sweden and Yucatan women have a part in the decisions relating to their deliveries. The Yucatan midwife emphasizes that "every woman has to *buscar la forma,* find her own way, and . . . that it is the midwife's task to assist with whatever decision is made."[17] This does not mean that births are painless, but that needless pain is avoided, birth is not treated as a medical event, and the woman's individual temperament and physique are treated with respect.

The artificially induced and stimulated labor, so common in this country, creates longer, stronger contractions with less relaxation-span between them than the contractions of normal labor. This in turn leads to the use of pain-relieving drugs; medical technology here creates its own artificial problem for which an artificial solution must be found. Moreover, these unnaturally strong and lengthy contractions often deprive the fetus of oxygen, while the analgesic drugs interfere with its respiration. If labor in the United States were induced only in cases of medical necessity, only about 3 percent of births would be induced. In fact, at least one in five births are drug-induced or stimulated, for the physician's convenience and with no medical justification whatsoever.[18]

Tucho Perussi, an Argentine doctor, crusades for a return to the obstetrical stool, pointing out that in the lithotomy position a contraction which pushes a fetus downward can be compensated against by the fetus sliding backward, thus lengthening labor, while in the vertical position gravity keeps the fetus from losing ground between contractions. Dr. Robert Caldeyro-Barcia of Argentina puts it succinctly: "Except for being hanged by the feet . . . the supine position is the worst conceivable position for labor and delivery."[19] Vertical delivery prevents loss of oxygen to the fetus which results when the uterus is lying on the largest vein in the body (the *vena cava*). The chief objection to the use of the obstetrical stool or chair seems to be that obstetricians believe it would be inconvenient for them in attending births.[20]

The writers cited above have concerned themselves with the labor and birth process, though they criticize the hospital practice of separating child from mother immediately after birth, often for hours. Frederick Leboyer assumes that the mother's problems have been solved by modern obstetrics, including analgesia, and concentrates on the child's birth trauma. He evokes the experience of being forced through the birth canal by powerful contractions, in highly charged language:

> An intransigent force—wild, out of control—has gripped the infant. . . . The prison has gone berserk, demanding its prisoner's death . . . this monstrous unremitting pressure that is crushing the baby, pushing it out toward the world—and this blind wall, which is holding it back, confining it—These things are all one: the mother! . . .
> It is *she* who is the enemy. She who stands between the child and life. . . . The infant is like one possessed. Mad with agony and misery, alone, abandoned, it fights with the strength of despair. The monster drives the baby lower still. And not satisfied with crushing, it twists it in a refinement of cruelty. . . . And the infant's head—bearing the brunt of the struggle . . . why doesn't the head give way? The monster bears down one more time. . . .[21]

After this cataclysmic struggle, Leboyer insists that the handling of the infant should be rhythmic, tranquil, and as respectful as possible. The child is to be placed on the mother's belly, on its stomach, and slowly, gently massaged by hands that recall, in their rhythmic stroking, the "peristaltic wave" of the womb; hands that "make love to the child." (These hands, apparently, belong not to the mother but to the obstetrician; Leboyer seems to assume that mothers have to be taught how to touch their children for the first time.) The umbilical cord is not to be severed until the child breathes naturally through its lungs and is no longer receiving part of its oxygen supply from the mother. The child is then placed in a bath warmed to body temperature where it can re-experience the amniotic waters and sense of weightlessness.

According to Leboyer, the expression on the face of an infant whose transition into life is eased by this procedure is relaxed, alert, even smiling. The eyes open and seem to focus, the hands play as the child unfolds in the warm bath. And certainly the photographs accompanying his text show infants encountering life with a rapt, thoughtful gaze instead of the anguished mask of the newborn.

Respect for weakness and vulnerability is so rare, both within and without the medical establishment, that Leboyer's book (actually an inflated pamphlet, and, at $7.95, an expensive rip-off), with its concern for the newborn's acute sensitivity, may appear more original and radical than in fact it is. With the exception of his preference for a semidarkened, hushed delivery room, in which even the mother is urged to utter no loud or sudden sound, his methods, described and defended in oracular tones, have been standard procedure for midwives in various parts of the world. In the heavily technologized, physician-centered ambiance of hospital obstetrics, his proposals indeed seem radical, and have been under heavy attack.

But what is disturbing in Leboyer's presentation of these methods is not simply his didactic tone but his identification with the infant to the virtual exclusion of the mother. She appears as the "monster" of the uterine contractions, as a belly on which the child is laid, hands that hardly know how to touch her newborn; but the physiological and psychic bond between mother and child is all but dismissed. The heroes of this obstetrical drama are Leboyer and the baby. He goes so far as to observe that each person attending a birth undergoes a kind of transference to the newborn, a return to their own birth struggle, and he believes that the obstetrician's haste to cut the cord and hear the child cry vigorously has little to do with good midwifery or the child's needs, being an unconscious identification with the child's fight for breath.[22] (But is this true for women? Does a woman attending a birth identify exclusively with the child?)

Leboyer himself seems possessed both by this transference and by a male need (seen in *couvade* also) to take over the *mana* of birth. Assuming as he does a physician-controlled hospital birth, a mother drugged for an "almost painless delivery," his "birth without violence" is already violent. He fails to recognize, for example, that the infant's torment in the birth canal can be increased and lengthened by the obstetrical "solution" he accepts for the mother. The limitations of Leboyer's approach can be appreciated when it is compared to Suzanne Arms's much more comprehensive view of childbirth. She matter-of-factly describes how in the Amsterdam Kweekschool the midwife bathes the newborn in lukewarm water

> very much like its earlier nine-month home. Then she patted the baby
> dry, wrapped it, and placed it in the mother's arms, generally just
> three minutes after birth. . . . Perhaps most amazing of all was the
> peaceful yet alert way in which the newborn infants adjusted to their
> first hours after birth. Even when the darkened nursery (used only
> at night) was more than half full, often not one baby was crying.[23]

Infant and mother are a continuum, and sensitive treatment of the one is incomplete without sensitive treatment of the other. *Immaculate Deception* both demystifies and pleads for rehumanizing the entire birth and postpartum, for the sake of both mother and child, whose psychic and physical welfare Arms, unlike Leboyer, sees as inseparable.

> Placed directly upon its mother's belly, while still connected to her
> placenta (by the unsevered umbilical cord), the baby finds the nipple

and begins its first suckling activity. The mere licking of the mother's nipple triggers the nerves in her breast to alert the uterus that the baby is out and safe. In immediate response, the uterus clamps down to begin to expel the placenta. Meanwhile, the suckling action of the baby stimulates its breathing and heat productivity. Most important, the newborn finds peace and calm in direct contact with its mother's warm body. This moment of security is the first it has known since the onset of labor.[24]

By contrast, in most American obstetrical units, the infant is immediately separated from the mother, with whom it may have no further contact until the hospital schedule permits it to be brought from the nursery. This separation not only violates a process still unfinished (the expulsion of the placenta, the natural stimulation of the infant's breathing) but, according to pediatric studies quoted by Arms, weakens the establishment of the "exquisitely important" early mother-child bond, on which the capacity to form intimate relationships strongly depends, and may lead to psychic stress in the child and even to the "battered-child" syndrome.

Of sixteen developed countries, in 1971 and 1972, the United States had the highest infant mortality rate; as of 1973 the rate of decline in these statistics was slower here than in nineteen other countries. *Immaculate Deception* is a gathering of concrete evidence that hospital delivery, always insisted upon on the grounds of its greater safety, actually contributes to infant mortality in the United States, not to speak of infant brain damage and retardation resulting from the oxygen deprivation caused by the lithotomy position, and toxic damage to the infant caused by drugs administered—most often needlessly—to the mother.

Through accumulated examples, Arms details how the requirements of the OB unit and its panoply of technology became the central issue. The mother's body is hooked to machines and intravenous units during labor; her belly may not be touched or massaged by human hands lest the fetal heart monitor be disrupted; contractions may be spurred or retarded by drugs in accordance with the doctor's lunch hour or the delivery room schedule. She is attended by no single person throughout her labor; shifts change, nurses, interns, anesthetists, technicians move in and out; often even her husband is denied access to her.

Arms has also studied home births and midwifery in other Western countries and in the few parts of the US where home-midwifery (as distinct from hospital nurse-midwifery) is practiced. She reports that even as women in the United States are beginning to demand home births, American obstetrical super-hardware is selling itself in countries like England, Holland, and Denmark which have a long tradition of midwifery, maternity clinics, and home births, with a complete backup system of emergency obstetrical care. Despite the much lower infant mortality in Western Europe, the promise of "quick and easy" technological obstetrics is making inroads. Meanwhile, in the United States, "American doctors resist any move to take birth out of the hospital or to make it a woman's event."[25]

But the most moving and impressive parts of her book are those in which the midwives and mothers speak, or in which midwife-assisted births are described. Arms does not, of course, claim that the hospital alone is the creator of pain in childbirth, although she does point out that hospitals are associated with "disease and disorder" and that when a woman in labor enters one her tension is increased by the atmosphere of medical emergency. Fear, she insists, rather than "pain," is the real barrier separating women from birth. And she rightly observes that "after centuries of ingrained fear, expectation of pain, and obeisance to male domination, she cannot easily come to childbirth a 'changed woman' after a few classes in natural childbirth or a heavy dose of Women's Liberation."[26] What we bring to childbirth is nothing less than our entire socialization as women.

It can be objected that, just as there may be individual obstetricians who are compassionate and flexible, so there may be cold and unsympathetic midwives.[27] But the question here is not really one of individuals, any more than in the prison system. Medical tradition schools the doctor to the role of officer of an army, one increasingly technologized. Success, in that tradition, has involved (in the United States especially) embracing the drug industry, the technological solution. Above all, the hospital is a place for disease, and childbirth is not an illness.

Midwives, undoubtedly, vary. But the question is really whether a woman can freely choose to give birth at home, attended by a woman, or at least in a maternity clinic which is not a hospital. It is a question of the mother's right to decide *what* she wants: to *"buscar la forma."* At this time it is extremely difficult and usually illegal for a woman to give birth to her child at home attended by a self-described professional midwife. The medical establishment continues to claim pregnancy and parturition as a form of disease. The real issue, apart from economic profit, is the mother's relation to childbirth. To change the experience of childbirth means to change women's relationship to fear and powerlessness, to our bodies, to our children; it has far-reaching psychic and political implications.

Suzanne Arms provides a patiently reasoned, documented indictment of the American hospital as a place for normal births (and 90 percent of all births are normal ones). But taking birth out of the hospital does not mean simply shifting it into the home or into maternity clinics. Birth is not an isolated event. It has been a central experience in which women have historically felt out of control, at the mercy of biology or chance. If there were local centers to which all women could go for contraceptive and abortion counseling, pregnancy testing, prenatal care, labor classes, films about pregnancy and birth, routine gynecological examinations, discussion groups through and after pregnancy, women would be encouraged to think, talk, and read about the entire process of gestating, bearing, nursing their children, and about the alternatives to motherhood.

Childbirth is (or may be) one aspect of a woman's entire life, beginning with her own expulsion from her mother's body, her own sensual suckling or holding by a woman, through her earliest sensations of clitoral eroticism and of the vulva as a source of pleasure, her growing sense of her own body and its strengths, her masturbation, her menses, her physical relationship to nature and to other human beings, her first and subsequent orgasmic experiences with another's body, her conception, pregnancy, to the moment of first holding her child. But that moment is still only a point in the process if we conceive it not according to patriarchal ideas of childbirth as a kind of production but as part of female experience.

Beyond birth comes nursing and the physical relationship with an infant, and these are enmeshed with sexuality. Mary Jane Sherfey has shown that during pregnancy the entire pelvic area increases in vascularity (the production of arteries and veins), increasing the capacity for sexual tension and greatly increasing the frequency and intensity of orgasm. Moreover, during pregnancy the system is flooded with hormones which not only induce the growth of new blood vessels but increase clitoral responsiveness and strengthen the muscles effective in orgasm. Thus a woman who has given birth has a biologically increased capacity for genital pleasure, unless her pelvic organs have been damaged obstetrically, as frequently happens.

Many women experience orgasm for the first time after childbirth, or become erotically aroused while nursing. Frieda Fromm-Reichman, Niles Newton, Masters and Johnson, and others have documented the erotic sensations experienced by some women in actually giving birth. Since there is a strong cultural force which attempts to desexualize women as mothers, the orgasmic sensations felt in childbirth or while suckling infants have probably till recently been denied even by the women feeling them, or have evoked feelings of guilt. Yet, as Niles Newton reminds us, "Women . . . have a more varied heritage of sexual enjoyment than men";[28] and Alice Rossi observes,

> I suspect that the more male dominance characterizes a Western society, the greater is the dissociation between sexuality and maternalism. It is to men's sexual advantage to restrict women's sexual gratification to heterosexual coitus, though the price for the woman and a child may be a less psychologically and physically rewarding relationship.[29]

The divisions of labor and allocations of power in American society demand not merely a suffering Mother, but one divested of sexuality: the Virgin Mary, *virgo intacta,* perfectly chaste. Women are permitted to be sexual only at a certain time of life. The sensuality of mature—and certainly of aging—women has been perceived as grotesque, threatening, and inappropriate.

If motherhood and sexuality were not wedged resolutely apart by male culture, if we could *choose* both the forms of our sexuality and the terms of our motherhood or non-motherhood freely, women might achieve sexual autonomy (as opposed to "sexual liberation"). The mother should be able to choose the means of conception (biological, artificial, or even parthenogenetic), the place of birth, her own style of giving birth, and her birth attendants. Birth might then become one event in the unfolding of our diverse and polymorphous sexuality—not a necessary *consequence* of sex, but one aspect of liberating ourselves from fear and the loathing of our own bodies.

Patriarchal childbirth—childbirth as penance and as medical emergency—and its sequel, institutionalized motherhood, is alienated labor, exploited labor, keyed to an "efficiency" and a profit system having little to do with the needs of mothers and children, carried on in physical and mental circumstances over which the woman in labor has little or no control. It is exploited labor in a form even more devastating than that of the enslaved industrial worker who has, at least, no psychic and physical bond with the sweated product, or with the bosses who control her. Not only have conception, pregnancy, and birth been expropriated from women, but also the deep paraphysical sensations and impulses with which they are saturated.

PART THREE

INSTITUTION-ALIZED MALE-PRACTICE

Barbara Seaman

THE DANGERS OF SEX HORMONES

Birth-control pill users are not the only women at risk from hormones. As Dr. Sheldon Segal of the Population Council stated at an FDA meeting in 1975:

> The use of synthetic sex hormones has grown to an extent that makes this class of drugs a significant part of the chemical environment. The under-thirty generation has been raised on beef fattened with estrogen-laced feed, lambs born of estrus-synchronized ewes, chickens caponized with estrogen paste or pellets. They are the first generation to include a large percentage of post-pill babies born to mothers who used steroidal contraception prior to planned or unplanned pregnancies and are themselves prodigious consumers of steroidal estrogens and progestins on a steady basis . . . steroidal and non-steroidal sex hormones . . . could reach and effect the gamete, embryo or fetus . . . one serious hazard—the use of high doses of stilbestrol during pregnancy—has been disclosed . . .

Stilbestrol during pregnancy—DES—is a carcinogen (cancer-producing agent) that is everywhere, even in our meat. From World War II until 1971, it was given to millions of pregnant women as a preventative for miscarriages. By 1953 it was established that DES didn't work, and not long afterward it was also revealed that it could produce a kind of hermaphroditism in some infants. But that didn't stop doctors from using it. What finally stopped most of them, in the 1970s, were reports that some of the

DES daughters were developing rare forms of vaginal and cervical cancers in their teens. (Some did not have to wait that long. The youngest victim is only eight years old.) Male children, as we are just discovering, may also be affected, but in less ominous fashion.

It is the 15th of December, 1975. Inside FDA headquarters at Rockville, Maryland, the Advisory Committee on Obstetrics and Gynecology is meeting to evaluate reports that hormones cause cancer. Outside, a group of about 40 women, men and children gather quietly. They are wearing black armbands, and carrying signs with slogans like "Feed estrogen to the rats at the FDA." They have come from as far away as California to mourn the thousands of women who died from various estrogen therapies, the Pill, DES and menopause treatments. Episcopal Minister Betty Ann Rosenberg opens with an invocation. Terri Clark, a black, feminist musician, sings a song she has composed for the occasion.

Jim Luggan from Dayton, Ohio, describes the death of his 24-year-old wife Dona Jean, from a Pill-related blood clot in the lung. "I watched her die—helplessly holding her hand while I watched her eyes roll back in her head, watched her face turn blue and saw the foam bubble out of her mouth."

Susan Adams, from Queens, New York, whose late daughter Cathy's liver was destroyed by the Pill, has tried to attend the meeting of the Advisory Committee that is taking place inside. She is ejected, on the grounds that her presence might "disturb their scientific deliberations."

Sherry Leibowitz, a Boston health worker, wears a green-and-white button that asks "Did Your Mother Take It?" The button refers to DES. Sherry is one of the millions of young women who were exposed to it in the womb. She is eager to spread the word about the urgency of regular check-ups starting at age fourteen or earlier. Those who have DES cancers that were found early are alive and well, whereas many of those who waited until symptoms developed have died.

Obstetricians are being urged to check through all their old records, and contact any patients who had DES so their daughters can be evaluated. Many obstetricians are not cooperating (perhaps out of fear of malpractice lawsuits) and yet the mothers themselves may never have been told what they had been given.

Dr. Robert Pantell, a pediatrician, expressed his concern and outrage at Senate hearings held in January 1975. Dr. Pantell considers DES to be "far more sinister than thalidomide" because

it strikes more than a decade later. . . . In my experience as a practicing pediatrician in Idaho, there were a number of alarming events. . . . In August 1972 I began work as a pediatrician for a clinic system in southwest Idaho. . . . We routinely asked all women coming to us regularly whether they received drugs during pregnancy. It soon became apparent that the recollection of drugs taken during pregnancy was poor. . . . Many individuals have been so accustomed to taking numerous pills, they do not even question the purpose and content of medications. . . . In the winter of 1973, Mrs. A. G. came to our clinic. In 1971, she had received a medication from an obstetrician to help her maintain her pregnancy. Because of our concern that Mrs. A. G. had received diethylstilbestrol, a drug posing potential risks to her three-year-old daughter, we requested her records be transferred from her obstetrician.

After several phone and mail requests, a note was received from the obstetrician stating that her pregnancy was normal. No mention of drugs was made. "Upon further questioning, Mrs. G. recalled the pharmacy where the drug was dispensed. Mr. George Murray, pharmacist in Homedale, Idaho, identified the drug as des-Plex, a preparation manufactured by Amfre-Grant, containing 25 milligrams diethylstilbestrol, as well as eight different items.

I might add, at this point, that combining potent drugs with vitamins needlessly obscures the purpose for which the preparation was given.

At the same time, another patient, Mrs. M.S., also came to our office for care.

Mrs. S. was currently being seen for prenatal care by the same obstetrician who formerly cared for Mrs. G. Mrs. S. was, at that time, taking des-Plex and had been on this medication continuously for the first six months of her pregnancy. Mrs. S. was unaware of the risks of diethylstilbestrol in pregnancy. She was taking this drug two years after the November 1971 FDA bulletin stated that diethylstilbestrol was contraindicated in pregnancy. Mrs. S. subsequently delivered a female child.

Because of our inability to establish an effective line of communication with the obstetrician who was prescribing diethylstilbestrol, a letter was sent, in conjunction with Dr. Thomas O. McMeekin, to Mr. C. E. Barnett of the Idaho State Board of Pharmacy, and to Mr. Armand Byrd, Secretary of the Idaho State Board of Medicine, on March 25, 1974.

We described our experience and suggested: (1) An independent party negotiate with the obstetrician to identify those patients at risk; (2) an effort be made by the board of pharmacy and/or medicine to educate this physician as to the dangers of diethylstilbestrol and current recommendations for its usage.

The reply from the State Board of Pharmacy was that this was not in their jurisdiction.

The secretary of the State Board of Medicine, at the time I left Idaho in the last week of June 1974, communicated to me that action had not yet been taken on the matter.

Neither Dr. McMeekin or I have received any further communication concerning this issue.

The physician under consideration, besides maintaining a private practice, was then, and to my knowledge still is, an obstetrical consultant for the State.

Only a tiny fraction of the DES daughters have thus far developed cancer, but many others have benign disorders of the reproductive organs which bear careful watching. Any further exposure to hormones, such as those in the Pill, or "morning after" contraception, may be inadvisable.

Unfortunately, several studies, such as those performed by Belita Cowan of Ann Arbor, Michigan, reveal that personnel at many student health services and clinics are now offering DES as a morning-after contraceptive without even *asking* the young women if they might be DES daughters. Thus, some of these young women are once again exposed to the same carcinogen.

They may also be exposed to it when they eat meat, especially beef liver. The FDA has twice tried to ban the use of DES in cattle feed, but the manufacturers have thus far succeeded, through legal manipulations, in delaying compliance. DES *has* been banned from cattle feed in more than twenty other countries, and some have altogether banned the importation of American meat. They want us to keep our carcinogens to ourselves. The reason that we go on using DES is to save money. It helps fatten up the cattle faster, reducing our meat bills by (according to the Department of Agriculture) $3.85 a year per person.

Until very recently, it was hoped that the sons of DES mothers had avoided injury, but now it seems that they too may be affected. At the University of Chicago, Dr. Marluce Bibbo has found that ten out of 42 young men whose mothers took DES have genital abnormalities, including undersized penises (two cases), variocele or enlargement of a vein in the testicle (one case), abnormally small testes (two cases), testicular mass (one case), and cysts in the epididymis, an area affecting sperm transport (four cases). In Winston-Salem, North Carolina, scientists have found that the male offspring of DES-treated mice have similar abnormalities of the reproductive tract. Six out of nineteen such mice were sterile, and it is presently feared that this will also prove to be a side effect in human males. As Dr. Bibbo has commented, "Our patients are still all single. The cysts might be of no importance, or they might cause some fertility problems. The proof will come after they are married."

Thus far, mercifully, there has been no indication of cancer in DES sons.

Who will bear the cost of the expensive check-ups required by the children of DES mothers? A New York attorney, Paul Rheingold, has attempted to bring a class action suit forcing drug companies to pay, but thus far he has been unsuccessful.

The Pill may cause *obvious* birth defects in some instances but, more than that, the children born to former Pill users—particularly those who conceived while taking the Pill or just after stopping—need to be watched closely for possible *latent* effects, as per DES. It cannot be stated often enough that all of these hormone products are related chemically, as well as in mechanism of action. A side effect produced by one kind of estrogen or progestin may well be produced by the others. Many doctors seem unaware of this, and they make comments like, "Oh, I'm against DES but the Pill, now, that's pretty safe."

All of these hormones are "safe" enough for the doctors who

prescribe them, but not for the women who take them.

There is only one group of hormone products which clearly cannot endanger unborn children. Estrogen Replacement Therapy (ERT), including brands such as Premarin—is used to treat menopausal symptoms, or as an "anti-aging pill." Millions of women take ERT—for ten years on the average—and most have little idea of the hazards of the drug they swallow. In New York City, WCBS-TV news recently interviewed more than a dozen ERT users and could not find *one* whose doctor had truly informed her of the risks. Researchers at the University of Washington in Seattle have just published an even more startling fact. Out of 75 women who first answered "no," they had never used such estrogens, twenty women, on closer examination, turned out to be ERT users after all. Apparently, they had no idea *what* their doctors had given them, much less what the side effects might be.

But, while some women may not know what they are getting, others do *ask* for ERT which has been sold to us, hard, like a used car. Ayerst, the largest ERT manufacturer, maintains a public relations outfit located in New York City called, euphemistically "The Information Center on the Mature Woman." The Center plants pro-ERT articles in magazines and newspapers, as well as booking speakers onto TV and radio programs. Often these propagandists present ERT as a youth pill, which it is not. There is *no* evidence that ERT inhibits facial wrinkles, sagging breasts, gives extra energy or "femininity" but all of these bonuses have been suggested. The Information Center's activities are contrary to the ethical code of the Pharmaceutical Manufacturers Association, which states that prescription drugs must not be promoted directly to the public. The PMA has not taken any action against Ayerst, although they are aware of the situation. There is no evidence either that ERT controls depression or nervousness, although some users may sincerely believe so because, frequently unbeknownst to them (the users), some of the popular ERT preparations are combined with mood or mind-altering ingredients. Two such brand names are PMB-400, which combines estrogen and Miltown, and Mediatric, which combines estrogen with (we kid you not) vitamins, testosterone and methamphetamine, also known as speed. Mediatric in liquid form provides 15 percent alcohol as well.

For any of you who may be wondering whether you are getting straight estrogen or estrogen-plus, Ayerst's pure Premarin tablets are, in ascending strength from 0.3 to 2.5 mgs., dark green, brown, yellow and purple. Premarin with testosterone is either brown or yellow, and is round instead of oval like the straight product. Premarin with Miltown is green or pink, and Mediatric, appropriately enough, comes in a black capsule or a big red tablet.

Certain doctors, as well as drug companies, shill ERT to vulnerable women. One such doctor is Robert Wilson, author of a bestselling book called *Feminine Forever,* which makes ERT sound like the Fountain of Youth Ponce de Leon came to the new world to seek. Dr. Wilson heads an outfit he modestly calls "The Wilson Research Foundation" which has received funding from Ayerst, Searle and the Upjohn Company. According to Morton Mintz of the *Washington Post,* Wilson has also promoted the Pill, specifically Searle's Enovid as a "menopause preventive."

The FDA has notified the Searle Company that they deem Wilson an "unacceptable investigator."

Wilson's book, in paperback, is still widely available—and widely read.

ERT is heavily shilled to doctors also. When findings concerning ERT and cancer were published last winter in the *New England Journal of Medicine*, the Ayerst Company, manufacturers of Premarin, sent a letter to doctors trying to minimize the seriousness. Incidentally—and curiously—the Ayerst Company was informed of these findings long before most prescribing doctors, or reporters. For several months before the studies appeared in print, rumors flew concerning them. Many doctors and journalists tried to learn the details, but failed. One worried gynecologist, Dr. Marcia Storch of New York City, called the Ayerst Company directly and got the information from them. They had it, when most doctors and patients did not.

This gave the Ayerst Company plenty of time to tool up its propaganda machine, and try to assuage the fears of doctors and women. Its letter to doctors was a masterpiece of innuendo. At Senate hearings on Birth Control Pills and the Use of Estrogens in Menopause, held on January 21, 1976, the following dialogue ensued between Senator Edward Kennedy, and Commissioner Alexander Schmidt of the FDA:

> K: First of all, tell me your reaction to that letter. You are familiar with the letter itself, I know.
> S: Yes, I read that letter several times, and each time I read it, I come to the same conclusion that the letter is misleading, and we believe that it is an irresponsible letter. . . . The intent of the letter is to reassure—and I do not think that what we know today is reassuring at all.
> K: What can you do about it? What have you done about it? —
> S: Well, it was our judgment that that letter was a series of correct, legally correct sentences which, when put together the way they were, was misleading, but that we could not easily make a case that the letter was illegal.

The point which concerns Senator Kennedy—and me—is that the Ayerst letter was so subtle that the FDA Commissioner, who deplored it, said he felt he could not demand a retraction. The average prescribing doctor may have been left feeling that the Ayerst Company successfully "answered" the *New England Journal*'s reports. These legal and verbal games may suit the FDA and drug manufacturers but what of the Premarin-using women who have cancer at stake?

The average age for menopause in the United States is 50. For many women it is not a dramatic event. Their periods grow lighter and/or more irregular, and then stop. Sometimes the cessation of menses is abrupt, however.

Pro-ERT propaganda often suggests that the body's natural production of estrogen "shuts off" like a faucet. This is untrue. Ovarian function changes, but the adrenals and other sites in the body continue to provide this hormone.

Some women, a minority, feel temporary discomfort while their body is going through these changes. We have mentioned that the ovaries and the pituitary are in a delicate balance constantly signaling each other. When a woman's ovarian function changes at menopause, the pituitary must also readjust. She may have hot flashes and sweats, temporarily. These are not alarming or dangerous symptoms, but can be likened to the unexpected voice-register changes some boys evidence at puberty, when *their* bodies are shifting gears.

In a few women these flashes are truly uncomfortable, and embarrassing. ERT, as a temporary measure, is effective to help tide them over. It is effective also for women troubled by dryness and thinning of the vagina, and painful intercourse, but locally applied creams serve this purpose too.

The National Academy of Science—National Research Council has rated ERT as "probably effective" for osteoporosis, a disorder producing fragile bones in some women over 60. Osteoporosis is not in itself uncomfortable, as a rule, but may lead to fractures if falls occur. The National Academy of Science—National Research Council states that *if* ERT is an effective treatment for osteoporosis, this is "only when used in conjunction with other important therapeutic measures such as diet, calcium, physiotherapy and good general health-promoting measures. Final classification of this indication requires further investigation."

Some scientists fear that in the long run ERT may actually be bad for osteoporosis. There may be a temporary improvement at first, but then there is a rebound, they say, and the bone-thinning proceeds more rapidly than if the patient had not taken ERT. This may be a consequence of the fact that estrogens can deplete essential vitamins.

The estrogens in most ERT products are different from the Pill and DES. They are synthesized from natural sources "blended to represent the average composition of material derived from the pregnant mares' urine." Nonetheless, ERT may inhibit pituitary function and produce side effects similar to the Pill. As noted, the association between ERT and cancer of the endometrium was established in studies published last year.

ERT is the fourth or fifth most popular drug in the United

States. Half of our women in the pertinent age groups are taking it. Some younger women take it too, if they have had a hysterectomy, or for certain medical conditions. Some doctors start women on it at 30, just to "prevent aging." Dr. Sheldon Cherry, author of *The Menopause Myth,* affirms that menopause is a normal process, not a "deficiency disease." "Women have been sold a bill of goods," he says. "Aging is built in. It's in the cell. It's bad enough we all have to die but why hasten the process by taking extraneous drugs!"

Yet even Dr. Cherry prescribes ERT occasionally, for women who have physical symptoms that warrant it. He tries to limit its use to two or three years. Some doctors advise their patients to take it only as needed, if hot flashes occur.

Women who have suffered from severe hot flashes are understandably grateful for ERT, and may maintain that the personal benefits outweigh the risks of cancer or gall bladder disease. One woman who *got* cancer told me she would do it over for the relief ERT gave her. Still, many others who didn't need it, who took it not for medical purposes but on the false assumption that it would keep them young, are furious at the outcome. One such woman, aged 53, developed estrogen-associated blisters on her face, neck, chest and hands, which, although they went away when she stopped ERT (after eight years of use), left her with permanent scars. An 83-year-old woman having taken ERT for three years, hemorrhaged from her vagina, and barely survived an emergency hysterectomy.

Sir Charles Dodds, whose basic research helped make estrogen products possible, deplored the use of them for frivolous indications. When he saw how popular they'd become he used to shake his head and say, "If a clock is working, you don't tinker with it."

It would be nice if we had a carefree contraceptive, as Margaret Sanger dreamed, and a pill against aging. It would be nice if we could all save money on our meat without risking cancer. It would be nice, but we don't.

Amanda Spake

THE PUSHERS

Langley High School in Northern Virginia, near Washington, D.C., looks like any other suburban, brown-brick set of classrooms. Langley has its prom queens, cheerleaders, and sock hops, its football games and jocks. It is not an unusual high school. But the birth and death of one of Langley's brightest students, Marilyn Malloy, had unique significance.

Marilyn's story could be played out in any high school in this country, and it undoubtedly will be in some. It is the story of America's pharmaceutical industry, too quick to sell doctors on prescribing drugs, and its physicians, too quick to believe in the drug houses. There is no way of knowing how many stories like Marilyn's are yet to be told, but a conservative estimate would be 2,000.

Marilyn Malloy was an attractive seventeen-year-old with long, dark hair, wide eyes, and a desperate love for horseback riding. At Langley, Marilyn was an honors student, at the top of her senior class. She was serious about her studies; had she graduated, a wide range of colleges and career choices could have been hers. But Marilyn Malloy did not make it to her Langley graduation ceremonies. Early in the summer of 1974, while her friends celebrated their own commencement, she died.

Grace Malloy became pregnant with Marilyn in 1955. Early in the pregnancy, she noticed bloody spotting, a sign that she might be losing her baby. She telephoned her gynecologist to tell him she feared a miscarriage, and her doctor prescribed a drug to insure the pregnancy. "I had no reason to believe there might be anything wrong with it," Mrs. Malloy says. The miraculous pill was diethylstilbestrol or DES, and Mrs. Malloy took it throughout her pregnancy with Marilyn.

"I was reading the morning paper," Grace Malloy recalls, "and I saw this little article about DES and cancer." It was a cold, November day in 1971. Marilyn was fourteen years old. "I was worried. I took the drug with two of my girls." She hustled Marilyn and her sister Patti off to a gynecologist; her former doctor who had prescribed DES was now dead. Her physician said that Patti, then twenty, was in good shape, but the verdict was not so rosy for Marilyn. Barely a teen-ager, Marilyn Malloy had advanced cancer of the vagina.

"Then we went through the operations," Mrs. Malloy remembers. "You know, they think they've 'got it all.' This is the tragic part. Marilyn was well after the first operation for a year and a half. We sat back relieved and thought it was over. The doctors told us that it was."

Grace Malloy's voice broke into a husky bitterness as she recalled the false hopes and bright promises of the doctors. "They were wrong. They were all wrong," she said. "It had already gone into her lung."

Adenocarcinoma of the vagina, Marilyn's disease and that most commonly found in affected DES daughters, spreads to the lungs in about 35 percent of the cases discovered so far. The disease used to affect, primarily, women past the age of fifty. When an upsurge of cases was discovered in teen-agers in 1966, Dr. Arthur Herbst, a gynecologist at Massachusetts General Hospital, began to put the pieces of the DES puzzle together. By 1971, he was able to show a link in seven cases between DES taken during pregnancy and vaginal or cervical cancer in female offspring.

Since 1971, the number of DES-related cancers has escalated dramatically. Dr. Herbst reported in the *American Journal of Obstetrics and Gynecology* in 1974 that 138 DES-induced cancers had been recorded and that twenty-four of those young women, like Marilyn, were dead. Thirty-seven cases in the study experienced a cancer recurrence in less than two years. A spokesman for the National Cancer Institute said that by last year "at least 400" DES cancer cases had showed up in young women.

The drug was widely prescribed for threatened miscarriage between 1945 and 1965 and by some doctors until 1971. Only in the late 1960s did studies show DES was ineffective in preventing miscarriage. Dr. Herbst noted in his 1974 *Journal* article that "the peak incidence of these tumors may not have been reached." A study at the Mayo Clinic to determine DES-induced cancer rates shows that there may be four cancer cases for every 1,000 women who took the drug. All doctors who see women born between 1945 and 1965 should ask them if their mothers took DES, but they do not. DES daughters should be checked for the disease as soon as they reach puberty; millions of women took the drug during those years, and some half of them delivered girls. The scope of the DES tragedy is as yet undetermined.

"And it was all for nothing," Grace Malloy says. "DES doesn't even prevent miscarriage. I didn't want to say or do anything while my daughter was living, for fear it might embarrass her, but now that she's gone, I want people to know about Marilyn."

The nation's drug firms spend about $1 billion each year in prizes, trips, samples, and medical journal advertising to promote drug sales. In 1973, physicians received more than $14 million worth of gifts and reminder items from the pharmaceutical manufacturers. In addition, the companies gave doctors more than two billion free samples to encourage drug use; 18 million oral contraceptive packets were handed out by the twenty leading drug firms alone. The firms also control most of the drug information doctors receive, and physicians admit that drug salesmen are their first source on the uses of new drugs. As a result of this promotion, some pharmaceutical products become "best sellers"—like tranquilizers, oral contraceptives, and, in the past, DES. As one doctor put it, drugs are "merchandised like detergents or vacuum cleaners" and the patients pay at the pharmacy for the cost of marketing.

Each year, women visit physicians 25 percent more frequently than men. With the burden of contraception and pregnancy, women fill about 50 percent more of the prescriptions doctors write than do male health consumers. It is women, more often than men, who bear this advertising cost both in drug-induced illness and cold cash. What do they get for their money?

The Ortho Pharmaceutical firm, a division of Johnson and Johnson, is one of the largest pill pushers in the country. Ortho runs a "bonus point competition" for drug salesmen who successfully convince doctors to prescribe the company's oral contraceptives. In the competition, sales personnel selling the most contraceptives can participate in the "diamond award program" and receive valuable art works and other prizes. Ortho also engages in "prescription surveys," in which the salesmen, called detailmen, are allowed to riffle through pharmacy files to see which doctors are prescribing contraceptives for their patients and what kinds. Ortho has said it may discontinue the practice but a detailman for Lederle (another producer of oral contraceptives) doubted the company would be able to enforce it. "Detailmen *have* to do 'script surveys' to sell drugs. I do them, everybody does them," he said.

Pfizer Pharmaceuticals relies in part on a "dinner program" for physicians, where doctors and spouses are treated to elaborate meals and an evening of drug promotion. When the company launched a campaign for one of its antibiotics the sales staff was told, "One of the most successful methods of quickly establishing Vibramycin intravenous has been the Vibramycin dinners. . . . Your district manager will be receiving fifty Vibramycin IV dinner kits. Each kit contains Vibramycin IV, reprints . . . and a small bottle of perfume." Presumably, the perfume was for the physician's spouse. Pfizer's president, Gerald G. Laubach, claims, "The dinner program is the heart of the informational and educational part of the thing." Yet a former Pfizer salesman told U.S. Senate investigators reviewing these promotional practices that the presentations were often unbalanced and reprints were seldom unfavorable to the product.

But the dinner programs are church socials compared to the almost 40,000 factory tours and seminar trips sponsored annually by drug firms. Food, entertainment, and transportation are often provided free to physicians and spouses and accommodations are never less than deluxe. On a plant tour of the Eli Lilly Company, one doctor commented, "We were afforded every luxury of bed and board," and on the Lederle tour, the doctors stay at the Waldorf Astoria in New York City.

One doctor, a dermatologist from Philadelphia, recounted his experiences at the generous hands of the drug companies: "I am chagrined to recall being a guest of a pharmaceutical house at the beautiful mountain retreat above New York City. Being wined and dined and then touring a plant. I also attended a symposium in a vacation spot, and I remember hearing at least five times that the meeting was a result of the Ciba-Geigy Pharmaceutical Company, as was our expensive roast beef dinner. I realized, on the way home, that it wasn't Geigy that was giving us all this, it was our patients."

The dermatologist also talked of gifts from the companies. "I remember accepting a tape recorder from a pharmaceutical company as well." Companies give tape recorders, books, or watches to doctors or pharmacists to convince them to prescribe or stock their brand of a drug that is similar to a competitor's, such as an antibiotic or oral contraceptive. The Lederle detailman added, "All drug companies have some incentive programs for physicians, pharmacists, and hospitals. If they say they don't, they're lying."

The G. D. Searle Company, makers of Ovulen, Demulen, and Enovid, decided one of its most effective sales tactics was to persuade nurses its oral contraceptives were superior. Realizing women often talk with gynecologists' nurses, the company directed its sales force to "Sell the nurse. Now talk to that gracious nurse, and tell the doctor she is well informed. She could better aid his patients. . . . She is as important in moving your product as gas is to moving a car. You cannot go far without either." Searle's training brochure next focuses attention on the physician: "He wants to be sold. He expects to be asked for the business. He is going to give it to the best sales person." Drawbacks of various oral contraceptives take a back seat to sales, when drug houses clearly feel the physicians' concern is "to be sold."

The pharmaceutical manufacturers may be right. One Maryland

physician, commenting on this Madison Avenue operation, said, "It certainly influences prescribing practices and the patients might get the drugs prescribed to them which ordinarily would not have occurred had it not been for the impact of the detailmen."

Searle's promotional efforts have been extraordinarily successful in pushing a drug for the treatment of vaginal infections, Flagyl. Each year, 2.2 million prescriptions are written for Searle's Flagyl, the only drug used to treat trichomonas vaginitis, a minor disorder marked by itching, discharge, and sometimes burning during urination. Most women have had it at one time or another, and probably most have received Flagyl to correct it. Doctors often ask women if their husbands or lovers can take the pills as well, since some medical authorities believe males carry the tiny, one-celled organisms and women will be re-infected. Many women live with the protozoa all the time with no ill effects until there is an overgrowth and sometimes even the overgrowth symptoms disappear. Hot baths, loose clothing (air kills them), and relying on sanitary napkins instead of tampons can prevent overgrowth and eliminate the need for Flagyl.

Naturally, this old remedy is not promoted by Searle. Medical journal advertising proclaims Flagyl as "the only systemic Trichomonacide." But in the fine print, the company recommends white blood cell counts be taken before and after administration of Flagyl in both partners, and stresses that proof of the presence of trichomonas, verified by tests, should be present in both males and females before prescribing. Gynecologists rarely follow even these minor precautions, since the drug has been available for more than ten years and is considered safe. I have received the drug three times and never had a white cell count taken, nor have any women I have known, yet all but one have taken Flagyl. Only once did a gynecologist bother to take a smear to test if the organisms were actually there.

There is good reason for the blood counts, were doctors to read the warning. Flagyl reduces white cells, the body's main agents to fight all diseases. Furthermore, the drug causes tumors in rats and mice. When Searle submitted studies on the drug, about ten years ago, to the Food and Drug Administration for approval, the company apparently "misinterpreted" the results. The FDA overlooked the mistake. An article published in 1971 showed the drug caused lung and lymph tumors in mice. When the FDA pulled out the data submitted by Searle, the agency had one of its statisticians, Dr. M.A. Gross, look at the results. He concluded that Searle's findings, showing the drug was not cancer-inducing, were wrong. The drug caused twice as many breast tumors in rats when the animals were fed a dose comparable to that women receive, but over a longer period of time. "It is quite clear," Dr. Gross reported, "that the evidence of increased risk of development of mammary tumors as a result of treatment with this agent is overwhelming." The FDA is now considering criminal prosecution of Searle for "falsifying" its original animal tests.

Flagyl has not been used long enough to determine if the animal studies apply directly to humans as well, but most medical authorities agree that anything that causes cancer in animals could have the same effect on humans. Flagyl may turn out to be another DES in ten years, when the results of its massive administration are evident.

Anita Johnson, a lawyer with Ralph Nader's Health Research Group, is working to compel the Food and Drug Administration to pull Flagyl off the market. "With more than two million prescriptions each year, I think nearly every woman in the country has received Flagyl," she says. She points out that Ortho, eager to cash in on Searle's cornered vaginitis market, has started testing a related drug, Tinadazoil. Ortho animal tests showed that the drug, like Flagyl, caused cancer in mice. But under pressure from the company, the FDA is allowing Ortho to do tests on women.

"That is unprecedented," Johnson adds, "and very anti-female. They're saying it doesn't matter what the animal tests show, even if it's the worst. Now that they've gone this far, the FDA is going to be obliged to approve Tinadazoil." If Tinadazoil is approved, Ortho will undoubtedly move the drug into its promotional apparatus with full-page, glossy ads in the medical journals which now show only the glowing claims for Flagyl.

Medical journal advertising is an art in itself. Physicians' first information on new drugs may come through the companies' detailmen, but their second source, according to the FDA, is company ads in journals and by mail. Mailed ads are usually reprints of the journal ads. The drug houses invested $9 million in 1973 on advertising in the American Medical Association's journals alone.

The featured players in these medical advertising dramas are often women, and the most common disease in America today, one would guess from reading the ads, is female depression and anxiety. A wide range of drugs is promoted to physicians to "cure" depressions. Next to depression, the biggest "disease" in the journals is pregnancy, and it is in advertising contraceptives that the drug houses find their forte. Contraceptive ads usually appeal to a physician's paternalism, casting women as uninformed children. But the Lederle pharmaceutical company went one better in promoting its new, sequential oral contraceptive, Zorane. Here, women were chastised for trying to gain information about their bodies.

The ads featured two attractive young women, both with long, dark hair and dressed in slacks. They were pictured talking with one another in what was almost surely a food cooperative. One woman, gesturing and speaking, was obviously telling the other something that disturbed her greatly. The copy read: "Because her 'medical consultant' alarms her about 'the pill' . . . and because she runs to you for her answer—Lederle presents: Zorane. For her peace of mind . . . and yours."

This ad ran in medical journals for months before the FDA cracked down on it; it forced Lederle to change the copy and seized twenty-five million Zorane pills. The company's promotion, according to the FDA, was "not supported by substantial evidence" that these drugs are safer than any other birth-control pill—a Madison Avenue style nuance that physicians who prescribed Zorane may have missed.

This promotional steamroller brings the drug houses more than $6 billion in prescription drug sales a year, about $30,000 per doctor. It also sends half a million people to the hospital with adverse drug reactions, and an estimated 30,000 to 160,000 unfortunate patients to the morgue. If the 160,000 figure is close, as indicated in studies from hospitals in Florida and Massachusetts, prescribed drugs could be the fourth largest killer in the nation. There are no exact figures on the numbers of Americans who die each year from overprescribed or misprescribed drugs, and no figures could reflect the pain these drugs can cause. (Significantly, the FDA recently banned the production of three sequential oral contraceptives—Oracon, Ortho-Novum SQ, and Norquen—because of new evidence that they may be harmful.)

Legislation has been introduced by Senator Edward Kennedy, Massachusetts Democrat, to curb the pharmaceutical companies' voracious advertising appetite. His bill, S. 1282, would require licensing of detailmen, provide doctors with a drug compendium, and force sales personnel to present both the side effects and advantages of their products. The bill would also ban expensive gift-giving and limit trips and tours. If his legislation is supported by women (as it should be) and the bill passes, it is a start. But women will also have to inform themselves about the pharmaceutical products they take, realizing that the prescriptions may be the result of journal ads, gifts, dinners, free trips, or a detailman's efforts to earn a "diamond award." It does not make much difference now to Grace Malloy's former gynecologist that he was undoubtedly receiving his share of gratuities from DES manufacturers. It does not make much difference to him now that he was merely following the prescribing practice of an era, a practice supported and promoted by the drug houses. It does not make much difference because he died a successful old man. But it could have made a great deal of difference to Marilyn Malloy.

Rose Kushner

THE POLITICS OF BREAST CANCER

One day in January 1975, Marge Stone's* fiancé found a seed-sized lump on the side of her left breast. She wanted to wait; he insisted on calling a cancer specialist friend of his right away. He won. The oncologist referred Marge to a surgeon who assured her that it was a tiny, benign cyst.

"You're only twenty-eight," he said confidently. "I'll take it out for your peace of mind, but I'm sure it's nothing."

Because he was so certain that it was "nothing," he suggested that she have the cyst removed in a hospital emergency room under a local anesthetic.

"There's no point in tying up a whole operating room and staff for a thing like this," Marge's doctor explained. "I can do the biopsy and have you out in half an hour."

Marge was out of the hospital in half an hour. But the "benign cyst" turned out to be intraductal adenocarcinoma—the most common type of breast cancer. Two weeks later, her left breast was amputated, along with thirty lymph nodes from her left armpit.

"All the doctors I saw after the biopsy told me that having a modified radical mastectomy was the safest route to take," she told her surprised friends. "I'd rather be alive with one breast than dead with two."

*Although the names have been changed, the case histories are real.

Barely two years later, in December, 1976, Ruth Miller's fiancé found a seed-sized lump on the side of *her* left breast. (Lovers are often the best breast examiners!) Ruth wanted to wait; he insisted on calling a friend in medical school. He won.

Because Ruth was only twenty-nine, the surgeon she was referred to suggested the same out-patient biopsy Marge had undergone. And, as in Marge's case, the diagnosis astonished the surgeon: intraductal adenocarcinoma.

However, instead of amputating Ruth's breast and cutting out all the axillary lymph nodes in a modified radical mastectomy procedure, Ruth's surgeon removed only the tumor and a band of healthy tissue around it. As soon as the incision was healed, he prescribed a series of X-ray treatments for her left breast and the area under her arm.

This may sound like medical heresy, but, according to many breast cancer experts, both the young women named above have identical odds for living ten years after surgery—the usual yardstick for measuring the effectiveness of any treatment of breast cancer.

Although nothing new regarding breast cancer had appeared on the scientific horizon since January 1975, the difference between the breast cancer treatments of Marge and Ruth was the result of widespread publicity, women's liberation, and consumers' rights activism.

Also, during the intervening two years, a wave of flexibility swept through the medical profession regarding the treatment of minimal breast cancer. Even some physicians who are hardline believers in radical mastectomy have become reluctant to amputate an entire breast because of the presence of a minute, seed-sized cancer.

Of course, the physicians who do not favor automatic amputation are still a minority—they are isolated experts who take into account emerging scientific knowledge about the biology of breast cancer. If a surgeon is not aware of this knowledge, he or she almost instinctively believes that the only course of action is to cut off the whole breast immediately. Almost all the surgeons in the United States today belong in this category.

As a matter of fact, many surgeons still advocate the Halsted radical mastectomy—a turn-of-the-century operation that excises not only the breast and the lymph nodes, but also the pectoral muscles of the chest. Women who are unfortunate enough to undergo the Halsted radical mastectomy lose everything between the skin and the bone in that area of the body.

And a few oldtimers still insist on performing the extended radical mastectomy—a mutilating procedure in which not only are the breast, the lymph nodes, and the pectoral muscles removed, but a section of the ribcage is sawed out, leaving a rectangular cavity.

Thus, Marge was lucky to have had a modified radical. Like Ruth, Marge lived in a large city where several fine hospitals and dozens of oncological surgeons were available to explain different treatments and offer choices—because both women had found their symptoms early.

Given the choices for treatment that her doctor recommended, all of which required the removal of her breast, Marge opted for the modified radical mastectomy. Ruth's surgeon, however, believed that removal of her breast might not be necessary. He believed that X-ray would destroy any remaining cancer as effectively as the scalpel would, so Ruth opted for local excision followed by irradiation of the breast and the axillary nodes.

But no one knows what the "best" treatment for breast cancer is, and there have *never* been long-term studies of large groups of women—"matched samples"—in order to compare the survival rates of all the numerous treatments available today. This is particularly vital in dealing with minimal cancers that are smaller than half an inch.

The only long-term study available was published in July 1975, by Dr. Vera Peters of the Princess Margaret Hospital in Toronto. This study compares two of the available treatments: local incision (segmental resection) with radiation, and the Halsted radical mastectomy with post-operative radiation. This report was impressive enough to influence Ruth's surgeon; for Marge, it came too late.

Women's liberation and consumer activism, combined with the

publicity about breast cancer, have brought the issue to the point where women have demanded the opportunity to have some say in their destinies. In large cities, where medical competition is keen, this kind of consumer pressure has resulted in a change in attitude by some surgeons. In one-doctor towns, women must still accept whatever that physician is willing and able to do.

Pressure by patients has not, however, pushed physicians into performing unsafe procedures. What it has done is to send physicians and surgeons back to their books and classrooms to learn more about the biology of breast cancer—an umbrella name that describes at least fifteen different malignancies that can grow in that organ.

Each type of cancer cell has a different rate of growth and a different tendency to metastasize (spread) to other organs. So, unlike a case of appendicitis, where there is a single treatment, a number of procedures can be used in treating a breast tumor.

The most important reason for this multiplicity of procedures is that breast cancer is a systemic disease that is truly "local" for only a short time. By the time a fast-growing tumor is large enough to be palpated (felt), it is at least two years old; a slow-growing tumor can take as long as nine years to become the size of a pea.

During this time, the tumor is shedding both living and dead cells into the body, and oncologists estimate that, in about 50 percent of all cases, there are already micrometastases—microscopic clusters of malignant cells—scattered in other organs. Some of these clusters continue to grow and show up months or even years later, while others are destroyed by the body's own immune defense system.

In addition, in mammary carcinoma, a malignancy can develop in many places—in a duct, between ducts, in breast fat, in lymphatic and blood vessels, in the nipple, or in the pouchy lobes where milk is manufactured.

Some cancers spread quickly throughout the breast and the lymph nodes, and invade other organs, even though the primary tumor remains tiny. Others develop *in situ*—they are true cancers, but the cells seldom stray from their home base. Most mammary carcinomas vary between these two extremes, living near their birthplaces for certain periods of time and then traveling to other parts of the body.

There's another factor that must be considered. Many experts have shown that breast cancer is a multicentric disease. This means that if one malignancy is found, there is a high probability that there are others scattered in that breast. And, since there is a crossover between the two breasts beneath the sternum (the central bone of the chest), many specialists feel that the multicentricity theory applies to both breasts.

There is a difference of opinion about this, and no one knows anything with certainty, but the multicentricity theory accounts for the belief that the entire breast must always be removed or irradiated, even if the only palpable symptom is a small lump. It is also the reason why many surgeons insist on doing a routine biopsy of the second breast.

These are only a few of the bizarre aspects of the biology of breast cancer that, so far, have made it impossible for physicians to prescribe a universal treatment for the disease.

When Marge faced her crisis in January 1975, this kind of information about the biology of breast cancer was available, although it was seldom discussed outside major cancer centers. Of course, the information was catalogued in medical libraries, but it was as inaccessible to most women as the files of the CIA and the FBI.

Marge had heard about a physician named George Crile, Jr. and had read his book about mastectomy procedures, *What Women Should Know About the Breast Cancer Controversy,* and she had read a news article about the work of Dr. Eleanor Montague in Houston. But she felt that these reports were still experimental and she wasn't willing to gamble.

Because Marge's tumor was smaller than half an inch, some of her friends had recommended doctors in certain parts of the United States and in Europe who routinely perform lumpectomies, wedge excisions, segmental resections, and partial mastectomies— with and without X-ray.

But when she was told that she had a cancerous lump in her

breast, Marge was not able to find any information supporting the biological reasons for these lesser procedures. The modified radical mastectomy seemed to be the safest, most effective way to treat the seed-sized mammary carcinoma in her left breast. And it seemed to her that keeping her breast was not worth the risk of dying of cancer.

By the time Ruth discovered her breast cancer in December, 1976, more information about the disease was available to the average woman. Many specialists had published results of clinical trials showing that just removing the lump and some healthy tissue around it, followed by X-ray treatments, was as successful in terms of that ten-year survival rate as was extensive amputation.

Probably the most impressive of these reports was the result of the thirty-year study mentioned above published in 1975 by Dr. Vera Peters of the Princess Margaret Hospital in Toronto. Soon after that, Ruth had to make her decision, and she chose lumpectomy.

Since then, the media have reported leaks from laboratories which hint that the "buckshot" theory of multicentricity may not be as common as earlier data had indicated. If this is true, automatic mastectomy may be unnecessary much of the time, and many X-ray treatments may also be needless.

Some pathologists have pointed out that many women have such slow-growing cancers that if they can be treated by minimal surgery, they may die of old age long before the disease can spread to a vital organ.

More recently, immunologists have offered evidence that once the primary tumor—the lump itself—is removed, a woman's immune system can destroy any microscopic cluster of cells that may have been left behind. Their studies seem to support the opinion that when a cancer is minimal, removing it, along with some healthy tissue and a few of the axillary nodes (in order to detect a possible metastasis), is more than enough surgery.

Endocrinologists have reported that a test can be done to see if a tumor is estrogen-dependent, that is, if the tumor depends on female hormones (estrogen) for growth. This knowledge may be important in deciding how to treat the disease at the very beginning. And plastic surgeons have reported a wide variety of techniques and materials to reconstruct the breasts of women who already have had mastectomies.

As a result of all this information, this is where women stand on the subject of breast cancer: If a woman is aware of her tumor at a very early stage, and receives prompt treatment from a breast-cancer specialist, she may not have to lose her breast; if she does undergo a mastectomy, she can make plans to have her breast reconstructed.

The permutations and combinations of possible procedures for minimal breast cancer are difficult to count, and what is done depends on the size and location of the tumor, its cell type, the presence of enlarged axillary nodes, and whether or not the tumor is estrogen-dependent. Women must also remember that a lumpectomy or a local excision in a large breast might be called a partial mastectomy in a small breast.

Most experts agree that whatever the procedure, ten or twelve lymph nodes should also be removed from the armpit nearest the cancerous breast. This is to make sure that the nodes have not been invaded by malignancy, even if the primary tumor is minimal. If one or more of the axillary nodes is malignant, some specialists will insist on performing a modified radical mastectomy.

However, many radiotherapists feel that using X-ray on the breast and underarm area is just as effective; other experts would preserve the breast and give a node-positive patient some kind of chemotherapy (the type would depend on the number of nodes that have cancer cells).

If an estrogen assay is done and the tumor is found to be hormone-dependent, then the treatment would probably involve removing the ovaries in premenopausal women and prescribing a new kind of medication—anti-estrogens—for postmenopausal women.

If there are no signs of cancer in the axilla, specialists would either use X-ray to irradiate these nodes, or prescribe anti-estrogens or an anti-cancer drug. However, if the symptom is found in the middle or inner sections of a woman's breast, this would affect the choice of treatment because tumors found in these areas frequently spread via the mid-chest nodes.

Before any treatment is done, however, the physician must first be positive that there are no metastases already visible in other organs of the body. Although the technology for finding distant colonies of cancer cells is still primitive, certain examinations known as "staging tests" should still be done.

These tests include scans (painless radioactive photography) or X-rays of the skeleton and skull, chest X-rays, liver function studies (simple blood tests) and, perhaps, scans of the liver and the brain.

The latter two tests are still unreliable, and many experts feel that they are not worth the added expense and time. However, the chest X-ray is excellent for detecting early lung metastases, and scanners can frequently find bone malignancies when they are still too small to show up on X-ray film.

Women must remember that the only reason for removing a breast is to prevent cancer from spreading beyond the axillary lymph nodes. If staging tests show that the disease is already in another organ, amputating the breast is useless.

There are so many options for treating minimal breast cancer that most anxious and agitated women simply give up and let their doctors make the decisions. In the United States, this usually means that a biopsy that shows cancer is immediately followed by a modified radical mastectomy, and, as a rule, the final decision to amputate is made while the patient is unconscious.

Thus the woman has no choice; her options are taken away from her. For this reason, the first step of any breast-saving treatment is simply to insist that the biopsy be performed as a separate procedure.

Arrangements for an estrogen assay must be made in advance because, if a malignancy is found, the specimen must be quickly frozen and sent to a laboratory which has the equipment and personnel to do this vital test.

Once the diagnosis is made, the woman can get a second, third, or fourth opinion from various specialists. The opinions may be conflicting and they may be confusing. But each opinion is an option.

Most physicians will say that a woman is committing suicide if she waits, but this is a myth. Women can safely wait as long as two weeks after a biopsy to get opinions. However, the prohibition against waiting for a breast examination and a biopsy is even more valid than ever. Women who procrastinate while a seed-sized lump becomes the size of a pea, then of an almond, and then of a plum are letting their breast-saving options disappear.

Early detection is not a shopworn cliché, it is an absolute prerequisite to any treatment that might save a woman's breast, as well as her life. To have minimal surgery, a woman must first have minimal cancer. There are few breast-saving techniques for women who merely wait and watch.

Deborah Larned

THE EPIDEMIC IN UNNECESSARY HYSTERECTOMY

A year and a half ago Mrs. J., a forty-seven-year-old Queens' schoolteacher, ran out of birth-control pills, and because her regular gynecologist had retired, she made an appointment with another highly recommended Ob/Gyn in her neighborhood. She was feeling fine, just needed a new Pill prescription, Pap smear and pelvic. As things turned out, she got all that and more.

"After my examination," Mrs. J. recalls, "the doctor told me to come into his office. I sat down, and in the most nonchalant manner he told me that I had 'a uterine fibroid the size of a lemon' and needed a hysterectomy as soon as possible. He, of course, was going to do the operation."

The doctor neglected to tell Mrs. J. that fibroids are almost always benign and are so common (1 in every 5 women of child-bearing age) that some doctors would go so far as to say that it's normal to get them. "The only thing I heard was the word 'tumor,'" says Mrs. J., "and when I asked, 'Are these things always cancerous?' all the doctor said was, 'Sometimes when we go in we find them to be cancerous.' I was so upset I could hardly talk. My husband was furious about the casual way I had been treated. When he suggested to the doctor that we get another opinion, the doctor just said, 'That's up to you.'"

Mrs. J. never had the hysterectomy. Two subsequent consultations proved that she had only a "tiny" fibroid, which was nothing to worry about. Like most fibroids, it would probably shrink as she approached menopause.

Looking back on it now, Mrs. J. feels lucky. "I'm forty-seven and very healthy. I feel and look younger than I am. I was happy with the Pill and had no interest in sterilization. The last thing I needed was an unnecessary operation." But she worries about the women who might not be so lucky. And she should.

American women are experiencing the effects of a mysterious and highly contagious epidemic. But it's not the disease that's gotten out of hand; it's the treatment. We're having a hysterectomy outbreak and though doctors have been aware of it—even promoting it—for several years, most women still believe that hysterectomies are performed rarely (after all, it is major surgery), and then only to alter the course of some critical disease like uterine cancer.

Hysterectomy, the surgical removal of the uterus, is in fact the fourth most commonly performed operation in the United States today—after tonsillectomy, hernia repair and removal of the gall bladder. And though this procedure is still used as a cure for uterine cancer, over the last 30 years hysterectomy has come to be regarded by many gynecologists as a "simple" solution for everything from backaches to contraception. Once considered a surgical last resort, hysterectomy is now put forth as "the only logical approach to female sterilization." American women are being sold an attractive, albeit expensive, all-purpose surgical package—no more periods, cramps, babies or bother—and if they do not readily accept the medical recommendation, they are often bamboozled into sterilization on highly questionable grounds.

While hysterectomy as a means of sterilization is a relatively new phenomenon, the controversy over hysterectomies is an old one.

For nearly a century doctors have been arguing over which "female conditions" warrant the removal of the uterus. In the mid-1800s hysterectomies were performed for such symptoms as general "troublesomeness," "eating like a ploughman," "erotic tendencies" and even "simple cussedness."

By the early part of the twentieth century science had replaced superstition, and only so-called medical problems were considered adequate reasons for performing a hysterectomy. To name just a few—uterine cancer, inexplicable menstrual bleeding, small non-malignant tumors (fibroids), dysmenorrhea (what most women just call "cramps") and vaginal laxness (a condition in which the vaginal walls lose their firmness, often as a result of childbearing).

Even then, many doctors weren't convinced, claiming that for most of these symptoms, rest, relaxation, hormones or scraping of the uterus (D+C) were all treatments that should be tried before major surgery. When a cancerous condition existed, or when a woman had a severely disabling pelvic disease that did not respond to less drastic treatments, no one quibbled over the necessity of a hysterectomy. But would a conscientious surgeon remove a woman's uterus because of simple backache? They've been doing it for years and, needless to say, not everyone is happy about it.

Out of the estimated 2 million unnecessary operations performed in the United States each year (a "conservative figure," according to Dr. Sidney Wolfe of Ralph Nader's Health Research Group), hysterectomies are one of the biggest offenders. Several medical studies—one as early as 1946—have shown that at least one-third of all the hysterectomies in the U.S. have been performed on women with *normal* uteri. In many cases women who underwent hysterectomies had not presented any symptoms prior to surgery.

So for years, gynecologists have been recommending major surgery for women who don't need it—and that's bad enough. Lately, however, doctors have simply abandoned the question of which medical symptoms warrant surgery and have wholeheartedly endorsed this operation for the sole purpose of sterilization—which is a clever and disarming move since such labels as "necessary" and "unnecessary" no longer apply. Doctors are off the hook. They've even changed the name. Now a woman may elect to have a "hysterilization." If she has an additional pelvic problem or two, all the better.

In hospitals throughout the country sterilization by hysterectomy, once unthinkable, has now become routine. At the Los

Angeles County–University of Southern California Medical Center, for example, the total number of hysterectomies performed for any reason increased 293 percent between July 1968 and the end of 1970. If only elective hysterectomy for the purpose of sterilization is counted, the increase was an astounding 742 percent.

"Up until the last few years," says Dr. Lester T. Hibbard, author of the L.A. County–USC Medical Center study, "no hysterectomies were performed at this institution unless functional or organic pathology was documented. . . . In 1970, sterilization by hysterectomy had become a commonplace and widely accepted operation . . . both for women with normal pelvic function and women with relatively minor abnormalities which otherwise would not justify a major operative procedure."

Although the general public is largely unaware of the sudden upsurge in hysterilizations, physicians have been quietly arguing about it in professional journals for the last five years. Finally in 1971, Hibbard's report and other indications of the soaring hysterectomy rate—California Blue Cross announced a 79 percent increase in hysterectomies for the last half of 1970—forced a showdown between the pro and anti factions.

At its 1971 annual meeting held in San Francisco, the American College of Obstetrics and Gynecology sponsored what is now fondly remembered as the "Great Debate" on the merits of hysterilization. Following the exchange, physicians were asked to register their approval or disapproval of this procedure by their applause. The acclaim for hysterilization lasted a full 25 seconds: the applause for the "no" position, only 10 seconds. What's more, according to *Audio Digest's* decibel meter, the intensity of the advocates' applause was double that of the opposition.

Though this victory may well have been pulled off by a rowdy band of partisans, there's no denying that hysterilization generates extraordinary enthusiasm among many gynecologists. It seems to have a lot going for it.

Contrary to popular belief, a hysterectomy does not bring on menopause, hasten the aging process, or physiologically interfere with sexual enjoyment. The ovaries continue to produce eggs and hormones each month, but because the uterus has been removed, menstruation and any accompanying discomforts are eliminated. As Dr. Joseph H. Pratt Jr. of the Mayo Clinic rather overenthusiastically pointed out at the Great Debate. "No more monthly curse, no napkins, no Tampax, no accidents, no embarrassment, no poring over a calendar to see when a trip is feasible."

Other hysterilization promoters point to the fact that hysterectomy is 100 percent effective in preventing pregnancy, whereas tubal ligation (a less complicated procedure involving tying of the Fallopian tubes) has a failure rate of from 2.2 percent to 1 percent. The removal of the uterus also eliminates further pelvic disorders, an important consideration since recent studies have shown that many women who undergo tubal ligation develop an unusually high percentage of pelvic problems in later life. (Whether these disturbances are a direct result of the ligation, however, is unclear. Some experts suggest that women who are no longer able to conceive are simply unwilling to tolerate even minimal discomforts.)

It all adds up to an attractive proposition, and yet for most women the nuisance of menstruation, the chance of contraceptive failure, or the remote possibility of future pelvic problems do not provide enough of an incentive to undergo major surgery. By far the most persuasive medical argument—for many women the real clincher—is that hysterectomy will prevent uterine cancer. As one woman who underwent a hysterectomy recently said, "I went into the hospital to get my tubes tied. When the doctor suggested that I have a hysterectomy instead, the whole idea was horrifying to me. But when he told me that I wouldn't have to worry about cancer of the uterus, I decided that maybe that was the best thing to do after all."

Dr. Ralph C. Wright, a Connecticut gynecologist and perhaps the most outspoken advocate of routine hysterectomy, views the possibility of cancer as fundamental. "When the patient has completed her family," Wright contends, "total hysterectomy should also be performed as a prophylactic procedure. Under these circumstances, the uterus becomes a useless, bleeding, symptom-producing, potentially cancer-bearing organ and therefore should be removed. . . . To sterilize a woman and allow her to keep a useless and potentially lethal organ is incompatible with modern gynecological concepts. Hysterectomy is the only logical approach to surgical sterilization of women."

Even ignoring Wright's apparent view that it is now the gynecologist's prerogative to decide which organs a woman may be "allowed" to retain, it is the "lethal organ" argument that has provoked the most heated debate. This view, says hysterilization detractors, not only appeals to an unreasonable fear of cancer but is patently misleading.

According to Washington, D.C.'s Health Research Group, which recently concluded a study of surgical sterilization practices in federally funded clinics, what hysterilization advocates fail to tell their patients is that the death rate for hysterectomy itself (1,000 out of every 1 million women annually) is, in fact, *higher* than the death rate for uterine/cervical cancer. The American Cancer Society estimates that of the approximately 44,000 cases of uterine or cervical cancer reported each year, 12,000 are fatal (or 100 out of every 1 million women each year). In addition, the Cancer Society claims, a majority of these deaths could be prevented if regular gynecological exams and Pap smears were available to all women.

Hysterectomy will, of course, prevent cancer; if you don't have a uterus you can't get uterine cancer. However, many cancer experts regard this procedure as a risky exercise in "surgical overkill." Dr. Sidney Arje, a gynecologist and vice-president of professional education for the American Cancer Society, points out that there are cheaper and, in the long run, safer ways of preventing death from uterine cancer. A simple Pap smear is 95 percent effective in detecting the earliest signs of cervical cancer, and though the same test is only 60 percent accurate in diagnosing cancer of the uterus, symptoms such as excessive irregular bleeding followed by a diagnostic D+C provide an early enough warning signal for successful treatment. "If the only reason for performing a hysterectomy is sterilization," says Dr. Arje, "you are probably exposing a woman to a danger equal to or greater than the risks of uterine cancer."

Planned Parenthood Federation, along with many others, takes issue with what they call "hacking 'preventatively' at future possibly offending flesh." For most women, the chances of *not* getting cancer far exceed the chances of getting it. "Preventative lobotomies," says Planned Parenthood in an effort to point out the absurdity of the argument, "for young people at statistically high risk of developing violent psychoses or opthalmectomy for those populations found most likely to get cancer of the eye at some future time have not been suggested by physicians writing in psychiatric or ophthalmologic specialty journals." They might also have pointed out that though cancer of the prostate frequently occurs in men over 50, male urologists are not suggesting routine prophylactic prostectomy.

Medicine is a complicated business and no single explanation can account for the high rate of hysterectomy or for the growing acceptance of hysterilization.

Many gynecologists blame their patients for insisting upon the operation. And yet the evidence does not bear this out. At the L. A. County Hospital, one-third of all the patients who received hysterectomies had originally requested tubal ligations. In another hospital in Florida, where hysterilizations outnumber tubal ligations 2 to 1, tubal ligations are "discouraged by general staff agreement."

Women are not clamoring to have their uteri taken out, but they are demanding more reliable birth-control methods. Hysterectomy is sold as a fail safe and if physicians are unable to "persuade" a woman to undergo hysterectomy, more devious methods can be used.

Dr. Bernard Rosenfeld, a California physician who is currently studying sterilization practices in the United States, describes one doctor's tactic that is especially employed among Third World women.

"I remember treating a young black woman with several children who was having trouble with her IUD. She was interested in trying another type of device and was referred to the family planning clinic of the hospital to have her present IUD removed. About two weeks later I accidentally ran into her at the hospital. She looked upset and I asked her why. She said, 'They just told me I needed a hysterectomy.' I knew from having examined her that she did not *need* a hysterectomy, so I went and looked up her file. On her medical chart the doctor had recorded, 'Patient *requests* hysterectomy.' "

Black women have long been aware of this kind of medical practice. In the old days it was called a "Mississippi appendectomy." You'd go into the hospital to have a baby and come out minus your uterus. Now doctors are more subtle, but the results are the same. When the doctor decides you've had too many children, he tells you that you "need" a hysterectomy and then writes down that you "asked" for it.

So the question remains: why are doctors "electing" hysterectomy for their female patients?

To begin with, 97 percent of all gynecologists in the United States are men, and to some extent their attitudes toward their female patients inevitably reflect the current view of women held by society as a whole. A woman medical student, for example, remembers this winner from her Ob/Gyn lecturer: "The only significant difference between a cow and a woman is that a cow has more spigots."

One of the more obvious reasons for unnecessary hysterectomy is that medical students need operating experience. Dr. James Ryan describes an exchange which took place while he was a medical student at Boston University Medical School.

"When the student asked the resident why this woman was having a hysterectomy instead of a tubal ligation, he was told, ' . . . We like to do a hysterectomy, it's more of a challenge . . . you know, a well-trained chimpanzee can do a tubal ligation . . . and it's good experience for the junior resident . . . good training.' "

But over-zealous residents account for only a fraction of unnecessary hysterectomies. It's out there in the world of private practice where it's happening and the reasons, many experts say, can be summed up in one word: greed.

Dr. Norman F. Miller, author of the earliest study of unnecessary hysterectomies, first hinted at it in 1946. Referring to the fact that 30.8 percent of all the hysterectomy patients he studied showed no uterine pathology following their operations, he could not help but conclude that a substantial number of women had undergone "acute remunerative or hip-pocket hysterectomies." The now famous "hip-pocket" theory of hysterectomy—an operation performed primarily to fatten a doctor's wallet—still holds true today. There's a joke going around the medical schools— Professor: what are the symptoms for a hysterectomy? Student: A Blue Shield card and $200. But only the doctors are amused.

For a "relatively easy" operation, hysterectomies aren't cheap. Prices run from $1,500 to $2,000 (five to seven times more expensive than a tubal ligation), not to mention the additional loss of a patient's income due to a four to six week recovery period. Like most of us, doctors have to make ends meet. And with a host of borderline justifications to choose among—from the population explosion to the patient's need for dependable contraception— hysterectomies are a tempting solution to inflation.

"It seems inevitable," says Dr. Charles E. Lewis, professor of preventative medicine at UCLA, "that in any occupation where considerable income is available on the basis of events called operations, a small percentage of people can well identify this as a marvelous, income-producing device. . . . Medicine is one of the few fields . . . where, if your wife wants a new coat, all you have to do is a couple more hysterectomies and she can buy it." Or, he might have added, if the doctor wants a Ferrari.

Other critics take a slightly less cynical view. "Human beings," says John R. Knowles, former director of Massachusetts General Hospital, "rationalize what they do without any conscious effort to be dishonest or greedy. Doctors are human. A significant number of them—20 to 30 percent—are de facto fleecing the public while 'knowing they are doing good.' "

Conscious or unconscious, most experts agree that what makes the hysterectomy business so lucrative and what may influence the high rate of needless surgery is the hospital-oriented, fee-for-service system of payment that dominates U.S. medical care. Comparative studies of fee-for-service medical practices (financed largely by insurance plans such as Blue Cross/Blue Shield and Medicaid) and prepaid medical plans (such as California's Kaiser Permanente or Health Insurance Plan of Greater New York) suggest that the incentive of fee-for-service medicine not only fosters more hospital admissions in general but as much as 50 percent more hysterectomies than prepaid plans that employ salaried physicians. Add to this a surplus of surgeons in many U.S. cities and you have a situation ripe with surgical possibilities.

"There are twice as many surgeons in proportion to population in the United States as in England and Wales," says Stanford anesthesiologist John P. Bunker, "and they perform twice as many operations." Consistent with these overall figures, U. S. gynecologists perform proportionately twice as many hysterectomies as their British counterparts.

Are American women sicker than British women? Some flatly say no, claiming that the United States is just experiencing a medical version of Parkinson's Law: the more surgeons you have, the more surgery is performed simply because the surgeons are there and need to make a living. Bunker's own study, "Surgical Manpower" (and here, as it applies to gynecologists, the choice of the word *man*power seems particularly appropriate) attributes discrepancies in the rate of surgery not to differences in U.S. and British health needs but to differences in the organization of health care.

One of the crucial factors—important to the hysterectomy controversy—can be found in the consultant system.

"The British surgeon is a true consultant," Bunker notes. "He sees patients only as they are referred to him by a general practitioner or internist, and he is hospital based. The American surgeon by contrast . . . may be the primary physician/general practitioner referring the patient to himself for surgery and thus creating his own demand."

What women tend to forget (and it's not surprising since in the majority of cases a woman isn't sick when she sees her Ob/Gyn) is that gynecologists are trained surgeons. Perhaps more than any other single group of medical consumers, women rely upon gynecological specialists, not as consultants but as their primary physicians. More than likely, if gynecologists had no vested interest in recommending surgery, fewer unnecessary hysterectomies would be performed.

But at present, with the childbirth business drying up, we have a lot of super-trained gynecologists running around with nothing to do. From the point of view of a physician who may benefit from "self-referral," hysterectomy may be the ideal form of birth control. For a woman to see a gynecologist under these circumstances, says Dr. Ed Stim, medical director of a New York women's clinic, "Is like sending a fly into a spider's web."

The case for hysterectomy has not been made. Despite the claims of gynecologists that surgical advances have made hysterectomy a "relatively easy" procedure—it may now be done through an incision in the vaginal wall as well as through the abdomen—it remains a major operation and, thus, all the complications of anesthesia, bleeding, infection, pneumonia and blood clots may occur. Moreover, there is always the possibility of serious local complications, such as injury to the intestine, vagina, bladder or the tube that connects the bladder to the kidney. Although the death rate for hysterectomy is commonly accepted to be equal to or only slightly higher than tubal ligation (.18 percent), the total complication rate for simple vaginal hysterectomy is 10 to 20 times higher than the complication rate for tubal ligation.

Beyond the cancer argument in favor of hysterectomy—in most cases a scare tactic—is the more fundamental question of how "useless" the uterus really is. Many American physicians would agree with hysterilization advocate Dr. Ralph Wright: the uterus functions primarily as an "incubator" and when conception is either no longer possible or no longer desirable, it loses its function. And yet such unsolicited remarks as "You're forty-two and don't need your uterus anyway," or "When you're finished with your family come in for your birthday hysterectomy," are regarded as cavalier and presumptuous by many women.

But even granting that at some point in a woman's life her uterus becomes something akin to excess baggage, the medical profession largely ignores the emotional impact that a hysterectomy may have on a woman's life.

Psychiatrists agree that a hysterectomy is often a blow to a woman's identity, yet doctors continue to discount the evidence—chalking it all up to female neurosis or sentimentality. "Gynecologists persist in believing," says Sylvia Oliver, a psychotherapist in Seattle, "that most women feel relieved by no longer having to suffer the nuisance of menstruation, and that with adequate counseling a 'well-adjusted' woman will be able to realistically cope with her hysterectomy. On both counts gynecologists are often wrong."

Dr. Peter Barglow, a psychiatrist on staff at the Michael Reese Hospital in Chicago, finds "that hysterectomy is clearly and immediately visualized as an irreversible, drastic procedure, which removes an organ with high value in the ego's image of the body, as well as with considerable conscious value in the woman's sense of identity and femininity. Surely, the loss of an organ whose presence was reaffirmed monthly cannot easily be denied." By contrast, Barglow and his associates suggest, "tubal ligation . . . involves a less drastic change to the body image. . . ."

Of course, depression following a hysterectomy is not a universal reaction. With strong support from friends and family and with a clear understanding of the possible physiological and psychological effects of the operation, most women can handle the loss of their uterus. Many women who have had hysterectomies for severe medical problems *and* who do not plan to have any more children have an easier time of adjustment. "The uterus," says one woman who recently underwent a hysterectomy for chronic pelvic infection, "is not a sacred organ. After what I went through, worrying about my femininity is the furthest thing from my mind. I'm just so relieved to feel like a *person* again."

The story is a little different, however, for women who have been rushed into elective hysterectomy with little preparation. A thirty-six-year-old mother of three says her operation was first suggested by her gynecologist.

My doctor somehow convinced me that a hysterectomy would solve the contraception problem and that I wouldn't have to be bothered with my heavy periods. I am embarrassed now at how reluctant I was to ask questions. I still find it hard to believe that I went along with it. Afterwards I became depressed. Even though I didn't want to have any more children, I realized that I wanted to have the option.

I finally went and saw a counselor. In one sense, the whole thing was good because I could no longer think of myself as only a 'mother.' I had a chance to figure out who else I was. But I still feel upset and angry. All my life I was valued, sometimes overvalued, as a mother. Then I had my uterus removed and everyone, especially my doctor, expected me to go along like nothing happened. It seems you just can't win.

The best way to "win" is for a woman to learn as much as possible about the reasons for her hysterectomy and the alternative forms of treatment. If there are medical indications for surgery, a second opinion is advisable.

If a woman is considering hysterectomy as a means of sterilization, or, as is often the case, it looks like her physician is electing it for her, she should ask her doctor to explain not only the risks of the procedure but also the alternative forms of contraception, including tubal ligation.

"It is the prerogative of the patient," states a recent precedent-setting California Supreme Court decision, "*not* the physician, to determine for himself the direction in which he believes his interests lie." A physician may not remain silent about risks or alternatives to proposed surgery, the court states, "simply because divulgence might prompt the patient to forgo the therapy that the physician feels the patient really needs. This attitude assumes instability or perversity for even the normal patient."

So, at least in California and now more recently in the District of Columbia, informed consent is a patient's right (not her privilege), and she may sue a doctor not only for physical damages but for failure to state the alternatives to proposed treatment. And it's about time.

With a hard sell, half-truths and a leave-it-to-me-dear, thousands of women have been buffaloed into major surgery, and hysterectomy has become one of the fastest growing and most questionable elective medical procedures in the U.S. The gynecological profession, led by such devotees as Dr. Wright, has a real headstart and women have a lot of catching up to do. But with the California Supreme Court ruling in hand and a raised consciousness in mind, at least women can give the doctors a run for their money.

Rosetta Reitz

WHAT DOCTORS WON'T TELL YOU ABOUT MENOPAUSE

1. The doctors didn't tell me there are 37 million sisters in this country today who have had, are having, or will soon have their menopause. The knowledge of this statistic makes me feel strong. How dare this culture try to shove that huge a number of us under the rug?

2. They didn't tell me to talk about menopause. It's the best thing a woman can do to demystify it. Talk to sisters: your own age, older, and younger, too. There is no shame in it, it happens to over 50 percent of the population, even though our culture finds it embarrassing and men call us hysterical or neurotic because they know so little about what is happening to us. The more talk about menopause, the sooner the veils of mystery shrouding it will be torn away. The sooner men doctors (or men-tracked women doctors) will stop automatically telling every woman over forty to take estrogen and tranquilizers.

3. No doctor told me a hot flash is harmless and is the dilation of the blood vessels, which usually lasts for about a minute.

4. They didn't tell me my estrogen supply continues even though

I'm not producing eggs. They imply it stops cold in order to sell me their estrogen-replacement therapy. But I'm not buying that, in the same way I'm not buying rouge to replace the blush I had at seventeen. You'd think the doctors are working on a commission from the drug companies. I know if I don't put any foreign estrogen into my body, my endocrine glands will regulate my hormonal activity and my adrenals will step up their estrogen production. The doctors don't know how this works or which unidentified glands also rally into this activity, but they admit that it is so when they speak among themselves. (If some of the medical-research money that went into studying men on the moon could have been used to learn about the women on the earth during menopause, I would consider the money better spent.) It is unbelievable to me that with the sophisticated medical technology (particularly for heart attacks, predominantly a male medical problem) that exists, my hormonal balance is treated like one of the Eleusinian mysteries.

The profession readily admits they don't know what is "normal" for whom; therefore, each woman's dose of hormones is an experiment. Experiment with my body, which could produce sore breasts, nausea, vomiting, bloating, cramps, or nervous tension? While they are guessing and charging me besides? Never.

5. My doctors didn't tell me estrogen-replacement therapy can create the possibility of uncomfortable enlargement of my breasts as well as cysts and benign and malignant tumors in them and in my uterus, or irregular bleeding and overstimulation of the uterine lining. Nor can they predict how much longer one's menstrual periods will be extended from this artificial input. I want to be through with the mess, the sooner the better, instead of prolonging it unnaturally. They think women feel "younger" or more "feminine" if their periods continue. They should ask women.

6. My "change of life" happened the day I decided I'd never pick up another dirty sock other than my own, and that had nothing to do with my ovaries releasing eggs or not.

7. My "climacteric" came from my bank balance, not from my hormonal balance. Ovulation had nothing to do with it for me. The

minute I had enough money in the bank to live for a year without working (and remain financially supportive to my three daughters), I became a different person and my performance on my job improved. That financial security gave me the confidence to make decisions and recommendations much easier, without the old fears of over-stepping or appearing aggressive.

8. My doctors didn't tell me my menstrual mechanism takes about five years to settle into a new cycle.

9. They never mentioned the importance of sex. If no one is handy, masturbation will do as well. Your sex glands don't care who's creating the action, and the activity is healthy for the total complex, particularly to keep the vaginal walls lubricated. The books they write don't go into this at all, except to speak of "dry vaginas," but the menopausal and postmenopausal women I have spoken to have told me about sex and many other things the doctors haven't reported on. Could it be because I asked?

10. And finally, the doctors didn't tell me I am smack on the national average, 49.2 years old, for the onset of menopausal symptoms. My body is going through its normal functions for my age, and I accept that. I totally reject their cock-and-bull medical term for my condition: "deficiency disease." The deficiency I am worried about is in these doctors' minds for trying to treat me like a dummy.

Kay Weiss

WHAT MEDICAL STUDENTS LEARN ABOUT WOMEN

Medicine, like the Constitution, is for men. For centuries, women were burned at the stake as witches for practicing medicine,[1] but now the focus of the punishment is reversed. It is when women are *sick* that they are most "evil," most threatening to the egos of male doctors. This is because many doctors cannot admit error, and increasingly, women are asking them to. The retaliation takes its form in a carefully constructed body of myths that passes for gynecological science and in the rituals of humiliation that pass for the office visit. The male-dominated practice of medicine is often a practice of selective mistreatment where women and so-called women's diseases are concerned.

One of the cruelest forms of sexism we live with today is the unwillingness of many doctors to diagnose people's diseases with equality. To let a patient's organic diseases go undiagnosed and refer that patient to a psychiatrist just because she is a woman is not medicine, it's punishment. Yet in 1972, it is estimated that 20 percent of the U. S. adult female population were given tranquilizers for the same diseases men were given medicine for.[2] Examples are migraine headache, abdominal pains, and fatigue.

The education of doctors, for and by men, can explain this. Many of the obstetrics and gynecology textbooks used in medical schools focus more on how neurotic women might be than they do on the etiology and treatment of disease. When reading them, it is easy to see why women are serving the medical industry almost as much as it is serving them. The low esteem for women results in more than discriminatory or negligent care. Last year three thousand experimental techniques were tested on women, most without their knowledge.[3] In some instances, the results were so tragic that congressional hearings were called to investigate the damage done to their bodies and minds.[4]

§ She Needs Pain

The use of women in experiments is usually rationalized by society with an ideology of the inevitability of women's passivity and suffering in intercourse, contraception, pregnancy, and labor. In *Obstetrics and Gynecology,*[5] a leading medical textbook, it is justified with a belief in women's need for pain and masochism. Freud's theory that pain is mere nourishment for woman's masochistic nature[6] is the dominant theme of its 55 *descriptions of women's minds,* which, in an otherwise adequate medical textbook, explains much about doctors' attitudes toward women.

The portrayal of doctors and women in many gynecology texts parallels the ancient Chinese principles of Yin and Yang. The female principle of Yin stood for earth, the moon, darkness, and evil, while the male principle of Yang became elaborated into heaven, the sun, light, fire, and goodness. That this attitude was held by at least part of the medical profession in the past can be seen in the 1968 text *World of a Gynecologist,*[7] which states:

> If like all human beings he (the almighty gynecologist) is made in the image of the Almighty, and if he is kind, then his kindness and concern for his patient may provide her with a glimpse of God's image.

But the condescension expressed in this 1968 text is in fact surpassed by the recently revised (1971, 4th edition) text *Obstetrics and Gynecology,* which is used this year in sixty of the nation's medical schools.[8]

In *Obstetrics and Gynecology,* women are childlike, helpless creatures with animallike or "instinctive" natures, who can't get through intercourse, pregnancy, labor, or child-raising without "enlightened" physician intervention. He is an omnipotent being capable of making infertile women pregnant, absolving "past sins"; he can even help mothers "transmit knowledge" to their daughters. The physician's will is so powerful and the woman's psyche so sensitive to suggestion that he can make an infertile woman conceive by performing an operation that will cause her to think some mythical blockage to pregnancy has been removed:

> The inability to conceive has many organic, etiologic factors, but not infrequently emotional problems may be . . . the cause. This is readily apparent in the case of previously "infertile women" who become pregnant after a D & C that has been done for diagnostic reasons. The physician has reassured and helped her in her emotional conflict. As he continues to care for this woman, he should be aware that an emotional problem exists and that this woman is under additional emotional strain during her pregnancy. Any operation can have symbolic meaning to the patient. This is especially true of surgery performed in the pelvic region.

The implication is strong that surgery might be performed for its psychological effect. No mention is made that unnecessary pelvic operations are performed on women each year.[9]

§ She's a Child

In the text, the woman in childbirth is just a child herself. Her doctor, even if he is a novice and she is an old pro, is a fount of knowledge while she is "anxious," "fearful," afraid of "getting messy" and may feel "ashamed" and "guilty." The medical student is taught to believe that many symptoms of illness in pregnancy (excessive nausea, headache) are really a result of her "fear of pregnancy" rather than any physical condition he (all medical students and physicians are "he" in *Obstetrics and Gynecology*) need test for. She "may have fears of death during childbirth" but these fears are always neurotic, never justified. They are most often caused by guilt: she may "fear that the rewards (of pregnancy) will be damaged or denied because of past sins." It is easy to see why maternal mortality is still a problem when women in childbirth are still referred to as sinners in medical texts.

By their acceptance of the text, medical schools indicate their acceptance of the Doctor as God, Woman as Child principle, and teach their students to use it as the basis for medical practice on women.

Nowhere does the stereotype of woman as hysteric have more damaging implication than in the text's warning that the woman's fear of injury in childbirth might be so neurotic that it could interfere with the normal progress of labor: the medical student is persuaded that he will have to administer a labor-inducing drug to "most" patients. Yet research has shown that labor-inducing drugs can lengthen contractions causing fetal respiratory distress, one of the causes of infant mortality.

The text says that women in the menopause may be even more neurotic than women in childbirth. With facile prejudgment, the text explains, "The patient may seek treatment for these conditions (headache, malaise) without realizing that her basic problem is emotional." Yet these symptoms can be signs of serious disease. In one particularly dangerous example the student is told, "Post-menopausal women who have been separated from the significant men in their lives . . . may have vaginal bleeding," although vaginal bleeding in this age-group is one of the signs of uterine cancer.

§ She Loves Rape

Many gynecology texts reveal a greater concern with the patient's husband than with the patient herself and tend to maintain sex-role stereotypes in the interest of men and from a male perspective. But *Obstetrics and Gynecology* clearly spells out the attitudes that other texts only imply:

> The normal sexual act . . . entails a masochistic surrender to the man . . . there is always an element of rape.
>
> The traits that compose the core of the female personality are feminine narcissism, masochism, and passivity.

Every phase of a woman's life is influenced by narcissism. Women then love in a different way from men. The woman falls in love with the idea of being loved; whereas the man loves an object for the pleasure it will give. She says, "I am valuable, important, etc. because he loves me . . ." This type of narcissism finds expression in . . . her interest in clothes, personal appearance, and beauty. Too much feminine narcissism without masochism produces a self-centered woman.

The idea of suffering is an essential part of her life.

Since the dictionary defines "masochism" as an "abnormal condition in which sexual satisfaction depends on being subjected to abuse or pain," this text is teaching our future physicians to define the *normal* patient in terms of what is clinically *abnormal.* Further, the text's requirement for narcissism, masochism, and passivity in the "normal" woman leaves women who aren't beautiful, women who don't have children, and women who aren't married outside the realm of normalcy.

The (normal) woman gives up her outwardly oriented active and aggressive strivings for the rewards involved in identification with her family . . . and sacrifices her own personality to build up that of her husband.

One wonders how many women are referred to psychiatrists each year for not fulfilling these requirements for servitude.

One can hope that Freud's belief that women have a "lust for pain"[10] does not really cause careless and painful treatment on the part of today's physicians. But a male medical student is a young impressionable person who knows little about women. *Obstetrics and Gynecology* tells medical students that "mature" women don't react to pain. And that women who suffer from dyspareunia (acutely painful intercourse) are "fearful" "anxious" women whose frustration has led to "unexpressed anger." If their pain is caused by a thick, rigid hymen, surgical incision of the hymen is recommended, but this acutely painful procedure should be done *without anesthesia* for the purpose of "demonstrating to the patient that she is quite capable of withstanding the discomfort . . . pain . . . is usually a valuable part of therapy." This prescription for sadism on the gynecologist's part follows nicely with the prescriptions for masochism on the patient's part. If cutting the hymen doesn't relieve painful intercourse, the problem could be caused by pro-lapsed ovaries, endometriosis, or retroverted uterus, the text ad-mits, but it is more probable that "intensive psychotherapy is definitely indicated. This therapy is directed toward helping the patient uncover unconscious fears and/or hostility relating to men."

§ She Feels Like an Animal

Women are described in the text alternately as psychopathic and idiotic: "She is likely to feel that she is animallike . . . to think of the vagina as a 'dirty cavity.' " "Black patients will think that the source of sexual desires is in the uterus; white patients think that it is in the ovaries." "Orgasm represents the woman's ability to accept her own feminine role in life." "Many women equate or-gasm with loss of bowel control. . . ." "Menstruation symbolizes her role in life. . . ." "To the immature girl menstrual blood comes from the same area as feces and urine; this causes her to transfer to menstruation the feelings she has toward these excretions." It seems that the text is equating women's role in life with feces. Apparently the state of medical science for women has not pro-gressed from the seventeenth century, when all illness was thought to arise from black bile, or from ancient Greece when illness was thought to arise from womb gases, and thus was termed "hysteria" meaning "of the womb." The medical student is persuaded by the authors that women with dysmenorrhea (menstrual dysfunctions including painful uterine contractions) have no organic disease they need test for; these women simply have "personality disor-ders," "emotional difficulty in the home," or "neurotic predisposi-tions." They need "sex education" and *"mental hygiene"* (does this mean their minds need cleaning?) if not "intensive psychotherapy." When treating such women "the husband can be helpful by not being too sympathetic and increasing the woman's guilt." A brief concession is made to the possible physical causes for menstrual pain, but the authors then quickly return to the problem of diagnosis:

> It is important to ascertain how crippling the symptom and how much emotional gain the patient is deriving from it. For example, does the whole household revolve around whether or not the mother is having menstrual cramps? Is the dysmenorrhea the locus for the expression of depression, anger, or a need to be dependent?
>
> The adult woman who presents this symptom very often is resentful of the feminine role. Each succeeding period reminds her of the unpleasant fact that she is a woman. . . .

Medical diagnosis is being made on the basis of myths about women rather than on any scientific understanding of painful menstruation. Rather than examining the physical causes of the problem, the text prefers to psychoanalyze in a cheap, unscientific way. Only after convincing the medical student that a woman's uterine cramps are really in her head, do the authors sheepishly admit that hormone therapy will usually result in a painless menstrual period. Another menstrual dysfunction, amenorrhea or complete cessation of menstrual periods, is often caused by endometriosis or pituitary failure. Yet the authors declare that it is more likely the result of an unconscious conflict between the woman's desire to become pregnant, and her desire not to become pregnant. That she might know her own mind on this subject is not even considered!

The authors make no effort to document these "facts," give no references that scientifically support them, and cite no case histories. Without even mentioning the grave danger of mistaking organic disease for psychosomatic illness, they brush over the serious physical causes for disease and quickly return to its more probable location—the woman's head. The mythology goes in gear when the woman first enters the doctor's office:

> The very act of coming to the physician puts the patient in a parent-child relationship . . . by the patient's dress, walk, makeup and attitude in answering questions, a judgment of her personality begins. . . . The physician notices whether the patient is reacting to the interview in a feminine way or whether she is domineering, demanding, masculine, aggressive.

§ She Needs a Psychiatrist

The clear implication is that if the patient asks too many questions, she is abnormally demanding! "The patient should be questioned about the sexual aspects of her life . . . when the patient fails to respond and seems to be unduly emotional about the discussion her transfer to a psychiatrist is indicated." If she is not "relaxed" during a pelvic examination with an *"unlubricated* speculum," she might also be referred to a psychiatrist. One wonders how she can relax when she is on trial for her makeup, walk, dress, attitude, and has been offended with questions. That she be branded as emotionally unstable by psychiatric referrals is unreasonable. The student is told that women may feel sexual about pelvic examination, but not that doctors have been known to feel sexual about it as well.

Only two paragraphs in the text are devoted to the hormonal role of female sexual response: one of these enlightens us about female dogs in heat and the other informs us that the sex drive of females can be increased by giving them testosterone (male sex hormone). According to the authors, trichomonas (vaginal parasitic infection) is probably a result of sexual tension! This is not more than an unsophisticated version of the medieval belief that women with the unbearable itch really just need a good screw. "The physician can help the woman discover how she wishes to relate to men in a more meaningful manner," an incredibly pompous statement in juxtaposition with 55 pages of medical ignorance about female sexuality! Frigidity is defined as "occasional failure to obtain orgasm" placing 99 percent of women in the category of abnormal. If pleasure is only felt from clitoral stimulation, she may be referred to a psychiatrist. The doctor may have trouble curing frigidity because of "too deep a degree of pathology in the woman," never because of her husband's poor technique. Her frigidity may develop because she "resents her husband's preoccupation with his work or his recreational activities." The physician, a "parental figure" should "discover the problems in the patient's personality" and "encourage her to mature sexually."

In sum, *Obstetrics and Gynecology* tells us that women are inherently inadequate, that most can benefit from psychiatric care, that if they react to pain they are not properly resigned to femininity, and that their doctors are inherently superior. Unfortunately, it is not an unusual book in its field.

Twenty-seven gynecology texts written over the past three decades were reviewed by Diana Scully and Pauline Bart in the *American Journal of Sociology* in January 1973. They confirm the idea that medical science has made little advancement for women. No text Scully and Bart examined incorporated Kinsey's 1953 findings that orgasm without stimulation "is a physical and physiological impossibility for nearly all females"[11] or Masters and Johnson's 1966 findings that portions of the vagina have no nerve endings and lack sensation and that although orgasm is felt in the vagina, the feeling derives from stimulation of clitoral nerves. A 1956 gynecology text even states that when sensation is limited to the clitoris this "is apparently due to habit (masturbation) and aversion to normal cohabitation."[12]

§ She Doesn't Need a Clitoris
In the nineteenth century under the influence of Freud, doctors instructed husbands to avoid the clitoris during lovemaking; Freud thought that clitoral pleasure retarded the women's ability to experience a "mature" orgasm, that is, one deriving solely from the penis. In 1962 we still read "if there has been much manual stimulation of the clitoris it may be reluctant to abandon control, or the vagina may be unwilling to accept the combined role of arbiter of sensation and vehicle of reproduction."[13] Several texts said that most women were "frigid" and two instructed gynecologists to teach their patients to fake orgasm. Scully and Bart concluded that "these texts used Kinsey's report selectively; findings which reinforced old stereotypes were repeated, but the revolutionary findings significant for women were ignored. For example, one often finds in the textbooks that the male sets the sexual pace in marital coitus, but nowhere is it mentioned that women are multiorgasmic." Nine of twelve texts published in the last decade preferred the traditional female sex role: in 1967 we read "an important feature of sex desire in the man is the urge to dominate the woman and subjugate her

to his will; in the woman acquiescence to the masterful takes a high place."[14] And a 1970 text states, "The frequency of intercourse depends entirely upon the male sex drive . . . the bride should be advised to allow her husband's sex drive to set their pace and she should attempt to gear hers satisfactorily to his. If she finds after several months or years that this is not possible, she is advised to consult her physician as soon as she realizes there is a real problem."[15] Again, no call for the man to act on the problem.

One can easily see the influence of patriarchy on medical knowledge. It took medical science several centuries to discover that the clitoris is the female organ of sensation although people in prepatriarchal societies knew it. Even when the supremacy of the penis and the myth of the vaginal orgasm did *not* reign over anatomic knowledge, the recognition of clitoral control was simply used to manipulate women: in an 1899 gynecology text we read "It is advisable to use electricity or an exhaust pump to enlarge the size of the clitoris in cases where it is deficient in excitability. This procedure has been successful in making satisfactory wives . . ."[16] In a 1926 text, doctors were instructed to expose the clitoris to x-radiation to "diminish the hypersensitivity of women suspected of excessive sexual activity."[17] Around the turn of the century, hundreds of American women were treated for "self-abuse" in the most barbarous fashion—clitorectomy.[18] This was justified on the basis of medical opinions about the proper appearance of female genitals— those of a virtuous woman were thought to be pink and soft with a clitoris that was hardly protuberant.

If the attitudes of gynecologists make women paranoid, rushing to a psychiatrist may be of little comfort. Freud reigns there as well. In a recent article "Femininity and Paranoidism" in the *Journal of Nervous and Mental Disease,*[19] required reading in some medical school courses, Dr. Leonard Sillman explains to medical students that their role as future psychiatrists is to help women accept "reality," that is, sexual oppression, which exists because of women's biological inferiority. Women who have careers usually feel guilty, says the doctor, but "where the sense of guilt is weak, the woman vents her hatred of men by emasculating and rendering ineffective or impotent the individuals involved." The menopausal woman is a "shriveled shell of a woman, used up, sucked dry, de-sexed and, by comparison with her treasured remembrances of bygone days of glory and romance, fit only for the bone heap." Female anatomy is "designed to be attacked" and "female instincts invite it, . . . the woman's genital organ is designed to be a receptacle subordinate to the male's and from his and her exaltation of aggression and its symbol the phallus, she becomes turned by the unconscious into a thing to be "used," "enslaved," and subjected to the unjust social circumstances they must live with so that their bitterness does not rob their husbands of their right to love. Feminine paranoidism is best analyzed by "exposing the woman's narcissism and her sadism. A part of the woman is profoundly envious of the superior physical power and strength of the male." Analysis must focus on "her sadism, which longs for masculinity . . . and, with its urge to degrade and debase . . . seeks to macerate and consume the ego of her husband with incessant derogation, criticism, nagging." The good doctor concludes that a psychiatrist must "persuade a female patient to abandon her wish for a penis on the ground of its being unrealistic."

Admittedly, the psychiatric profession is undergoing changes in treatment of women. But reform in psychiatry will not help women who receive psychiatric referrals from their gynecologists for symptoms of uterine cancer!

With doctors like these for friends, who needs enemies?

Deborah Baker

THE CLASS FACTOR: MOUNTAIN WOMEN SPEAK OUT ON WOMEN'S HEALTH

Ever since I can remember, a mother has been responsible for the well being and the needs of her children—health-wise and everything else. . . . Mountain mothers has always had the responsibility of the health problems of their children and their husbands too, really. And they usually tend to neglect their own health . . . until sometimes it's beyond repair. . . . But that's the way it's always been in the mountains.

The words are Ethel Brewster's. But women everywhere find themselves with the special burden of being primarily responsible for their family's health care—and fighting the resulting battles against a health-care system that is often downright hostile to the persons that it is supposed to serve. Ethel Brewster, fifty-five, is white, the mother of sixteen children, twelve of them living. Madeline James, fifty-seven, is black, the mother of six children, five of them living.

Both women have been active in the West Virginia Welfare Rights Organization.

Ethel: You know, I was just a kid. I had two, and I didn't want any more children. I really didn't. I didn't want any more pregnancies. So I told the company doctor, look, there ought to be something that you could give me, I don't want to be pregnant all the time.

So I'd missed two or three weeks, and he said, "Drink you a big dose of turpentine." Well, I didn't know what a big dose of turpentine was. You know really now, a big dose of turpentine is ten or twelve drops. But I took a half a teacup full! I thought a big dose of turpentine was like a big dose of castor oil.

And I drank it, oh, you know, 11, 12, something in the day. And I went ahead and did my work, took care of my kids, cooked supper. No effects and you know, it made me awful sick. Yuck in my stomach. But when I started to sit down to the table it seemed like one of the bowls just scooted over across the table and it jumped and I grabbed at it. And my husband looked at me, and I said. "Didn't you see that bowl move?" and he said, "No, I didn't see no bowl move." Well, he was making him a churn of peach brandy behind the cookstove—you know we cooked with coal— and he run right quick to look at his peach brandy to see if I'd been into it. I hadn't. And it was funny really. And I started to sit down again and all the dishes started running across the table, you know, and I said, "Oooh, there's something wrong with me." And he said, "Woman what have you been drinking?"

And I said "Nothing," and ran and lay down across the bed. By then my stomach was acting up. He went ahead and eat and he come in there and turned me over, and honest to goodness, when he turned me over and I looked up at him, he was a horrible monster-looking thing! It looked like his eyes was that big and his teeth they stuck a way out, you know. And I thought I was screaming and fighting with him because I didn't know who he was, but I was only whining you know, whining like a puppy and wigglin' my fingers. I was almost gone I guess. But he called the doctor, and the doctor said, just make her vomit, so he aimed to turn me over to get me up. I was as limber as a rag and when he turned me over on my stomach I started vomiting—up came the turpentine. I was so glad. That's the only way it bothered me though.

I didn't know what a big dose of turpentine was! It's funny in a way. But, you know, I wonder . . . The doctor was old, real old. Looks like he would have told me how much to have took.

I didn't realize that life was life, no matter what, then.

Madeline: (Talking about her daughter who died last summer)

She died the fourth of November. She was thirty-two years old . . . the mother of one son. She'd taken this disease three years ago.

And when it first began she went to the Wilcoe Health Center and Dr. ——— told her she was allergic to washing powders and bleach, and told us to quit washing her underclothes in it. Well, she did, and instead of getting better, it continued to grow. Her breast turned red, and after turning red . . . it continued to spread and then she went to Dr. ———, and Dr. ——— told her she had milk breast. So I insisted—I told her anytime a girl is the mother of a five-year-old kid it was impossible for her to have milk breast, and I advised her, I begged her to go to a doctor. And the reason she didn't go to a hospital was because she did not have no medical [insurance], no hospital to go to.

And she went to a doctor and when he looked at her he told her to go to Stevens Clinic Hospital. (Later she was a Headstart driver and then got insurance through her employer.) She went to Stevens Clinic Hospital and they thought she had an abcess in her breast . . . and they put hot compresses on her breast. Well then it started to spread more, and she stayed there two weeks after that, and then they decided to do a biopsy on her . . . that's when they found out she had cancer.

They removed that breast and the muscle of her arm all over— they removed the complete breast . . . Three months after they removed that breast, then it went into her ovaries . . . and six months after, then they removed half the other breast. And then she done fine with it for over a year, but she never did stop work

—she had very good courage . . . she never complained about it, and when anyone would ask her what was it, and when she had to go to the hospital or anything, she would tease them and she would tell them, "Bring me some flowers, or a gown," and she would laugh . . . I don't care who asked her how she felt the whole three years she had it, she never did say in that time, "Well, I feel bad, I feel sick."

And so she went on and worked three years after she had those operations . . . they sent her to Maryland for her to take treatments . . . the doctor he did not believe that she did have cancer, because she held her weight from 257 pounds until a month before she died. And Dr. ————, he told her as long as she held her weight, that it wasn't eating her cells away, that she would do fine . . . But then after she'd taken 127 radium treatments from the Bluefield Sanitorium and 87 [other] treatments, she taken hepatitis . . . then she begin to swell and they couldn't get the swelling down. And this is when her son, his eighth birthday was on the 30th of September and so she asked the doctor could she come home for his birthday, and so she came home. I carried her back the eighth of October, and she became thirty-two the 10th of October, and nearly a month later she went into a coma on a Saturday evening at seven o'clock, and Sunday at eight o'clock, she was gone.

She died that quick, and her desire, her wish, was that if she couldn't live to raise her child that she didn't want to suffer.

It was eight months (from the time she went to the clinic to the time they discovered the cancer). I believe that if he had found out then, and she had that first operation before they did all that other treatment to her, I believe that she could be saved. And that's the reason I'm very bitter against birth-control pills . . . Because whenever she had her child, her baby, well they put her on birth-control pills and because she didn't have no hospitalization, she didn't have no check-up . . . it was five years before she finally had another check-up . . . she had a lot of side effects from these birth-control pills because she gained a lot of weight from it . . . They just gave them to her, told her not to have no more children, because when she was five years old she'd taken rheumatic heart trouble . . . After she'd taken the second operation, after they removed her ovaries, that's when she stopped taking them . . . That's the very reason I say that if they do put these girls on birth-control pills there ought to be some way for them to have a check-up every six months, or three months that it calls for.

§ Birth Control

Madeline: I may be wrong but I always say that the health care for young girls in this place is very poor. They put these girls on these birth-control pills and a lot of them have side effects on them, and a lot of them make them real sick. And then they tell them, "You're just not used to them, you continue to use them." And then when they do go back they have no kind of hospitalization. They can't go back—they got to stay home.

Ethel: I had six children in the hospital and ten at home. You know, a long time ago, doctors wouldn't even talk to you about no kind of birth control. It was just a hush-hush thing. The first time I heard anything about birth control whatsoever was after Patty (the youngest) was born.

(Describing her experiences as a family planning worker) Lots of times I'd go into a home and they'd say "You have to talk to my husband," and he'd say "No! Absolutely not, positively not. No family planning . . . don't talk about it." Well, you know, I had some little booklets that said For the Father and I'd say, "Well, why don't you read this little book." You know, nine out of ten fathers finally came across by clinic day, but it took a lot of visits.

The biggest part of the women wanted birth control, but a lot of them didn't want the pills. They were afraid of them . . . some women are naturally afraid of something you take by mouth . . . especially mountain women . . . They had been told that pills would cause them to lose their sex desire. And a lot of men thought that, too. Some women would sneak out to the clinic and take them (the pills) and their husbands didn't know they were taking them. I'd sneak (the woman) out when they asked me to. I never asked them to sneak out—I'd never dare do that.

(On birth control for unmarried women) Me, I think it's great,

I think that if girls are going to participate in sex—I don't care how much you talk to them, if they want to they will, regardless of what anybody says to them—they ought to get birth-control pills.

§ Prenatal Care

Madeline: If a child, a girl, gets pregnant, and if parents just don't put themselves in a lot of debt and try to take care of this girl, then this girl is just in a bad shape . . . And I think the law should be changed in this welfare . . . If you do get a baby, take care of it while you're carrying that baby and not wait til after you have a baby.

Pat Crozier, Madeline's neighbor, mother of four: You see it on TV all the time—the earliest possible, try to get your treatments the earliest possible. But if you don't have the facilities for it, the means for it, how you going to get there as early as possible? It's hard. You can't hardly get anybody to take you anywhere now, and you got to pay so much . . . It (childbirth) has never been explained to me . . . Why not let me know what I've got to go through ahead of time?

Ethel: When I had my fourth baby . . . I sent for a doctor and no doctor came and I had her with a midwife. And she was premature, seven months, and you know, I had a fallen womb for a long time till I couldn't walk around. Twenty years old and you know that was because not the right kind of care, no prenatal care whatsoever . . . You didn't have a blood test. And later on after I had all my children they said, "Look, you weren't supposed to have but three normal children, and I'd had sixteen. I have RH negative (blood) and Bill has RH positive.

§ Childbirth

Ethel: You know, back then coal miner's wives didn't get the medical treatment they should have because company doctors didn't—they didn't know then what they know now. And you had your babies at home. You didn't have no anesthetics. And I wonder what they would have done if you had to have a caesarean. They'd wait if you go into labor, and you know if you go into labor and you have to have a caesarean then sometime you and the baby both die. I don't know what would have happened to coal miner's wives.

There was a lot of women back then, their babies died and was sickly.

I had all mine at home except the last six . . . but really that's no big thing, because it was easier to have them at home than to have them at the hospital . . . I guess I'm just old-fashioned. They'd take me to the hospital and they'd strap me down. I'd like to never have the baby! When I was home you know, I'd walk til the pains got so bad that I had to lay down then I'd lay down and have the baby. Without any anesthetic, and never no stiches or nothing, because they waited til time. Now they cut you, you know, and they don't give you time to have it . . . That's what ruins women's health.

§ Doctors

Pat: To me, a doctor's supposed to be able to talk to you and tell you what's wrong with you. But half the time they look at you like you're crazy when you ask them what's wrong.

Ethel: I hate to go up to Logan General and use those doctors. I never go up there. They just don't explain anything, they don't even tell you what the prescriptions are for. They just say "Here" and they halfway examine you and stick you with a lot of prescriptions and you can say, "What are these for?" "Take them like directed" and that's it.

Like when I went up there when I was so sick a few weeks ago, got hurting in here (points to her chest). I got again now, I thought I was about to have a heart attack, it hurt so bad. He sent me to take an EKG . . . I waited and then I saw the nurse hand him the test and I said, "Well?" and he said, "Well what?" and I said, "What about the test? What about my heart, was there anything wrong with it?" And he said, "You'll be all right, you're heart's O.K.," like it didn't matter to him whether it was or not, you know. I was glad to hear there wasn't anything wrong with my heart, now, I didn't mean that, but he could've said something. And I asked about my blood pressure. "Do you want to know everything?" he said, "You're a little bit nosey." Yes I want to know if it's high or low, that's what I'm here for."

You know, I guess it's just prejudice on my part, but you know uneducated people, we can't understand people—foreigners—that doesn't talk good English, and that's the reason a lot of mountain mothers don't use the hospitals. Because they can't understand the doctors . . . I've had a lot of them tell me, well I will not take my child there, because I cannot understand what they are talking about.

§ Hospitals

Madeline: You go in there (Doctor's Memorial Hospital) and instead of them changing your bed, they let you lay in it . . . the doctors bought stocks in this hospital and they control this hospital altogether, and so if they want to take care and clean your bed they do it, and if they don't want to they won't do it. They don't care how much you report to them and tell them—they're not going to do more than they want to do for you.

They say there is an out-fee you got to pay . . . before you can walk out of that door . . . A lot of times 60 or 70 dollars that you got to pay just out-fee before you can get out of the hospital. And then if you don't pay it, they're gonna turn around and charge you for it. And things like that, there's too much of it. And not enough of care.

§ Clinics

Ethel: When I was working for the family-planning clinic, they put those paper dresses on the women and they had to sit out in the hallway. And in the hot summertime, they would slip open you know, they'd bust and that's all you had on, just paper wrapped around you. And the men—the prenatal clinic was on back in there, and men went through this hallway, and you had to move your legs around, it was so narrow, to let them by—and going to the prenatal clinic to see about their wives, and those women sitting nearly naked! And I put up a fuss about it I didn't like it. 'Cause some of the women said, "I'm not coming back no more. I'm not gonna put on those paper dresses and sit out there and show my ass." I said to the doctor, "Get a room for these women to set in, not out in the hallway half dressed 'cause whether you got any decency or not, some women has."

People still call me about family planning. They still call me and ask, "How can I get my pills?" because the clinic started charging them. Well, I didn't know that. So I called the doctor and he said yeah, they did. "For a while we charged people that we thought could pay. And," he said, "it didn't work out too good." And I asked, "You had a lot of pregnancy didn't you?" And he said, "That's right." So he said, "Now you tell people they don't have to have money." So I guess they thought they'd take the public for a few more dollars and it didn't work out.

§ Welfare

Madeline: Like this kid here (a grandchild). I don't have her on nothing. She is not on nothing. I can't even get them to add her on the grant in the welfare (unless) I go and have (a woman's) son arrested . . . If anything happened to this child, right this minute, if I ain't got 100 or 200 dollars to get this child somewhere, this child have to lay right in this house and die.

Ethel: The worst medical problems I've had really has been since I been on welfare. Trying to see the kind of doctors that's needed for the children and myself, and they don't take the card—needing to see the specialists, and the specialists don't take the card. That's the biggest problem I can find. Like when your children needs to see eye specialists—not just glasses—there's no one in Logan you can see. None of them takes the card. You have to take them to Williamson, Huntington, Charleston you know, and no transportation. That proves to be a great problem. And teeth. Until the last year or so you could get a tooth pulled and that was it. That's all you could get done to a child was get a tooth pulled. No caps, no braces, no nothing.

Madeline: (After talking about her troubles with the UMWA in regard to her husband's pension check, and with trying to get Black Lung benefits)

I tell you, you don't know who to fight, where to begin or where not to begin. Cause it's too much . . . If you sit down and think long enough about it, you almost lose your mind.

And you go out there and you ask the man that's supposed to know, "What must I do with this matter?" What help can they give? What do they tell you? "I don't know. I'm sorry for you Mrs. James, but there ain't nothing that we can do." But is that paying my bills? Is that feeding me and my children? It's not.

Ethel: I think that if the mothers could get together—even the old ones, the old ones has a place too, not just the young ones—and make a lot of demands, we could do something about this big health problem we have in the Appalachian mountains.

PART FOUR

WOMEN WORKERS IN THE MEDI-BUSINESS

Carol A. Brown

WOMEN WORKERS IN THE HEALTH SERVICE INDUSTRY

Health work is women's work. Over 85 percent of all health service and hospital workers are women. The largest occupation in health work—nursing—is almost entirely female.

The increase in health employment over the past decades has been primarily an increase in women employees. Weiss[1] showed that the occupations that were predominantly female were expanding fastest, and that most occupations were becoming increasingly female. He showed the reason to be that the greatest increase has been at the lower ends of the ladder, where there are more women. Between 1960 and 1970 the number of physicians in practice increased by only 25 percent, registered nurses by 39 percent, and practical nurses by 80 percent.[2]

The health service industry is run by a small minority. It is run primarily by physicians, who have traditionally held the power, but also by the increasingly powerful hospital administrators, insurance company directors, government regulators, medical school educators, and corporation managers. Most of these people are men.[3]

Aside from this top level in which industrial power is concentrated, men are found largely at the bottom—as kitchen helpers, janitors, and porters—and in a few technical fields such as laboratory and x-ray. Men at the bottom experience the same lack of power as their female coworkers, and, like the women, the further down the professional ladder they are the more likely they are to be non-white.

Health service is women's work, but not women's power. It is not unusual to find industrial power concentrated at the top echelon of an industry, nor to find the policy or practice of "men only" at the top echelon. It *is* unusual to find an industry requiring a complex mix of highly technical skills in which most of the skilled as well as the unskilled workers are women. In health service the conflict between "management" and "workers" is a conflict mainly between men and women.

Three main areas are dealt with here. First, why are health workers women? Second, how is the overlap of sexual and occupational status upheld, and with what effects on the field? Third, what struggles take place that may lead to change in the future?

Many apparent advantages to physicians and other elites in the health industry accrue to the hiring of women. First, women are an inexpensive source of labor. Health care is a costly but essential commodity, with labor constituting the biggest expense. Health service only became big business with the rise of hospitals. Hospital services are expensive and the biggest expense is labor. If costs are beyond the reach of consumers, the industry suffers, and with it the incomes of physicians and service organizations. Public financing has been put forth as one solution to high health costs; keeping labor costs low is another. A labor force composed mostly of women can be hired more cheaply than one composed mostly of men. Women can be paid less than men would be paid for the same work. In addition, women are believed to be dedicated to service and not self-interest,[4] and are expected to drop out of the labor force to raise families—thus obviating the need for promotions or increased pay for seniority.[5]

Second, women are available. Rapid expansion of labor requires an easily available labor force to draw on, and women are the last major reservoir of unemployment.[6]

Third, women are safe. They pose no threat to physicians who, in order to expand their own services and therefore their incomes, must be assured of subordinates who will stay subordinate. Women do not have the social power—that is, access to capital, access to specialized education, freedom from family responsibilities, and respect of political leaders—to become organized competition to physicians in the medical marketplace, whereas other men and other male-dominated professions such as optometry or osteopathy do provide competition to physicians.[7] Women's efforts to open medical schools to more women students have had limited success for the same reasons. At an interpersonal level, physicians are (or hope to be) assured of respect and willing service in members of subordinate occupations in part because they are men and the others are women.

Why do women accept the low pay and interpersonal subordination of the health service industry? If asked, many would say they went into health service to help people, to care for the sick, rather than to earn a high salary or to enjoy prestige. Caring for others is seen as women's work by society at large, and is seen by many women as their vocation. But physicians and surgeons also help the sick. The answer to women's acceptance of poorly paid subordinate occupations lies outside the health service industry in the economic opportunities available to women elsewhere. Women are "willing" to accept subordinate conditions of work because they have little choice in the matter.

Few occupations are open to women, whereas many are open to men. Out of 80 major occupational categories listed in the 1970 United States Census, seven occupations contain 43 percent of all women workers. One of these occupations is nursing.[8] Non-white women are concentrated in service and labor occupations. Discrimination is endemic, and few can afford to spend years pressing antidiscrimination suits at every barrier. When people need jobs they have to take what is open to them. When they need skill training, they learn what skills are offered. In addition, most women work because they need the money. The majority of women workers are single, are sole supports of households, or have husbands with incomes below $4000 a year.[9]

The low pay for high skills found in health service is only low compared to white *men's* opportunities elsewhere. From the point of view of women, the pay is relatively good. Pay rates are low in all occupations in all industries for women. Median full-time earnings in hospital employment are *above* the median for workers in all industries for the categories of white women, black men, and black women. Median earnings in hospital employment are well below the median only for white men.[10] One black woman from the South described to this author her entry into health service as a nurses' aide as an "incredible opportunity," because it was steady work and good wages. In getting further education, the average woman does not have a choice between nursing school and medical school, but between nursing school and, for example, computer programming school.

The lack of promotion opportunities in health careers over a lifetime does not compare unfavorably to the lack of promotion opportunities everywhere else for women. Of all the managers and non-farm administrators at all levels in the economy, only 16 percent are women and 1 percent non-white women.[11]

Women's low wages compared to men's make a wife-mother necessarily dependent on her husband for her livelihood and that of her children.[12] Her husband has the economic power to insist that she give up any other job. Thus, because of her tenuous position, long-term upward mobility opportunities within one organization, as much as she might want them, become unavailable to her. More relevant are good starting pay and certified skills for jobs that she can leave, reenter, and move to a new location. In many health occupations, one-half of entrants have left after five years; those who remain often change jobs for marginally higher pay, better working conditions, or family responsibilities, rather than for nonexistent promotion opportunities.[13, 14]

Women accept the interpersonal subordination assigned to them in health service for the same reasons they accept low pay: there is a lack of alternatives. Few women are in decision-making positions in the polity or the economy, making women dependent on men's decisions. A woman cannot afford to demand her rights or to walk off the job if she is treated like an inferior. She will be treated like an inferior everywhere else, and like an unemployed inferior to boot.

Thus the limitations on women's opportunities everywhere else make it possible for the health service industry to offer low wages for high skills and to keep women down. The outside limitations lead women to accept subordination within health service. Health service, at least, is an area in which they can get skills, get jobs, and have the self-respect of making an important contribution to society.

Health service, then, has a sex hierarchy as well as an occupational hierarchy. The decision makers are almost entirely males and the workers are largely female. It is generally assumed that women as workers are satisfied with their positions in both hierarchies within the industry, that women workers will not fight for their economic welfare as men would, and that as women they accept the leadership of the male sex. The assumption is false.

The labor force pattern of women is now changing. More women are able to continue working despite childbearing, or to drop out for shorter periods of time. More women have a long career ahead of them, and they are increasingly in a position to demand the opening of high-level positions to them. Women now fight for position when they can. The modern health service industry has been permeated with internal economic conflict since it began, and the conflicts have grown as the industry has expanded.

To understand the peculiar nature of some of the conflicts in health service, we should examine the way the system is maintained. Health service is somewhat like the construction industry in having separate specialized crafts, with work performed on a custom basis in a large number of small work units.[15], [16] Each health occupation above the unskilled level has a separate training program and special entry procedures, often culminating in registration or licensing procedures. Each occupation has a national professional society which tries to function like a craft union.

Unlike the construction industry, however, many highly skilled health occupations are relatively low paying and dead-end. In addition, the "crafts" are not independent of each other; they are hierarchically organized with rigid barriers between levels. The top male occupation—physician—controls the female occupations, not only on the job but in the educational programs. The American Medical Association and its affiliate medical societies have the right to set the curriculum, direct the training programs, control professional certification, and sit on the state licensing boards of (at last count) 16 other occupations. Through the Joint Commission for Accreditation of Hospitals, the American Association of Medical Colleges, the American Hospital Association, American Medical Association (AMA), and the Commission on Medical Education, for example, physicians can decide to create new occupations and control the division of labor. In the dental area the American Dental Association controls dental hygienists, assistants, and technicians. Bullough[17] has shown that historically the development of medicine as an elite profession depended on the patronage of socially powerful institutions external to health service, such as universities. This continues to be true. State legislatures, federal funders, government regulators, college and university administrators, and others support the power of physicians to control other occupations through, for example, hospital staffing regulations, Medicare funding regulations, rights of accreditation, and licensing laws.[18]

The nursing profession has escaped total medical control only by its self-conscious determination to be an independent profession, yet organized nursing has far less power in the health service industry than one would expect of an occupation of so many workers and so key to the industry. The American Nursing Association (ANA) and the National League for Nursing (NLN) are generally ignored by the health service industry elite and its outside supporters on questions of public policy with respect to health care. The ANA and the NLN have no voice on the Joint Commission for Accreditation of Hospitals in regulating occupations and hospitals.

On the job, nurses are very much subordinate to doctors. Although some of the middle-ranking occupations assert some controls over lower-ranking occupations following the physicians' model, they cannot assert power because they have little or none to assert.

The formal controls on occupations are reinforced by the personal relations between employers and employees, superiors and subordinates at the work site. Who is allowed to work and who is allowed to make decisions are controlled by the same interlocking mechanisms explained above.

Both the ranking system and the ranks of each individual are as obvious in hospitals as in the armed forces. The individual's position is identified by distinctive uniforms and name tags which list occupation and department. As in the armed forces, a superior rank carries weight across departments—a physician on one medical service can often endanger the job of a technician or assistant on another service. Since jobs are insecure, everyone knows not to cross a superior, even though many acts of arrogance or unfairness in superiors can be traced to sexism or racism rather than to mere bureaucratic superiority. Those who complain fear being charged with insubordination, bad work attitudes, or disrespect to the superior.

In case individuals might begin with bad attitudes, training programs for the subordinate occupations include "professional ethics," in which they are taught primarily how to respect the physician and be loyal members of "the team." One chief radiologic technologist at a training hospital complained to this author that the radiologic technologists allow themselves to be pushed around by the doctors, but then he said ruefully, "But I suppose it is our own fault—that's what we teach them to do in the ethics courses."

To a certain extent teaching such "ethics" is unnecessary. Individual placements in the occupational hierarchy reflect the placements in the social hierarchy—men over women, whites over nonwhites—and each has spent a lifetime learning how to act toward the other. When an intern is coached on how to handle nurses to get what he wants[19] he is simply relearning at a higher level his teenage lessons on how to handle girls.

The overlap between occupational and sexual status is so great it is sometimes hard to tell which is which. If a male physiologist ignores a female physical therapist's suggestion, is this because the physical therapist knows less, or because women don't know anything worth listening to? When she does not make the suggestion in the first place, has she learned her ethics as a physical therapist or has she learned her place as a woman? When a black nurses' aide talks back to a white nurse, is she being an uppity nurses' aide or is she being an uppity black?

Lest we think that the bureaucratic hierarchy is the primary reason for the superior-subordinate interaction, let us consider what happens when the two hierarchies do not overlap.

Nurses know how to respond to doctors because women know how to respond to men. But what if the doctor is a woman or the nurse a man? Suppose in our previous example the physiologist were a woman and the physical therapist a man? Suddenly the standardized behaviors that were presumed to flow from occupational hierarchies are thrown into turmoil. Much of the "natural" behaviors between occupations turn out to be based on the sex of the incumbent rather than the status of the occupation. Male doctors do not treat male subordinates the same way they treat female subordinates.[20] Studies of female doctors show that they often try to identify with their occupational superiority and are perceived as "arrogant" in trying to get the same assistance from nurses and other women subordinates that the men get automatically.[21, 22] Similar problems arise when a woman chief technician runs a partly male department, or a black therapist supervises white therapy aides. Male orderlies often resent orders given by female nurses. The behavior patterns seen in hospitals between women and men of different occupations are very much sex-status patterns, just as the interpersonal relations between blacks and whites of different occupations are racial relations.

While it would appear that male physicians and hospital administrators have the upper hand through their ability to control other occupations, their ability to go outside the system for support, and the deference imposed on subordinates, the apparently iron-clad control system does not necessarily work. Women do fight for opportunities, and have most commonly followed the physicians' model of a professional society fighting for the status of its members.

Because occupational and sexual segregation overlap, conflict often revolves around the shape and structure of the occupations and can best be characterized as maneuvering for "turf"—for control of occupational territory.

Historically, physicians fought hard to suppress midwifery, and by World War Two finally won for physicians the right to deliver babies.[23] Now general practitioners are being prevented from assisting at hospital deliveries by obstetricians. Both general practitioners and obstetricians have fought against public health nurses and nurse-midwives giving service in rural areas and urban slums, but this fight presents a dilemma for physicians. Maternity, like most medical specialties, is on a fee-for-service basis. Obstetricians may want to assure that they alone have the right to the fee for this service, but few want the reciprocal obligation of giving the service where there is no fee to be gained. As a result, there is an appallingly high maternal death rate from lack of medical care. Nurse-midwives, after years of struggle, have gained "permission," we might say, to become the inexpensive substitute for the expensive private practitioners, but only in the rural and urban areas that obstetricians do not want.[24] Organized medicine keeps a careful watch to see that nurse-midwifery does not expand into serving the more affluent population. Nurse-midwifery services are as yet a controlled threat to a lucrative medical specialty.[25] Similarly, nurse-anesthetists are a real threat to anesthesiologists, who have attempted without success to abolish the occupation.[26]

The nursing profession has developed other clinical specialists whose skills and training with that specialty are greater than the average physician's, and who can undercut the physician-specialists' high wage rates. Physicians on their part attempt to undercut the threat of nurse specialists by creating lower-skilled substitutes such as obstetrical technicians and operating room assistants who are under AMA control and physicians' authority.

The occupation of licensed practical nurse (LPN) or licensed vocational nurse was consciously created over the objections of the nursing profession by physicians in medical schools and university-affiliated hospitals, who sought a less-trained, lower-paid, and more controllable alternative to the registered nurse, and the LPN was quickly accepted by hospitals and state licensing boards for the same reasons. The nursing profession was not able to prevent the development of the LPN, but was able to incorporate LPNs into the National League for Nursing structure and to obtain some control over licensing. Simultaneously with the LPN movement the three-year registered nurse programs were terminated in hospitals and two-year community college programs were created, although the nursing profession favored and has developed four-year B.S. training for nurses.[27, 28]

With the shortage of physicians and the high cost of care by physicians, nurses began to develop nurse-practitioners, thus moving into the physicians' territory of diagnosing and curing. Physicians countered with the physician assistant, an occupation completely controlled by physicians, as nurses are not. The occupation was first advertised as a means by which physicians in private practice could increase their patient load and boost their incomes by letting someone else do the work. In this it was similar to the development by dentists of the dental assistant and dental hygienist occupations. The physician assistants were intended to be on a higher level than mere nurses—better paid and possessing medical skills and some decision-making power, but functioning only under the control and direction of physicians.[29] They were also intended to be men, especially Vietnam-veteran medics. However, men are expensive and not automatically respectful of the physician's male status, and men can get better-paying, more responsible jobs elsewhere. The physician assistant programs are now primarily training women, taking the same amount of time as nurses' training, and currently at issue is whether physician assistants, standing *in loco medicus,* can give orders to nurses or whether nurses, as independent professionals, can give orders to physician assistants.[30]

The sex identification of the occupations is an important component in many of the struggles. Physicians attempt to stamp out lower-level male professions such as podiatrist and optometrist, and attempt to develop women's occupations that can be controlled. Since women have little social power, men are assured of their own primacy. In any other industry a professional society or union which represents half the workers would not be as blithely ignored as is the ANA. Governments and educators simply do not pay attention to mere women. Although 40 percent of medical technologists are men, the American Society of Medical Technologists (ASMT) is collectively referred to by the clinical pathologist leadership as "the girls." The organization is treated as men treat women—as not very serious and not needing to be taken into account when decisions are made that affect them. When the ASMT elected its first male president, one prominent woman technologist wondered if the ASMT would now be called "the girls and boys."

The pathologists' belief in women's collective subordination has backfired, as did belief in the collective subordination of nurses. The men might not wish to take the women seriously, but the women find their situation to be no laughing matter. Conflict in laboratory technology is rampant.[31]

Although medical technologists, with college graduation and a year of clinical training behind them, are the official subordinate profession in pathology laboratories, pathologists have hired lower-paid technicians, usually with a year or two of college and no formal training. To protect themselves, the medical technologists attempted to create an occupation subordinate to themselves in the laboratory assistant, a high school graduate with one year of training who was intended to squeeze out technicians. The pathologists, however, refused to sponsor that level. Desiring a less troublesome but still skilled assistant occupation, the pathologists began to develop an official technician program, requiring two years of college and one year of training, which the technologists refused to sponsor. Pathologists subsequently sought tighter control over technologists' schools and registration. Technologists then sued the pathologists as a combination in restraint of trade. The best efforts of the AMA and out-of-court mediators have not brought a satisfactory solution. The ASMT has begun developing master's degrees in laboratory management, an area the pathologists consider to be their exclusive prerogative, and the American Society of Clinical Pathologists has withdrawn some financial support from ASMT and its related organizations.

The change to hospitals and clinics as the first line of medical defense has weakened the independent power of physicians, who no longer control the market. The AMA's lessened influence on national medical policy is indicative of this. Increasing financial involvement of government, insurance companies, and other corporations has inevitably brought increased power to those institutions at the expense of hospital administrators as well as physicians.[32] These third parties, as they are known in the trade, are not as interested in supporting the status quo as in providing inexpensive, efficient, and often profitable health service.

This increasing industrialization will clearly restructure the health occupational system, although if it follows current trends the structuring will be downward. Lesser-skilled and lesser-paid subordinates will replace the higher-skilled, higher-paid subordinates, just as the semi-skilled factory workers have replaced craftsmen in other industries. The current rigid occupational structure does enable women to retain some exclusive occupational territory and to attempt to move up by group mobility into the higher slots. However, the rigid segregation produced the high-skilled, low-paid, dead-end nature of health work in the first place. The likelihood of success through this strategy is questionable.

Other changes may be more productive of upward mobility. Clinics, hospitals, and Health Maintenance Organizations are now increasingly replacing the private physician even in formerly lucrative areas, and physicians more and more are adopting the role of backup personnel and paid staff rather than that of controllers of medical care. The administrative side of medicine then becomes more important, and produces a different potential for the lower occupations.

For one thing, the physician loses the personal incentive to keep down the training and wages of subordinates as he had in private practice. Since the wages are being paid by hospitals rather than by the physician, the physician wants the best assistants money can buy. Hospital-based physicians sometimes side with the upwardly mobile women's occupations against the hospital administrators and private practitioners.[33]

In addition, most physicians have not perceived administration as a career ladder to success or as a major means to industrial power.* Members of subordinate occupations are developing hierarchies within their occupations and are moving upward there and in the administrative hierarchy. This permits them a certain amount of occupational self-control and even some bureaucratic control over the practice of physicians. The subordinate occupations are taking steps to enhance mobility by writing administrative positions into their own staffing guides, adding management courses to their training programs, and adding articles about administration to their professional society journals.

However, these new bureaucratic opportunities tend to benefit the men and the whites within the lower occupations more than they benefit the women and blacks. Lower-level administrators are appointed from above and the top tends to choose its own kind. For example, chief radiologic technologists, who are promoted by administration, are twice as likely to be men as are radiologic technologists as a whole. The form of the stratification may change, but the membership composition by race and sex at each level may remain the same. As long as control flows from the top down, and the top is a small minority of white males in a system that fosters racism and sexism, the relative positions of white men, non-white

---

*A past governor of the American College of Surgeons perceives the development as follows: "Nurses originated as helpers for doctors but over the years they have assumed more and more administrative functions until they occupy a position midway between administrative and professional staff. Many doctors regret this development but it has come about because of the laissez-faire attitude of doctors so that they have no real basis for complaint. As long as nurses realize and remember their primary mission of assisting the doctor in the care of his patients, no real harm results."[34]

men, white women, and non-white women will (or may) remain the same.

As the private office and small hospital are replaced by the large hospital and clinic, there is not only an increasing number of occupations, but also an increased number of workers within each occupation, in national communication with each other. Health service has become a major form of employment. These are the ideal conditions for unionization. Both craft unionism, in which workers are organized by occupation, and industrial unionism, where workers are organized by employing unit, have increased.[35]

Nurses' strikes are an example of what craft unionism can accomplish.[36, 37] This kind of militance is only possible when there are enough members of an occupation in positions that can bring the hospitals to a halt. Hospital technicians on both the east and west coasts, mostly male, have attempted similar unionism and have largely failed, because their numbers are too small and the skills can be bought elsewhere. Nurses' strikes are aided not only by sufficient strength and number but also by the militance that the subordinate position of women can create. Having no future to lose, they can risk a strike, and they are brought together by their mutual identity as women as well as nurses. In addition, nurses who have carefully developed the identity of nursing as a profession giving service to patients are outraged by their treatment as assembly-line workers giving skilled labor to employers.

Industrial unionism is typified by hospital strikes, in which all the employees of one hospital or one city's hospitals are organized as a unit. Such organizing is aided by the development of large medical centers employing hundreds and even thousands of low-paid workers.[38]

There is tremendous hostility to strikes in the health sector, in part because strikes interfere with treatment but in part because of the sex and often race of the striking workers. The enormous hostility to the hospital workers' strike in New York City in the early 1960s resulted in large part from the fact that the strikers were mostly non-whites and women and identified themselves with the civil rights struggle. "How dare they?" would best characterize the response of hospital administrators and the informed public.

Similar upper-level sentiment against the San Francisco nurses' strikes was outrage that women would do such things. The California Nurses' Association sees its struggle as a woman's struggle. In many cases, hospital strikers realize that their problems within the work setting are based partly on their sex and race status in the community.[39]

Although people can unite around their sexual and racial oppression, these factors can also hold back organization, as can the segregation of occupations.[40] Workers often feel more solidarity with their occupational colleagues in other hospitals than they do with their fellow workers in their own hospital, some of whom are in competing occupations and some of whom are of occupations, races, or sex perceived as inferior.

Strikes have failed because white strikers ignored black workers and black strikers ignored white workers, or because of male-female hostility. All these differences are exploited by the upper level. One major hospital union was not able to organize the nurses, technicians, and therapists into an industrial union until they developed a separate professional guild for these higher-level workers. In one hospital I studied which was undergoing a unionism drive, a technician explained her opposition to the union with, "Why should I have to go on strike because a porter throws a broom against a wall?" This same argument was given me by the laboratory administrator as a reason "his girls" should not join the union, leaving me with a strong impression about where the argument originated. The objection to the porter was not merely occupational. All of the porters who might have thrown their brooms against the wall were black men; all the technicians were white women. Thus race, sex, and professionalism combined against the union.

Professionalism is often seen as the antithesis of unionism and is used in this way. Said the chairman of the radiologists' Committee on Technician Affairs:[41]

Better trained and better paid technologists have a more professional attitude and are less likely to seek unionization and licensing as solutions for their problems. They also more properly appreciate their role in medicine and their relationship to their radiologists.

Nevertheless, in the attempt to push away unions, the professional societies are themselves having to respond to the rising demands of their members, and have taken actions resembling those of unions, partially in fear that their members will desert them in favor of unions. The radiologic technologists instituted a salary study "to meet head-on the encroachment of unionization. . . ."[42] The resulting salary proposals were so far above prevailing wage rates as to resemble nothing so much as the bargaining demands of a union.

Unionism seems promising, and hospital unions have been successful in raising the wages and bargaining position of hospital workers across occupational, race, and sex lines, and many have been making efforts to open mobility channels for low-level workers. However, unionism as a whole in this country has been both racist and sexist and has tended to become subordinate to management. If unions are to solve the problems, women must have power within them.[43] The unions must remain aware of the need for equality for women and non-whites, and aware of the need to challenge management's right to rule.

A successful struggle against sexism in health service, as against racism, requires the unification of women and non-whites at all occupational levels in a common struggle not only against particular hospitals or occupations but against the entire structure of the health service industry that sustains low wages for the majority of workers and poor quality of care for the general population.

Claudia Dreifus

BUILDING A HOSPITAL WORKERS' UNION: DORIS TURNER, THE WOMAN FROM 1199

New York City, on a recent sunny April morning. Two gray-haired, gray-suited personnel executives from Manhattan Medical Center X* seat themselves uncomfortably in the small West 43rd Street offices of Doris Turner, aged forty-five, the executive vice president of New York's District 1199 of the Drug and Hospital Workers Union. There's something about the ambience of this office that makes the two gentlemen executives squirm. Perhaps it is the African sculpture that decorates the room. Perhaps the pictures of Martin Luther King and Malcolm X that stare down at them. Perhaps it is the endless collection of plaques that line the wall: awards to Doris Turner from the NAACP, the Central Labor

*This reporter agreed not to give the name of Medical Center X as the price for sitting in on usually confidential negotiations.

Council and the Black Trade Union Leadership Committee? Or perhaps it is the formidable reputation of the female they've come to do battle with that is leaving them so *unhinged.*

Within trade-union circles, Doris Turner is something of a miracle woman. While union leaders tend to come in packages that are white, male and elderly, Doris succeeds at being what she is: black, female and in her prime. She is the highest-ranking woman within the American labor movement. She has worked her way from ghetto poverty to her current position of power in sixteen short years. She is known to friend and adversary as the sharpest, shrewdest union negotiator since the late Walter Reuther.

And negotiate is what the Manhattan Medical Center X's personnel department are here to do. They've come to iron out the final details for implementation of a new contract between their institution—one of the largest medical centers in the nation—and the union.

Personnel Executive Number One kicks off negotiations with his idea of a funny. "Women's lib has just triumphed at our place," he jokes. "We've just hired two *lady* personnel assistants!"

Ms. Turner smiles. She couldn't care less about the gender of the administrators who'll be hiring and firing her members.

Undaunted, Personnel Executive Number One continues: "I remember my first lady labor lawyer. *She* was tougher than *I* was. Ha. Ha. Ha."

"Is that so?" replies Turner. "It sometimes happens that way. We have a woman lawyer on the staff here. She's very good."

For the next three hours, the gentlemen receive a first-hand lesson in female toughness. Doris controls every aspect of the negotiations. She pores through reams of legal material while dictating to her adversaries—ever so charmingly—exactly how grievances will be dealt with, when sick days will be used, what will be done with authoritarian supervisors.

A small on-the-job question comes up. A worker was suspended for refusing to talk with her supervisor without the presence of her delegate (shop steward). 1199 is taking the case to arbitration. "Listen, it's going to cost us both $250 a day to go to arbitration," says Turner. "It would save a lot of time and money on both sides if you'd just drop the matter."

"Well," says Personnel Executive Number Two, "we can't have employees constantly refusing to talk with their superiors without the presence of their delegates. The hospital would stop functioning."

"True," answers Turner. "But this was such a *gray* situation and a lot of your supervisors are having a hard time adjusting to the newness of the union. This is really a problem of transition."

Before the matter is tabled, Doris has convinced the management-men that she really exists to help them with their administrative problems; that her defense of worker's rights is a service to the hospital. The men agree to consider dropping the suspension; they leave the office looking dazed.

Later that day . . . after Doris has attended a meeting of the City Commission on Human Rights (of which she is a member), . . . after she's talked with a group of Brooklyn maintenance workers whose boss is attempting to increase workload but not payload, . . . after giving a peptalk to sales agents for "1199 Plaza," the East Harlem middle-income housing project of which she is construction director, . . . after all that, she gets into a car and heads to Plainview, Long Island for more meetings.

"Jeez," says Doris, "I'm sure glad I'm not driving. I've been up since six-thirty this morning, and I'm dead."

Our driver, however, is a young staff organizer from the Long Island area and he has no intention of letting his boss rest for the trip out. "We're having problems with intimidation at the nursing home I'm trying to organize," he complains. "The bosses keep taking pictures of the workers handing out leaflets."

"Two can play that game," Turner replies. "Why don't you get some cameras and get the workers to take pictures of the bosses takin' pictures of them?"

Logical, huh? Doris Turner knows her stuff about organizing. She's organized thousands of hospital workers—herself included—and helped them escape a life of extreme poverty; Doris's success as an organizer has resulted in her gaining more power than any woman in American labor history. In addition to her executive vice presidency of District 1199 (65,000 members in the New York metropolitan area), Turner is secretary of the National Union of Hospital and Health Care Employees (100,000 members in 17 states). What's more, bets are on Turner to replace current Hospital Workers' president Leon Davis, sixty-three, when he retires. If that happens, Doris Turner will be the first woman—black or white —to head a large national trade union.

As our car inches along the Long Island Expressway, Doris yawns, complains of lack of sleep and tells this reporter a little about her life: "My childhood . . . it was 'Doris against the world.' I grew up on the worst block in Harlem. West 114th Street. The City of New York *declared* it the worst block! Across the street from where we lived was a house for prostitutes. Our place was in such terrible shape that my mother died after breaking a leg by falling on a bad floor the landlord wouldn't fix. I lived on 114th Street from the time I was twelve till the time I got married."

Turner married at twenty, in 1950, retaining her maiden name. Of that marriage she says little. All I can pry from her is that her husband's name was "Moore," that he worked in a button factory, that the marriage lasted five years, and that they had two daughters, now grown. "I married against my better judgment," is her final comment on that episode in her life.

"In 1956, I took a job as a dietary clerk at Lenox Hill Hospital on the East Side of Manhattan," she says, changing the subject to something she's more comfortable with. "Lenox Hill had a very wealthy clientele. My salary was $30 a week. In those days, hospital workers didn't have anything. We didn't have minimum wage, disability, unemployment or health insurance. Most important, because we were working for 'charitable' institutions, we didn't have the automatic legal right that other kinds of workers have to force an employer to recognize a union. We were caring for sick people, but we couldn't afford to be sick. If you took time off to be sick, you'd be fired. There was racism and sexism on the job, too."

"Racism?" I ask, seeking an example.

"Yeah. I trained a white woman and she couldn't even speak English and she made five dollars a week more than me."

"And sexism?"

"They had a dining room that was set aside for the men to eat in, and the men got free meals. Women weren't allowed in it. If we ate a cracker from there and got found out we were fired. I used to watch them throw away enough food every day to feed an army. They'd throw it away rather than give it to us to eat. This was 1956, not 1936! You really had to like people an awful lot or be desperate for a job in order to work in hospitals in those days."

Dietary Clerk Turner's take-home pay was $29.71 weekly. How did her family survive? "It wasn't easy," she says. "You learn to do a lot of things when you have to. I used to shop in secondhand stores for clothing for my children. I'd walk twelve blocks to buy something for two cents less. Things were so bad at Lenox Hill that I once ran into a nurse I knew in this thrift shop not far from the hospital. I didn't think anybody but *me* came into those sorts of places. The nurse said, 'My dear, I raised my children from this very thrift shop.'"

Exactly how the union came into her life is something that Turner is sketchy about. It happened late in 1958. At the time, 1199 was a 5,000-member union of pharmacists. Hospital workers were excluded from basic labor legislation; they did not enjoy the automatic right to collective bargaining. "Some man from 1199," recalls Doris, "I don't remember who, came up to me and said, 'If you want to see some changes, get people to sign this yellow pad saying they want a union.' " I didn't know much about unions. All I knew was that they might make life better for us. I remember running around the hospital like a crazy lady and getting people to sign." In an hour's time, Turner had organized a hundred out of Lenox Hill's five hundred nonprofessional workers.

The Personnel Department at Lenox Hill was unenthusiastic about the activities of Ms. Turner and friends. But Lenox Hill wasn't the only nonprofit hospital in New York getting the 1199 treatment: organizing drives were simultaneously conducted at six other institutions around town. "We had a majority of the workers signed up by early 1959," Turner recalls, "but the hospital kept telling us it was illegal for us to have a union. It wasn't. The hospital simply wasn't bound to let us have one. The Administration was getting so uptight about 1199 that one day the boss called me down to his office to give me a talking-to . . ."

"What was his name?" I ask.

"Never mind his name," Turner snaps. "I have to negotiate with him these days. Anyway, the first thing he wanted to know was how my children were. *My* children! He couldn't care less about them, because they were starving on $30 a week. Then he said he'd heard that people were thinking about a union and that there was no point to *that* because the hospital was nonprofit and it didn't have no money. So I pointed to a new building they'd just built and he said, 'Oh, we get contributions for that.' So I said, 'While you're out there asking the left hand for money for buildings you better ask the right hand for money for workers. Otherwise, you ain't gonna have no workers to fill your pretty new building.' "

And that's exactly what happened.

On May 8, 1959, menial workers at seven nonprofit institutions made history by giving New York its first hospital strike. Their demand: union recognition. Doris Turner led the Lenox Hill action. "Oh, it was rough, rough," she admits. "No one had any savings. The union gave us a dollar a day 'cause that's all it had. It meant you had to chew a piece of bread several times. We ate so much bologna that I couldn't look bologna in the face for years."

After forty-six tumultuous days—during which mink-coated doctor's wives walked through picket lines so that they could scrub floors—the hospitals and the union came to a stalemate agreement. No official union recognition, but a permanent administrative committee to deal with workers' grievances. "It made it possible for us to build," explains Doris.

Shortly after the strike, Lenox Hill fired Doris Turner. "They said I was a terrible, terrible worker," Doris laughs. While the legality of the firing was debated during nine months of arbitration hearings, Turner went on staff as an 1199 organizer. "I didn't come to the union looking for anything," she says. "I just saw myself organizing hospital workers. If I organized ten today, I wanted to organize twenty tomorrow. It was a really good feeling—like being able to do anything you wanted to."

Moe Foner, executive secretary of the Hospital Workers, an 1199 veteran from the pre-1959 days, remembers Turner when she first went on staff. In an interview earlier that week he told me: "Doris was quiet, very inexperienced in a union setting. . . . She had a problem with the males here. I'd say she had to prove herself twice over. Even for Doris to emerge under the protection of [1199 president] Leon Davis, she had to claw her way over some people who resented her as a woman having leadership in a staff that was predominantly male."

As our car pushes on toward Plainview, Turner dismisses Foner's comment. "I never thought about that stuff one way or the other."

What Doris did think about were complaints from relatives that all her union work was resulting in her neglecting her children. "It was hard to make my family see," she says, "that I was making a better life for as many children as possible, mine included."

There was a brief return to Lenox Hill after arbitrators ruled Doris' firing illegal, but in August 1961 she quit Lenox Hill's kitchen forever and went to work full time for 1199. From then on, Doris Turner's life became completely intertwined with the idea of a union for hospital workers. Leon Davis, a man with the foresight to see that a union with a predominately black and female membership needed black and female leadership, made Doris his protégée. Doris, in turn, worked herself to the bone, achieving one victory after another for the union. A second strike in 1962 resulted in a new state law granting the right to union recognition. In New York today the average wage for a dietary clerk is $218 per week. Benefits include health insurance, pension, major medical and dental plans, vacations averaging four weeks per year, and a training program for job upgrading.

By the late 1960s, 1199 had organized the vast majority of hospital workers in the Metropolitan area; among the union officers, thoughts were turning to a national organizational campaign. In 1969, a call came to Doris from a group of nurses' aides in Charleston, South Carolina: they wanted 1199. "I went down there to see if the workers meant to stand behind their message," says Turner, as we turn off the Expressway. "Conditions were just like at Lenox Hill ten years before. But racism was the big thing. The blacks, both men and women, were really treated differently from the whites. It ended up in a hundred-day strike. . . . State troopers with bayonets. Coretta King and Ralph Abernathy came to help. It was at Charleston the National Union began. After that, we went on to Baltimore, Rhode Island, Boston, and Washington and . . ."

In the midst of all this empire building, with Doris running herself ragged simultaneously administering her section of the New York union and helping out with the National drive, she met a gentle-spirited, handsome young union member named Willie Keyes. "He was a comfort," she says. "He watched me in the crazy world of 1199 and thought it was great if that's what I wanted to do. He said, 'I'll help you if I can, but I won't ever hinder you.' I didn't have to fight for my identity with Willie. I may have to do that with other men, but not at home."

Doris Turner married Willie Keyes four and a half years ago. The wedding had to be squeezed into Doris's schedule as she dashed between two separate organizational drives. Today, they live in her pleasant Riverside Drive cooperative apartment. "With Willie," she says, "I don't have to be anybody but me."

Our car pulls into the parking lot of the Plainview American Legion Hall. "Mmmmphhh," humphs Doris, "the American Legion. We *are* getting respectable these days."

Inside, nearly a hundred new 1199ers are seated waiting for a union orientation session. Doris walks to the podium and gives a small speech: "It's up to you to make sure you have a clean, decent union. The union doesn't exist for me to have a job. It exists to make your life better. 1199 is the kind of union that's going to translate itself into better benefits for you, just as long as you stand up for yourselves. That means *you've* got to go out and organize workers in other institutions."

After Marshall Dubin, 1199's educational director, explains some of the organization's benefits, a CBS film about hospital workers is shown, *Countdown to a Contract.* Though the documentary is only five years old, I see something shocking in it: 1199's officers, Doris included, look a decade older. The strain, the exhausting tension of constant work, seems to age people in double-quick time. Doris stares at the film and becomes misty-eyed when the camera focuses on several 1199 staffers who've since died of heart attacks.

"Does the movie scare you," I ask.

"No! Absolutely not," Doris snaps—a bit too quickly. "Listen, I decided long ago that nobody lives forever. Besides, getting gray doesn't cause me to die, it just causes me to get gray."

Turner moves away from me. It seems I've said something terribly wrong. She walks toward a blond woman, neatly dressed in her hospital uniform. "I wanna know what you think about these meetings," Doris tells the new member, "because we have them all the time and we wanna know what you think."

"Well," the woman answers haltingly, "I liked what you had to say about getting involved and all . . . but I don't think . . . I don't think my husband would let me come to union meetings."

"Bring your husband along," suggests Doris. "That's what I do."

And then, as if on cue, in walks Willie Keyes, tall, handsome, with a warm sympathetic face; he's come all the way from the City to give his wife an easy lift home. "Honey," he says, kissing Doris on the cheek, "there's a blue Cadillac out back blocking all the parking. One of the workers seems to have left it there."

Doris Turner breaks up with laughter. "Well, we've come a long way if our people have got Cadillacs. . . . From holes in our shoes to Cadillacs . . . it ain't bad."

PART FIVE

TAKING OUR BODIES BACK: THE WOMEN'S HEALTH MOVEMENT

Ellen Frankfort

VAGINAL POLITICS

An old church basement, a long table, a woman, a speculum—and pow! In about five minutes you've just about destroyed the mystique of the doctor.

I saw it happen this week when Carol,* a woman from the Los Angeles Self-Help Clinic, slipped off her dungarees and underpants, borrowed somebody's coat and stretched it out on a long table, placed herself on top, and with her legs bent at the knees, inserted a speculum into herself. Once the speculum was in place, her cervix was completely visible and each of the fifty women present took a flashlight and looked inside.

"Which part is the cervix? The tiny slit in the middle?"

"No, that's the os. The cervix is the round, doughnut-shaped part."

"Have you had any children?"

"Yes, six, and two abortions and two miscarriages."

"My God, how old are you?"

"Thirty-eight."

"You know, it's changing. The cervix now looks more protruded and the os has opened slightly."

"Yes, we're very flexible inside."

*Ed.'s note: The two women mentioned here are Carol Downer and Lorraine Rothman of the Los Angeles Feminist Women's Health Clinic.

263

"How much of this can you see yourself?"

"Come, take a look from here."

Carol placed the dime-store mirror so the women could see from her vantage point. The cervix, as reflected in the mirror, was clear and distinct.

Before actually demonstrating the use of the speculum, Carol had talked about self-examination while Lorraine, another woman from the clinic, showed slides.

"This is what a speculum looks like, the thing the doctor puts inside. Except it doesn't feel cold because it's not made of stainless steel.

"Here's a picture of cancer of the cervix. There's the tumor— that bulbous structure attached to the bottom. It takes about ten years for most tumors to reach that advanced stage. Each year 13,000 women die of tumors of the cervix. And the so-called danger signs we're told to look for are usually associated with late stages. But if each woman had her own speculum and knew how to examine herself, she could note any changes immediately.

"At our self-help clinic, we believe very much in sticking to our own experiences. We don't talk about what we've read in books. For example, one woman said, 'We can have twenty-five orgasms.' 'Well, have you?' I asked. 'No.' Now I'm not saying it's impossible, I'm just saying I haven't personally met a woman who has.

"The same thing applies to health. For instance, doctors have been telling women they have tipped or retroverted uteri. They're at the wrong angle, they say. You know the picture the textbooks have of the so-called normal uterus. Well, now that we've been examining each other, we see that the 'normal' uterus is the least common. The uterus can assume all angles of flection. And they're about as relevant as the shape of a nose. Yet one woman had her uterus removed because of its shape and another had braces stuck up to force it not to be tipped.

"But what really gave us the biggest charge was hearing a doctor check an IUD [intrauterine device]. You know, doctors talk in real fancy language. The eleven o'clock position, he says. For that he had to go to medical school and we have to pay $15. Well, if you look at the cervix in this slide at the eleven o'clock position, you can see exactly what the doctor sees: a little string. Generally, you have cervicitis where the string is. We recommend that the string be longer so you can pull it out.

"Now in this slide, the woman has monilia, a yeast-like infection. It's the milky white area over the cervix. And if you put a cotton swab to it, it will be cheesy. The smell is not foul, which is one way you can distinguish it from other vaginal infections.

"Here is a woman with cervicitis, an inflammation. Most of us have it. Yet many women are cauterized for it by doctors. We say watch it by checking whether it is still there a week later. In most women it goes away. We found that the frequency increased in the summer. At first we said women don't have odors, that's a male myth. But then the warm months came and we found there was a distinct odor when we examined women.

"Here's a cervix of a woman who's had several children. It's slightly protruding. But if we touch it, it will retreat. Once we became tuned in to our uterus, we saw we had great control. What had previously been referred to as gut level, we now call uterus level."

"Do you notice anything different about this cervix?"

"Color." (It was very red.)

"Any idea why?"

"She's pregnant?"

"Right. She *was,* that is. By the next day, she wasn't."

"Right on!"

"If you look at your cervix every week, you can see when it's softer, when the os opens and the color becomes darker or blotchy or reddish. And then you can know you're pregnant before a test tells you."

I hesitate to use the word "revolutionary," but no other word seems accurate to describe the effects of the first part of the evening. It was a little like having a blind person see for the first time—for what woman is not blind to her own insides? The simplicity with which Carol examined herself brought forth in a flash the whole gynecological ritual: the receptionist, the magazines, the waiting room, and then the examination itself—being told to undress, lying on your back with your feet in the stirrups, looking at a blank ceiling while waiting in an overly airconditioned room (the doctor isn't the one without clothes, after all) for him to enter—and no one thinking that "meeting" a doctor for the first time in this position is slightly odd.

As Carol and Lorraine pointed out, not only does the drapery further depersonalize the woman by making her faceless and bodiless *except* for her vagina, it also prevents her from seeing what the doctor is doing. Carol and Lorraine advise women to discard the drape by throwing it on the floor when the doctor enters. If he replaces it, throw it on the floor again. If he questions your behavior, tell him that doctors in California are no longer draping. And if you're in California, tell him that doctors in New York have stopped this strange custom.

By now the Los Angeles self-help women had a captive audience. So deep is the feeling—the "uterus reaction"—that women are systematically denied any control over their bodies by the medical profession that any alternative to it is embraced with joy. I, too, wholeheartedly support women learning about their bodies. I even think that having a mirror next to your bed to see the outside of your body is good: it does away with the idea that a woman is to be looked at only by others. It also makes her more at ease with her body and does away with the shame that such practices as draping encourage. In addition, there is no question that a woman who examines herself regularly can spot a change at the earliest possible moment, which could lead to curative treatment that more-advanced stages of a disease rule out. I think women could learn to diagnose vaginal infections, screen themselves for VD (venereal disease), and take Pap tests, which would be a way to have women who can't afford routine checkups receive this kind of care.

But suppose every woman in the country reaches the point where she has her own speculum (as I and most of the women who were in the church basement that evening now do) and examines herself weekly or even monthly; what good is it to know how to recognize disease if we have a health system that remains unresponsive to prevention or to the need to provide adequate care for everyone? True, doctors who treat women informed about their bodies couldn't possibly get away with the unnecessary surgery they now perform; true, gynecologists couldn't so easily behave in their characteristically patronizing way; and, perhaps more important, women who understood their bodies would have a means of evaluating their doctors and of holding them accountable for their work.

Nevertheless, the mystique of the doctor, as profound as it is, is not the only negative feature of the present health system. Unfortunately, the women from the Los Angeles Self-Help Clinic, in their very real and legitimate disgust with American doctors, seemed to be focusing mainly on this aspect of the problem while ignoring the need for institutional change. Feminist politics cannot be divorced from other political realities, such as health care and safety.

The second half of the presentation by the self-help women was devoted to a period extraction device, a small collection bottle to which two tubes are attached. At the end of one tube is a plastic syringe about six inches long; at the end of the other tube is the Karman cannula, whose 4-mm diameter makes it narrow enough to be inserted into an undilated uterus. Pumping the syringe creates suction sufficient to draw material out of the uterus. According to Carol and Lorraine, this device could be used by any woman to end her period as soon as it began, or to terminate pregnancy; it thus would make all forms of birth control, including abortion, unnecessary. (Both Carol and Lorraine use the device every month; if their periods begin in the morning, they end them by afternoon. Neither woman has reported any change in her cycle.)

First the device was demonstrated using a glass of water. Then color slides were shown illustrating an actual period extraction (which turned out to be an early abortion of a woman six weeks pregnant). The procedure was performed in a private home; the woman wore street clothes and everything went normally. However, that was just one case. I saw the Karman cannula used this past year in New York City with the vacuum aspirator (which the self-help women claim is obsolete). I have also read reports about it, including a favorable one in the June 15, 1971 *American Journal of Obstetrics and Gynecology.* However, the authors, Dr. Sadja Goldsmith and Dr. Alan Margolis, worked out of a hospital, and in a film I saw of them illustrating the Karman cannula, both were in traditional surgical garb with masks.

What am I trying to say? That abortions should be performed only in hospitals and only by doctors? Certainly not. For a year I have been arguing just the opposite—that trained paraprofessionals, under the supervision of doctors, can safely perform abortions in out-patient clinics. (It should be noted that in its first year of legalized abortion, New York had a startlingly good record of safety, due in part to the efforts of women to have abortions performed in out-patient facilities which have a better safety record than hospitals.)

I am, like the Los Angeles women, appalled that doctors and clinic owners have been able to make abortion one of the biggest rip-offs of women's bodies ever known. However, I don't think the way to eliminate profiteering, as the self-help women stated with what seems like considerable naïveté, is to set up six-week courses at which women learn how to do period extractions. I would also hesitate to recommend what amounts to a method of early abortion (although it is not called that) to pregnant women who might not yet be finished with childbearing, as are Lorraine and Carol. It's too early to know what the long-range results of this kind of monthly tampering are. At the very least, introducing foreign parts every month to a germ-free area like the uterus raises serious medical questions about infection. Women can't rail against drug companies using them as guinea pigs and allow self-help clinics to do the same thing (although I think it an improvement to use white, middle-class women rather than poor, nonwhite women, since at least if something goes wrong the former can usually get to a hospital and treatment; in addition, middle-class women usually are healthier to start with).

Another way in which I think that feminist politics interfered with medical realities at the session in the church basement was in the omission of some of the negative findings about the Karman cannula. When I asked about the high number of incomplete extractions doctors have reported with this method, my question was viewed as an attack on feminism. They said, "Incompletes are a problem only when abortion is done in different states or cities. But if you do a period extraction at home, then you can just repeat it if you don't get everything out." This all sounds very reasonable, except that many women discover that they have an incomplete by way of developing an infection. Sometimes an incomplete can mean that the egg has been left in and the pregnancy continues; sometimes an incomplete results in a continued pregnancy *and* an infection. I would be less cavalier about incompletes.

When it became clear that all such questions were seen as an attack on an ideology, I began to feel sad. What had begun as such an innovative evening had become dogma-ridden. To set up a program that specifically aimed at educating women, to do a dazzling demonstration that immediately won their trust, and then to fail to give out information or to receive questions in a cooperative spirit seemed to me plainly exploitative. After all, women who were told, "No more Kotex, no more tampons, no more pills, no more IUD's, no more abortions," were going to be pretty receptive to just about anything and deserved to have all the information made available to them.

The self-help clinic intends to do some studies about diseases of the cervix, sexual habits, contraception, and so forth. This is fine and could be of great help to women. But to believe that self-help clinics can offer an alternative means of delivering health services seems foolish. The United States has more hospitals and doctors than most countries. However, they do not offer the services people need; nor is the distribution of services they offer rational. But doctors, hospitals and drug companies are not going to be affected by having small groups of women learning how to examine themselves or how to extract their periods. Nor will such self-help improve health care for the people who lack the kind of movement experience that leads to feeling at ease with lay women working in homes without supervision. And it will not help the women (and men) who are too sick for self-help and who have no alternative but to go to a hospital.

Rather than push the psychologically very appealing but medically questionable period extraction method, I would like to see women organize around the institutions where the power lies. Period extraction kits are not going to do away with abortion. But women could do away with the profiteering by winning real control of the medically excellent abortion clinics. However, in order to do that, women must overcome their naïve response to technology. Machines per se are not bad. Those foreign countries and areas of the United States where babies are born without the benefits of scientific knowledge and where abortions are done in the most primitive way possible are also the places which have the highest infant and maternal death rates—medical technology could only help the women there. But if those currently in charge of the machines and hospitals don't respond to people's needs, let's replace *them,* not the machines.

Any group genuinely interested in self-help clinics ought to look at the People's Republic of China. There, one million paraprofessionals, half of whom are women, have been trained. These health workers, fetchingly called "barefoot doctors," would find it absurd to discard a modern, effective method of abortion because it contradicted some notion of sisterhood, just as they would find it absurd to dismiss acupuncture because there is as yet no "scientific" explanation for it. Something that works speaks for itself. And, as of this date, this cannot be said of the period extraction kit, whether used for periods or pregnancies.

In order for women to receive the best care, they must receive not only dignified, nonpatronizing, nonsexist care, but also medically sound care that takes into account the latest scientific knowledge. If happiness is, as the Los Angeles self-help women claim, "knowing how your uterus looks," then health may be using that knowledge to force the system to keep our uteri the way we like to see them.

Rachel Gillett Fruchter, Naomi Fatt,
Pamela Booth and Diana Leidel
of the HealthRight Collective

THE WOMEN'S HEALTH MOVEMENT: WHERE ARE WE NOW?

In many towns and rural areas and in almost every major city in the country, groups of women (both patients and health workers) are working to make changes in a health system that does not serve their needs. The purpose of this article is to describe the background and work of those local groups which have grown out of or identify with the Women's Movement. These hundreds of groups together constitute what we are defining as the "Women's Health Movement." Their work falls into three categories:

- Changing Consciousness.
- Providing health related services.
- Struggling to change established health institutions.

Groups may focus all their energies on one of these activities or may take on all three. But whatever their specific work, the groups also represent the attempt of thousands of previously isolated women to control their own lives, to develop their skills, and to gain strength through shared experience, work, and political activity.

Women's "Body" courses, self-help sessions, and workshops and discussions on women and the health system have become coast-to-coast phenomena. Held in women's centers, community centers, schools, and private homes, these sessions are important outreach activities of many groups. They differ from traditional "health education" in that they include strong elements of shared "consciousness raising"—and because in each discussion, the health system itself is seen as a problem as great as any infectious or degenerative disease.

Starting from discussion groups or classes, many groups now run speakers bureaus, prepare materials for local newspapers, and appear on radio and TV. The original focus on birth control, abortion, and maternity care has expanded to emphasize all aspects of preventive health, including nutrition and exercise, while certain groups have focused their work on respiratory problems, occupational health, and aging.

A combination of shared experience, health information, and political comment also marks the literature put out by the Women's Health Movement. Materials range from mimeographed leaflets on single topics by many local groups, pamphlets like those by the New York Health Organizing Collective, and booklets such as Circle One from Colorado or Feeding Ourselves from Berkeley, to comprehensive collective books like Our Bodies, Ourselves. This book, which has sold more than a million copies, is but one indication that the Women's Health Movement has struck a responsive chord in American women.

Traditional health education has also been affected by women's groups. Students have demanded new health education courses in colleges and high schools. Some are taught by students, some by faculty, and some by women's health groups. For example, the

New Bedford Women's Clinic in Massachusetts teaches a course on Women and Health at Bristol Community College. In a Catholic-dominated mid-western city, a group of women are bringing new perspectives to "Growing up" health courses for young girls in the public schools. In Cleveland, the NOW Task Force on Health is studying sex education within the school system.

Despite the millions of dollars spent annually in the health industry, there are still crucial services lacking. First, there is a lack of medical services: sometimes a certain type of service, or service in a specific geographic area, or for a particular group of people. Second, there is a desperate need for help in negotiating a health system that is not only increasingly specialized and institutionalized, but is also over-priced and notorious for over-treating patients.

No one knows how many underground groups quietly performed abortions when it was illegal to do so. "Jane," a group of about fifty women in Chicago, provided 11,000 abortions in the four years they worked together before legal abortion came to Illinois. Even after the Supreme Court decision, groups like the Emma Goldman Women's Clinic in Iowa City and the Vermont Women's Health Center set up needed above-ground abortion facilities in states with restrictive regulations or conservative medical establishments.

Many women's clinics provide primary care for common problems because, as a Tallahassee, Florida group states, "quality health care services for women are seriously lacking here." The Somerville Women's Health Project in Massachusetts and the Fremont Women's Clinic in Seattle are both located in poor areas of a large city where most medical services are unavailable to the community. Others, like the Women's Clinic at Evergreen State College in Washington, got started when establishment services were cut off. Several women's health groups work as women's caucuses in free clinics which serve a general community or a specific group such as teenagers or gay women and men.

Preventive health services often ignored by the health establishment are the basis of many of the "well woman" clinics that women's groups have established, working with little or no involvement by doctors. Groups, such as the Beach Area Women's Clinic in San Diego and the S.E. Portland Women's Health Clinic, provide check-ups and tests (Pap, VD, blood pressure, and others), counseling on nutrition and all aspects of reproductive health, and referrals where necessary, as well as exercise classes. The Feminist Women's Health Centers, spearheaded by the Los Angeles group, are notable for developing techniques of self-examination and in-depth counseling that are used not only by other women's health groups, but by some regular clinics and doctors.

All of these health services emphasize the use of paramedics, nurses, and lay counselors to provide care. Even when doctors are involved, the focus is still on health education, preventive care, and the sharing of skills and information. This work has motivated many women to train as health workers at every level. From a worker's viewpoint, these clinics are unique, not necessarily in what they do, but in how they are organized. Each worker has a major role in determining policies and activities, quite unlike the rigid hierarchical decision-making process within the health system. As a woman from the Elizabeth Blackwell Brigade in Bellingham, Washington, put it: "We see our clinic as a dual model: first, to women [as an example of] self-reliance, taking power through knowledge and sharing it with other women; second, as a model of a health care facility—a non-hierarchical, consumer run, low cost, quality care community clinic."

Women's Information Service in Pueblo, Colorado and Women's Counseling Service in Madison, Wisconsin are just two of the hundreds of groups that are providing referral, evaluation, and monitoring services across the country. So great are women's needs for good information on how to use health services that every women's center in the country has found itself actively engaged in helping women through the expensive maze of medical facilities, drug and medical technology, and government agencies.

Groups, like the Women's Rap Program in Tampa, Florida, discuss a woman's problem with her, talk about the services available at a price she can afford to pay, give information on essential tests and how to get them, how to avoid being overcharged, when and how to get a second opinion, how to make use of health insurance and Medicaid, how to complain and get recourse, and how to deal with sexist doctors and rip-off clinics.

Organized information of this sort, in the past a part of women's day-to-day conversations, is now becoming recognized outside the Women's Health Movement as an important part of patients' efforts to organize themselves. Most of the thousands of activists in the Women's Health Movement want to see major changes in the health system: changes in how and where health services are delivered, an end to profit-making, more preventive services, and more power to patients and workers in all aspects of health planning and delivery. Most groups have at one time or another engaged in some direct struggle or conflict with health institutions or agencies. Early widespread Women's Health Movement tactics demanded public attention for the central issue of a woman's right to control her own body. Initially, groups picketed and marched to get the right to abortion. WONAAC, the Women's National Abortion Action Coalition, organized across the country. Later on, groups took to the streets again to protest clinic abuses on the one hand, and harassment of abortion facilities on the other.

In January, 1970, the D.C. Women's Liberation group disrupted Senator Nelson's hearings on oral contraceptives, and raised loud and clear the issue of a woman's right to make decisions about her own medical treatment. For several successive years women asserting their rights as patients picketed or disrupted conventions of the American Medical Association or the American College of Obstetricians and Gynecologists, in New York, Chicago, and San Francisco. More recently, women's groups have disrupted Planned Parenthood conferences in Texas and New York.

Today, most groups see these tactics as a few of a number of possible tools to gain publicity for issues, reach the general public, and challenge those in power.

Although women were working actively to change abortion laws before the Women's Liberation Movement developed in the late sixties, the movement gave new energy to many women. Women vs. Connecticut, from New Haven, was one of many groups that lobbied and brought lawsuits to change restrictive abortion laws. Despite the Supreme Court decision, work to protect women's abortion rights is still necessary. Recently, in Chicago, several women's health groups participated in a lawsuit to force Cook County Hospital to perform second trimester abortions.

Groups are taking on other areas of patients' rights. In Los Angeles, a group is forming to end forced sterilization practices. Others have been winning suits that give a woman the right to voluntary sterilization. Still other groups have documented instances of poor care and abuse and feminist lawyers have taken up the issues.

Women's health groups probably represent the most widespread health referral system outside the health establishment. While most groups have been successful in helping individual women, many have also set out consciously to try to improve or change the services to which they refer. In abortion, their power has clearly lain in their ability to channel fee paying patients to abortion clinics that meet the group's standards. A coalition of women's referral groups in the mid-west was particularly successful in monitoring and evaluating services in New York. In other cities, women's health groups have exposed substandard practices. The Health Evaluation and Referral Service in Chicago was instrumental in closing down a clinic that did unnecessary abortions. While other areas of medicine are less grossly profiteering than the abortion business, individual doctors have been successfully "persuaded" to lower their fees or change their practices by referral groups such as the Woodstock New York Women's Health Collective or the Women's Crisis Center in Ann Arbor. In several instances New York women's health groups collected complaints about care in hospitals from patients and health workers, evaluated clinics as patients themselves, and with some success, pressed for changes in in-hospital doctor's practices, emergency room care, and counseling.

Using their resources in referral, counseling, or health education, many women's health groups have documented cases of abuses, poor care, and over-treatment that have been important in public hearings, commissions of inquiry, and health planning sessions. A Troy, New York group directed its demands to a state agency; a Washington group, to a comprehensive health planning committee.

Since the mid-sixties, some legislation has made provisions for consumer and community participation in community advisory boards, health planning and standard-setting committees. Because of their base in the community, Women's Health Movement activists from Boston, Chicago, Washington, and elsewhere have acted on such committees.

Whatever their specific areas of work, each women's health group is contributing to the growth and development of a movement which is not limited to United States boundaries. Extensive work is being done by Canadian groups like the Women's Information and Referral Center in Montreal, which, among other things, has set up a women's clinic and organized a rape crisis squad, and the Community Women's Center in Regina, Saskatchewan, which emerged from a campus based center to become a group serving the larger community. In Europe also, active groups have formed in England, France, Spain, and West Germany.

All this work reflects the insistence that patients have the right to determine and control the health care they receive and that health workers have the right to share in the decision-making of the health system in which they work.

Since this article was written in the fall of 1974, the Women's Health Movement has continued to grow and to expand its activities and perspective.

Most of the groups mentioned still exist, although there have, of course, been changes. For example, the Somerville Women's Health Clinic is now totally run by women from the community it was set up to serve. The Feminist Women's Health Centers, now numbering almost a dozen, have trained many women who have set up clinics of their own. HealthRight's quarterly newsletter, in which this article first appeared as the lead article in its first four-page issue, has expanded to twelve pages and plans to become a bimonthly publication in 1978.

While the work of most Women's Health Movement organizations remains firmly based in local communities, greater nationwide coordination and activity has marked the growing sophistication and strength of the movement.

•1975   1300 women attended the first National Women's Health Conference in Boston.

•1975   A caucus of women from many organizations lobbied in Washington against continued widespread use of cancer-inducing estrogens such as DES.

•1976   The Washington-based Women's Health Network was established to provide a nationwide clearing house on health policy and legislation.

•1976   HealthRight was joined on the national scene by the journal *Women & Health*.

•1977   Movies such as *Healthcaring from Our End of the Speculum,* books and a plethora of pamphlets have been produced. The second edition of *Our Bodies Ourselves* has been on the best-seller list for almost a year, is being translated into Spanish and is selling widely abroad.

Locally and nationally, groups have spearheaded action around sterilization abuse, woman-battering, unnecessary surgery and home birth.

From the first tentative gatherings of women sharing experiences and new-found knowledge, and the excitement of the early demonstrations and illegal abortion work, women's health groups have matured and coalesced into a strong and viable movement that is clearly dug in for the long haul.

Elizabeth Fee

WOMEN AND HEALTH CARE: A COMPARISON OF THEORIES

The women's movement has generated at least three forms of social criticism. These may be labeled liberal feminism, radical feminism, and Marxist feminism. These three branches of the feminist movement each differ in their approach to the analysis of women's situation, and in their prescription for the ailing American health-care system.

§ Liberal Feminism

Liberal feminism is the most widely diffused and generally acceptable version of feminism. The liberal feminist position was crystallized by Betty Friedan's now classic text, *The Feminine Mystique*, and given organizational form in the National Organization of Women (NOW); the movement demanded equal opportunity for women to enter the upper reaches of the job market and equal treatment once they got there. Liberal feminists do not seriously challenge the hierarchical structure of American society; they simply want access to the same choices as are available to men. NOW fought to "bring women into full participation in the mainstream

of American society *now*, exercising all the privileges and responsibilities thereof in truly equal partnership with men."

During the economic flush times of the sixties, the liberal feminist movement made considerable headway. The case for equality
gained widespread publicity and seemed compelling to many
women and men; concrete legislative victories reinforced the belief
that gains toward equality were possible "within the system"; they
moved on toward a constitutional amendment that would embody
their central demand in the fundamental law of the land as their
predecessors had done with the women's suffrage amendment fifty
years before. The resistence to apparently reasonable demands has
proved stronger and more stubborn than the theory would seem to
predict, particularly on the part of other women, some of whom
cling to women's roles as housewife and mother in preference to
the free labor market. Liberals counter with the explanation that
women are to have a free choice whether to stay at home or go out
to work, but the ideal of free choice seems increasingly implausible
in the face of growing unemployment and inflation. Indeed, as the
state of the economy has begun to restrict and erode some of the
hard-won gains of the last decade, many have begun to search for
a more penetrating analysis of the roots of their oppression. For
many more, however, the direction already marked out seems
sufficiently correct, and they continue with the struggle to win
women's rights and equality within the established system.

§ Liberal Feminism and the Health Care System

Liberal feminists see the social subordination of women reflected
in the sexual structure of the organization of medicine, i.e., in a
field where women are the majority of health workers, the upper
reaches of the medical hierarchy constitute a virtual male monopoly. The imbalance of the sexes here is more extreme than in most
other areas of employment, a situation which seems particularly
ironic since the practice of medicine requires personal characteristics compatible with those traditionally ascribed to women. The
case of the Soviet Union, where the majority of physicians are
female, has been frequently cited to show that no social or biologi-

cal necessity enforces the rule that men become doctors and women, nurses. The demand for sexual equality in education and employment should rather result in approximately equal numbers of men and women in each occupational category.

Another area of criticism concerns the nature of the patient-doctor interaction. Physicians heal (or do not heal) from a position of power; they relate in either a paternal or an authoritarian manner to their patients. They may withold information about a diagnosis, be deliberately vague and obfuscatory, or be simply incapable of explaining the problem in nontechnical terms: they seem to doubt that patients have a right to an explanation of their illness. Aware that these attitudes are also directed at men, liberal feminists correctly argue that they are exaggerated when the patient is female: well or ill, women are accorded less respect. Many women feel that their symptoms are treated less seriously than those of men because doctors harbor the secret suspicion that most of the medical problems presented are psychosomatic.

"Specialist" is a more accurate term than "doctor" to describe the focus of the liberal feminist critique of medical attitudes. Middle-class women usually do not see a general practitioner, but rather a series of specialists: a gynecologist for birth control and Pap smears, a pediatrician for the kids' fevers and a psychiatrist for depression and anxiety. The disaffection with medical care, already directed at the upper strata of the profession, tends to further concentrate on two specialties: gynecology and psychiatry. These are the medical areas in which contempt for women is most evident; each has a long history of explicating the disadvantages of a female body and a female mind. Surveys of gynecological and psychiatric textbooks reveal the contribution of medical education to the reproduction of these attitudes in new generations of medical students.

The criticism of the sex-typing of health occupations and that of the sexist attitudes of physicians intersect in the call for more women to be admitted to medical schools. Women physicians should be more capable of treating the health problems presented by women patients with respect, if only because the female body would be less alien and the female mind less mysterious. The overwhelmingly male bias of gynecology and psychiatry would be difficult to maintain if even half of the pracititioners were female. Medical research might become less male-biased if the research teams were composed of equal numbers of each sex. Rigid distinctions between medical skills and "caring" functions should weaken if these were not reinforced by sexual differentiation; the widespread desire for such an integration is attested to by the popularity of the Marcus Welby image, fictional though it be. Then, too, a feminization of the medical profession and a corresponding invasion of nursing by men would erode the artificial income and status distinctions between doctors and nurses; this relation is now maintained as a traditional male-dominant, female-subordinate one.

This liberal critique thus approaches the problem of medical care at the point most visible to the middle- and upper-middle-class consumer, the private office of the physician or specialist. From this vantage point, the giant medical institutions, clinics and hospital emergency rooms tend to fade from view, although it is here that the health needs of most women are met—or, more frequently, not met. In speaking to the attitudes of male doctors, it centers on the tip of the medical iceberg and tends to ignore the majority of health workers—medical technicians, orderlies, household workers, and practical nurses, over 70 percent of whom are women. In emphasizing the need to equalize the upper ranks of the medical profession by sex, it may implicitly acquiesce in a hierarchical structure that rests on a base of exploited female labor. The liberal position offers most to those who can afford a view from the top, to women who might have gone to medical school had admissions been equal to both sexes, to women who would be able to pay for feminist therapy if it were available. It offers less to the woman who cleans the floors of the hospital or is sick because medical care is unavailable or too expensive.

§ Radical Feminism

Radical feminist goals are not to achieve equality with men under the existing social and economic structures, but to entirely transform those social institutions. They do not want to perpetuate a society which is perceived as fundamentally inhuman.

Many of the women oriented toward radical feminism shared certain ideas and attitudes with radical men: a profound alienation from American culture, a distaste for formal hierarchical systems, a contempt for traditional political forms, and a commitment to the radical restructuring of both values and institutions. It became apparent however that existing left organizations—for all their disaffection from the dominant culture—yet shared one important characteristic with it: sexism.

Some of these women abandoned left organizations, formed independent movements and developed alternate theoretical perspectives. Radical feminists then began producing studies of specific aspects of women's oppression in the United States. They analyzed and attacked the patriarchal family, which not only directly oppressed women, but socialized children into an artificial and destructive sexual polarization. They attacked Freudian psychoanalysis as the ideological basis of patriarchal control. They undermined the conventional model of female sexual passivity, another prop to patriarchalism.

These approaches shared an implicit or explicit theoretical assumption—that the central oppressive agent of society was the patriarchal family and the set of psychic and cultural structures it created. Feminists planned to attack the psychic structure itself; as Kate Millett said: "the arena of sexual revolution is within the human consciousness even more pre-eminently than it is within human institutions. So deeply embedded is patriarchy that the character structure it creates in both sexes is perhaps even more a habit of mind and a way of life than a political system."

For radical feminists the biological division of the sexes was the first and most fundamental class division of history; it provided the basis for the later division into socioeconomic classes. Feminist revolution should thus overthrow not only a specific form of social organization (capitalism) but nature itself. The difficulty with posing sex as the primary contradiction is that it becomes almost impossible to find any final solution to the problem; one may suggest the abolition of men, but usually without much conviction that such a step would be possible or practicable.

The emphasis on sexual oppression as the primary contradiction has served several essential functions. It has directed women's attention to their oppression as women and thus focused attention on precisely those areas where women's experience is different from that of men; it was a necessary precondition for exploring that half of human experience which had generally been ignored or passed off as inessential. Nevertheless, the theoretical difficulties of a perspective based on biological sex as the basis of women's oppression deserve to be emphasized. If women are everywhere oppressed by men on the basis of this biological difference, then how has this situation developed, how is it maintained and how is it to be overcome? How is a raised consciousness of patriarchal oppression to be translated into a public political movement dedicated to the transformation of concrete reality? Male supremacy can hardly be predicated on physical strength in a society where strength is not a noticeable characteristic of those in positions of power; the ability to have babies is woman's most obvious biological trait but not one that can carry the weight of women's oppression.

If the theoretical work of the radical feminists has been uneven, they have nonetheless been productive in actual struggles against an oppressive reality, and inventive in developing new forms of resistance. In addition to the ideological demystifications of paternalist ideology, women have created special organizational structures to combat specific symptoms of their oppression. Among these are the consciousness-raising group, the women's center, the rape crisis center, the women's commune, and the self-help group. Within these structures women have experimented with different organizational forms, with or without formal authority or recognized leadership; they have sought to break down barriers between women and base their relationships on collective responsibility and mutual support rather than on competition and individual isolation. The thrust has been not so much to demand equality of opportunity in a system known to be structurally oppressive, but rather to organize women collectively and arm them with ideological tools, so that they may resist their oppression politically. Their general solution is organized, knowledgeable self-defense, backed by a new-found pride in their sex, its history and its culture. A possible drawback to the small group strategy may be that it restricts the struggle to the margins of the established order, or leads to the development of alternative enclaves within it. As a political form, the small group may not allow development of sufficient power to confront or overthrow the dominant structures, but it aids the development of a collective consciousness and helps to break down the dominant ideology.

§ Radical Feminism and Health Care

Radical feminists see the medical profession as yet another system that conforms to the patriarchal pattern established in the family. The doctor-father runs a family composed of the nurse (wife and mother) and the patient (the child). The doctor possesses the scientific and technical skills and the nurse performs the caring and comforting duties; these roles, of course, replicate relations within the patriarchal family. This perspective helps both patients and medical workers make sense of the attitudes they encounter and the feelings they experience when they confront physicians. Visiting a doctor *is* indeed an infantilizing experience; nurses *are* often treated as wives.

What then is the radical feminist solution to health-care problems? It is not simply to change the sex ratios of doctors. Radical feminists would agree that it is difficult for a woman to be as authoritarian as a male doctor (if for no other reason than that patients will expect her to be more sympathetic and understanding). But they also realize that women doctors are likely to be socialized into the "physician role" as long as the role itself remains unaltered. Paternalism and authoritarianism are not genitally but structurally and culturally determined. Nor do radicals recommend the construction of health "teams" as an antidote. That solution might simply produce a polygamous rather than a monogamous family; if the patriarchal structure stays intact then each new health worker would be socialized into the submissive female role. Studies of the roles played by members of existing health teams bear out this suspicion. In addition to their criticism of the power of physicians and hospital administrators, radical feminists work to increase the knowledge and thus the ability of patients to resist their infantilization at the hands of those who possess that knowledge. Rather in the manner of the Naderites, they seek to inform and organize those who receive health care and thus indirectly bring pressure on the patriarchs of the system.

Radicals argue that women should understand their bodies and know what they can reasonably expect from physicians. Only then can they judge for themselves the competence of the care they receive. When dealing with physicians (as when dealing with auto mechanics) knowledge is power. Women are encouraged to press their doctors for information about the results of tests, to draw up lists of questions to ask gynecologists, to acquire their own medical records, to get names of drugs being given, to sit in on medical conferences. Aware that this path is a difficult one—the disparity in specialized knowledge is enormous—feminists call for the formation of medical consciousness-raising groups. The self-help groups of women meet regularly to explore health problems, to share knowledge and experiences about the health system, to become familiar with their own and each others bodies, to aid one another in following their own cycles by self-examination, to generate an understanding of the normal variations among healthy women in order to facilitate the recognition of symptoms of illness, and to break through the body-alienation imposed on females by patriarchal culture.

The self-help movement started with women's sexual and reproductive functions, the areas of maximum alienation between women and the health system. Members learned to view their own and one another's cervixes, using a simple and inexpensive technological device, the speculum. This simple self-(and mutual) examination proved a revelation for many women who had assumed that the impersonality of the routine gynecological exam—being draped with white sheets, probed by cold metal instruments, surrounded by secrecy and embarrassment—was somehow inherent in the process. The self-help groups in fact allow the potential patient to make great leaps in understanding her own body, and she becomes immeasurably strengthened in future dealings with professional physicians.

Another aspect of the radical Women's Health Movement was the development of protest against the American way of childbirth. Normal hospital procedures for expectant mothers are among the most inhumane of medical practices. The prone positions, the impersonality, the shaving and probing, the enemas and the drugging, the isolation and the labor inducement, the expense, the enforced passivity—all these lead to misery for the mother and often physical impairment for the infant. Feminists have been articulate critics of this system, have called for the legalization of midwifery, and many have argued that the best way to give birth is at home with husbands and relatives present.

As feminists confronted the intransigence of the health-care system, they turned increasingly from consumer resistance to the construction of alternate modes of health care—the women's health centers. These institutions, set up and controlled by women, seek to help women with their health problems *outside* the established institutions. In the women's clinics patients learn about their bodies; they are not turned into passive recipients of treatment. Information is shared and the patient retains control over essential decisions concerning her own health. Education, moreover, is reciprocal: the "providers" seek to learn from the "consumers." Patients may often keep their own records. Care is free whenever possible, or a sliding scale of fees is arranged. Many clinics are able to give free health care by charging for abortions; the income obtained pays for the running of the entire clinic. The Feminists Women's Health Center in Los Angeles was the model for many others. It offers self-help clinics, gynecological exams and treatment, pregnancy screening and counseling, and paramedic training programs. It has its own abortion clinic. All staff members participate to some extent in decision-making, and "directorship" depends on degree of commitment to the health center and the length of time worked. In line with the ideal of sharing rather than restricting medical knowledge and skills, there is a summer session to train women to staff other women's health facilities.

As radical feminists moved to develop the women's centers as a widespread alternative to the established medical order, they ran into a string of roadblocks imposed by that very system. Increasingly they began to confront the same sorts of problems that confronted the communes, problems inherent in any attempt to organize real alternatives while the old order remains intact, powerful, and in command of the wealth, resources, and political and legal mechanisms of society.

There are simply not enough women doctors to fill the demand. Many clinics have had to rely on male physicians to perform abortions while seeking to keep the control and policy-making power in the hands of women. There is a real tension, however, between the inherent power that comes from the possession of knowledge (in this case medical expertise) and the desire to keep power in nonexpert hands. More generally, the radical dictum that knowledge is power itself points to the difficulties inherent in a virtual monopoly of specialized knowledge by the established order. Lack of credentials and shortage of funds make it difficult to obtain access to sophisticated technology, difficult to obtain necessary drugs.

The profession, too, is not loath to defend itself from what it correctly perceives to be a threat to its power and perogatives. Legal charges of practicing medicine without a license are an available weapon; three women midwives were arrested in March 1974 for their work at the Santa Cruz Home Birth Center on such charges. The use of legal restraints to prevent women from carrying on self-help activities has generally failed, if only because of the difficulty of deciding the exact point at which an individual's control over her own body is superseded by the restriction of medical practice to licensed professionals. Nevertheless, economic pressures can be brought to bear. The Women's Health Clinic in Portland, Oregon was to have been partially supported by the Office of Economic Opportunity, but funds were cut because the women refused to set up the proper hierarchy, and had decided to operate the clinic without a doctor.

The most important limitation of the radical feminist program for remaking health care is that it deals only with those areas where women's health needs are different from those of men. But a woman's health needs are greater than the care of her reproductive system. The very advances of the women's clinics have only pointed up the obvious shortcomings of the rest of the system. Some clinics have attempted to move ahead, and have begun counseling in nutrition and drug problems, but it is manifestly impossible—without a nationwide reordering of health priorities for men and women—for these clinics, operating on the margin of a powerful (though ineffective) health establishment, to cope with all health problems. Women are thus forced back into reliance on the established and unsatisfactory order.

The various feminist alternatives have therefore practically demonstrated the depth of the difficulties; they have become—in addition to forms of self-help—arenas of political development. Thus Ellen Frankfort worried (in *Vaginal Politics*) that self-help was medically dangerous. The flood of congratulatory mail she received from doctors demonstrated to her that they were in fact much more upset by the potential independence these groups afforded women than by any potential medical dangers. On that score she realized that the doctors themselves had conflicting opinions—profound disagreements—about the medical "facts" in question. This forced her to question her earlier uncritical appreciation of medical expertise.

The potential of the Women's Health Movement depends not only on the extent to which it is able to provide a more human and less alienating context for women to learn about their bodies, but also in its influence as a model for general health care. Thus, its success may increase the awareness among health consumers of the deficiencies in other areas of health care and increase the pressures for a more human and humane reordering of medical priorities. The demand for more consumer knowledge and control over the health-delivery system develops as that system becomes increasingly alienated from the needs of the people whom in theory it exists to serve.

§ Marxist-Feminism

Marxist-feminists have tried to understand the position of women by utilizing the method of analysis developed by Marx and Engels, believing that this is the most effective tool available for understanding all social contradictions, including the oppression of women. They believe this approach can explain the changes in women's status and consciousness in relation to the development and organization of capitalism.

Sexism has historically been useful to capitalists. Patriarchal assumptions about women's special social role as wife and mother support and reinforce the system whereby women are almost invariably paid lower wages than men for the same work. This system has other functions: it has the effect of depressing wages in general, of increasing profit margins and of dividing the labor force along sex lines. Yet the very fact that women's labor can be bought more cheaply frequently leads to an employer's preference for female over male labor, especially in the newer areas of mass employment such as clerical and service work. Women are then increasingly drawn into the work force, a fact that in turn undermines the structure of the patriarchal family. Whether the woman has entered the labor force in search of a career and personal fulfillment, or whether she has been unwillingly compelled to do so by the pressures of inflation and male unemployment, the result in either case will be a weakening of the patriarchal family bonds. The wife who is no longer completely economically dependent on her husband can afford to challenge his authority when it runs counter to her own interest. In addition, those who are abandoning their earlier social definitions as protected and dependent wives and mothers are in turn led to demand equal pay and employment as the patriarchal ideology loses its force and social content.

As capitalist development shifts more and more areas of women's labor outside the family, it undermines the basis of home production. It therefore provides the material conditions for a future abolition of the distinctions between women's and men's work: the cooking of food and the making of clothes are functions which are increasingly absorbed by factory production while the state conducts the unprofitable business of the socialization of children. The development of contraceptive technology holds the potential for women to control their own reproduction. Juliet Mitchell said in *Women's Estate* that "as long as reproduction remained a natural phenomenon, of course women were effectively doomed to social exploitation. In any sense they were not 'masters' of a large part of their lives. They had no choice as to whether or how often they gave birth to children (apart from precarious methods of contraception or repeated dangerous abortions); their existence was essentially subject to biological processes outside their control."

The potential for the eradication of sexual inequality is however realized only to the extent that it serves the development of capital and women are the victims of the contradictory requirements that result. Domestic labor within the family serves the production, maintenance and reproduction of labor-power; this essential labor is unpaid yet socially necessary, and the arrangement serves the stabilization of capitalism. Yet women also serve as a convenient reserve labor force. The family burden puts a woman at a disadvantage when she enters the work force (which if she is working class she must frequently do if her family is to survive economically); she is unprepared, untrained and limited by the children's schedules, so she tends to have to settle for what job she can get. Women's wage labor is widely utilized during periods of economic necessity (*e.g.*, wartime) and the women are then pushed back into the family when no longer required. Thus day-care centers may be provided when an influx of women into the labor force is deemed necessary, only to disappear again when economic conditions change. Marxist-feminists conclude that although capitalism has developed a material base for the dissolution of the patriarchal family and the liberation of women, the final steps cannot be taken toward that goal as long as the production and property relations of capitalism remain intact.

To summarize, the relationship of capitalism and sexism has been a contradictory one. On the one hand capitalism has supported and drawn support from the subordination of women. On the other hand capitalism has eroded the material base on which that subordination rests.

Feminists have sought to strengthen and hasten along the development of the liberatory side of this dialectic. Marxist-feminists support this effort, believing with Marx that while history affords the possibilities, it is up to people to realize them in practice. But Marxist-feminists argue that although feminism may heighten the contradictions inherent in capitalist society, liberation cannot be attained within the framework of this system. Women's gains will remain contingent, dependent, and limited by the repressive side of the dialectic, by the fact that sexism remains useful for capitalism.

Capitalism, many Marxists argue, cannot free itself from dependence on sexism any more than it can transcend class oppression or the pursuit of private profit at the expense of the satisfaction of real human needs. So a necessary condition of the complete liberation of women, Marxist-feminists would say, is the rejection of capitalism and its replacement by a humane, democratic socialism.

§ Marxist-Feminism and Health Care

Marxist-feminists believe that the specific structures of the American health system that are oppressive to women—as workers and as patients—cannot be understood without an analysis of that system as a whole. That system, in turn, becomes fully comprehensible only when it is recognized as one component of a capitalistic economic and social structure. Many of the deficiencies of the modern American health system, like those of the education, transportation, and communication industries, flow from its commitment to the imperative of production for profit, rather than the fulfillment of peoples' needs.

The health system mirrors the priorities and organization of the larger system which supports it, and which it in turn supports, in a variety of ways: in its intense concentration of financial and political power at the top, in its thoroughgoing stratification of its work force by class, sex and race, in its division of labor and specialization, in its very definitions of health and illness, and in its inaccountability to the American population whom it theoretically serves. Let us consider these characteristics in turn.

As in other sectors of American society, power is concentrated at the top, in a handful of monopolistic institutions. One of them, the AMA, was once the undisputed dominant force in the health field. Times have changed, however. As the standard nineteenth-century capitalist enterprise—the small competitive firm—gave way to the giant monopoly corporation, so too has the undisputed power of the small fee-for-service solo practitioner been overtaken and largely surpassed by new forms of medical organization. As in other areas of the economy, the increasing reliance on large scale, expensive technology gave the competitive edge to those who could muster the capital resources to obtain the new equipment. Also complementing the pattern in other sectors, the enlightened wing of the rising corporate class in the early 1900s, the Rockefellers and the Carnegies, strove to nationalize, organize, and centralize the medical system; the Flexner Report (1910) was an important milestone in the process.

Power now rests with a coalition that includes, in addition to the AMA, the commercial insurance companies, the research and teaching hospitals, and the voluntary and public community hospitals. These institutions are themselves dominated by members of the corporate class, or of the upper middle class (middle management and professionals), who occupy commanding positions in almost all major American institutions.

At the top are the ten largest commercial health insurers (Aetna, Travellers, Metropolitan Life, Prudential, CNA, Equitable, Mutual of Omaha, Connecticut General, John Hancock, and Provident); between them they control nearly 60% of the multi-billion dollar industry. Their leadership is tightly interlocked with the corporate and banking sectors, and they exert decisive influence on state policy in matters of health care. In the current debate over how to deal with the financial crisis of the health delivery system, they have (with lavish expenditure of funds) managed to so dominate the discussion that nearly all the proposals for action are simply varieties of publicly supported insurance programs. Most would enhance the profit making capacity of the commercials and further shift the fiscal burden of the health system to working and middle class citizens via regressive tax structures.

The great teaching and research institutions are also dominated by representatives of the corporate class. In 1970, for example, Columbia Presbyterian Medical Center had a director of Texaco presiding over a major teaching hospital, the President of United States Steel chairing its finance committee, and the President of AT&T running its planning and real estate committee. These institutions train and socialize the people who staff the upper and middle echelons of the health system. They encourage the development of and reliance upon sophisticated medical technology, an extreme specialization and division of labor, and the flow of funds to esoteric research projects (often involving experimentation on poor, minority, or working class women).

The voluntary community hospitals are controlled by boards composed of upper-middle class professionals, rather than representatives of corporate capital; doctors, lawyers and smaller businessmen predominate. Women, minorities, representatives of organized or unorganized labor, are virtually excluded from access to any of these decision-making bodies.

Far below the capitalists and the professionals are the lower-middle and working classes of health industry. The former comprise the nurses and paraprofessional auxiliary and service personnel, representing 54.2 per cent of the total labor force. Both groups are predominantly female; the working class includes an overrepresentation of minority groups. These classes are often played off against one another. Middle ranking groups are given a degree of control over those below them (though they are excluded from the real decision-making bodies above them.) The employment of lower level workers may be used to undercut the bargaining position of the mid-level groups, as for example, in the mass employment of licensed practical nurses and nurses aides over the opposition of registered nurses.

The non-physician workers are divided into over 375 independent occupations, most of them narrow, specific, and rigidly defined, most representing one aspect of the work once done by a doctor or a nurse, most dead-end, low-wage positions, boring, repetitious, and firmly under someone else's control and direction. This process of breaking up labor into little bits, each of which may be parceled out to a single worker, is a general tendency of modern capitalism. The fragmentation, as Harry Braverman shows in *Labor and Monopoly Capital,* is not to increase efficiency, but to maximize management control over labor, and to replace highly paid workers with less skilled and thus less costly ones.

Seventy-five per cent of these health workers are women, doing modern forms of traditional women's work. The old female roles of nurturing, caring, cooking, educating and cleaning have become, under corporate medicine, such occupations as nurse, housekeeper, dietitian, clerk or technician. Ninety-eight per cent of nutritionists and dietitians are women.

If capitalist medicine fragments the organization of work it also fragments the delivery of health care. First it provides multi-level services based on a patient's ability to pay. It affords very high quality service to the wealthy, and shoddy, assembly line care for the poor. Specialization makes it difficult, at almost any level, to find comprehensive care. Medical fragmentation rests on the premise that the body is rather like a machine and can, like any mechanical system, be broken down into interlocking parts for purposes of repair. The patient (the whole) becomes invisible while parts of her or his anatomy engross the attention of different (and highly paid) specialists. Where the patient has no power over the forms of medical care, his or her experiences of pain or illness become much less relevant to the "case" than the pathologist's report. Where there are class, race and/or sex differences between the physician and patient, the situation becomes still more acute, personal communication still further hindered.

Capitalist medicine reinforces the capitalist order in still other subtle ways, in its very definitions of health and sickness. Health is defined in terms of the system rather than the individual. The central concern of medical institutions, is whether or not the patient is well enough to go to work. This orientation suggests why women's illnesses are taken less seriously than those of men; they are not as crucial to the production process. Their ills rarely interfere with their ability to do housework.

Capitalist medicine, moreover, prefers to concentrate (in research and treatment) upon the "scientific," "objective," organic basis of illness. Thus it evades the social causes of much ill-health, causes rooted in the structure of the capitalist system itself. Vast quantities are spent seeking the organic basis of cancer but it proves extraordinarily difficult to wipe out known causes of the disease, such as cigarette smoking, asbestos dust in factories, or coal soot in mines. Improving health in those areas would require confronting the powerful interest of tobacco companies, asbestos manufacturers and coal mine operators.

The process of ignoring the social causes of disease becomes self-legitimating. Disease which cannot be given a specific biomedical correlate is defined out of existence. The physician draws his own distinction between a "real" disease—one whose organic basis can be identified by the available technology—and functional or psychosomatic illness in which the patient's experience cannot be legitimated by a laboratory report. Complaints stemming from such environmental factors as poverty, sexism and racism, the nature of work outside and inside the home, crises in housing and education, problems in personal relationships, and the like, can be "treated" only by tranquillizers or placebos. American women consume large quantities of both. (If the patient has enough money, she, or he, may be able to obtain sympathy from a psycholanalyst, but this option is not generally available.)

In addition to defining many forms of disease as "not real," some forms of health are defined as medical problems. Pregnancy and childbirth are, or should be, considered natural and healthy aspects of human life. American medicine treats them as forms of illness, to be removed from the "patient's" control, a development which the radical Women's Health Movement is struggling to reverse.

In medicine, then, as in the condition of women generally, Marxists find crucial contradictions. On the one hand the possibility of extending superb health care to the entire population exists; we have the knowledge, the resources, and the need. But the social relations of health care, the way in which it is controlled and organized, act as fetters. The needs of the giant insurance companies, of the industrial corporations, and the professional organizations predominate.

Marxists believe that a thoroughgoing reordering of priorities is not possible within the present system. Capitalist medicine's internal dynamics point toward still greater concentration of control, still greater subordination of workers, yet more scientific research and sophisticated technology generating greater reliance on capital intensive medicine, and ever increasing specialization and dehumanizing division of labor—a poor prognosis for workers and consumers alike. Marxists believe that the only way to liberate the potential for improved care and better preventive measures is to retire and replace the capitalist order with a democratic socialist one.

A final note: many who are developing a Marxist analysis of health care are male. It is imperative that the specific concerns of women be further integrated into this developing analysis. Contributions to the advancement of Marxist theory must come from women, whether they define themselves as feminists or socialists. Men sensitive to the achievements and concerns of the women's liberation movements can also help oppose the systematic bias toward the male sex evident in much of the existing left literature, a bias that has operated as a barrier between Marxists and feminists.

Radical feminists are now increasingly confronting the issues of class and race. The theoretical development of both Marxism and radical feminism is aided to the extent to which each can benefit from the insights of the other. In the aid to create a healthy system, indeed a society, which exists to fulfill people's human needs, there is, after all, no contradiction between them.

NOTES

INTRODUCTION

1. Executive Office of the President, Council on Wage and Price Stability. Staff Report, "The Problem of Rising Health Care Costs," Washington D. C., December 1976, p. 72.

2. U. S. Department of Commerce, Bureau of the Census. *Statistical Abstract of the United States, 1976,* Washington D. C., July 1976, p. 402.

3. Executive Office of the President, *op. cit.*, p. 72.

4. David Kotelchuck, ed., *Prognosis Negative: Crisis in the Health Care System* (New York: Vintage, 1976), p. 5.

5. Robert J. Wilson, "Health Care for Women: Present Deficiencies and Future Needs," *Obstretrics and Gynecology*, Vol. 36, No. 2, August 1970, p. 178. Quoted in *Our Bodies, Ourselves*, 2nd edition (New York: Simon and Schuster, 1976), p. 338.

6. U. S. National Center for Health Statistics, "Facts of Life and Death," Rockville, Maryland: 1974, p. 7; United Nations, *Demographic Yearbook*, 1973, 25th issue, New York: 1974 pp. 94–100.

7. *Statistical Abstract, op. cit.* p. 79.

8. John P. Bunker, "Surgical Manpower: A Comparison of Operations and Surgeons in the United States and England and Wales," *New England Journal of Medicine,* Vol. 282 (January 15, 1970) pp. 135–44.

9. U. S. Department of Health, Education and Welfare, "The Nation's Use of Health Resources, 1976 edition," Washington D. C., p. 22.

10. *Health/PAC Bulletin,* March, 1970, p. 1.

11. Barbara Seaman, "Pelvic Autonomy: Four Proposals," *Social Policy,* September/October, 1975, p. 43.

12. *Ibid.*

13. Linda Gordan, *Woman's Body, Woman's Right,* (New York: Viking, 1976), pp. 40–46.

14. As quoted in *Witches, Midwives and Nurses* (Old Westbury, N. Y.: Feminist Press, 1972), p. 9.

15. *Ibid.*, p. 19.

16. Suzanne Arms, *Immaculate Deception* (Boston: Houghton Mifflin, 1975), p. 17.

17. As quoted in *Our Bodies, Ourselves*, Boston Women's Health Collective, 2nd edition (New York: Simon & Schuster, 1976), p. 343.

18. Barbara Seaman, *The Doctor's Case against the Pill* (New York: Wyden, 1969), p. 43.

19. Helen Marieskind, "The Women's Health Movement," *International Journal of Health Services*, Vol. 5, No. 2, 1975, p. 218.

20. From private interviews with Frances Hornstein and Carol Downer, January, 1977.

PART ONE
1 The Women's Health Movement

1. Palmer Findley, *Priests of Lucina: The Story of Obstetrics* (Boston: Little, Brown & Co., 1939).

2. Sophia Jex-Blake, *Medical Women* (Edinburgh: Oliphant, Anderson and Ferrier, Source Book Press, 1886). This anecdote is vouched for by Hyginas, Pliny, Martial and Celsus, among others.

3. Kate Campbell Hurd-Mead, *A History of Women in Medicine from the Earliest Times to the Beginning of the Nineteenth Century* (Connecticut: The Haddam Press, 1939).

4. Geoffrey Marks and William K. Beatty, *Women in White* (New York: Charles Scribner's Sons, 1972).

5. Eileen Power, "Some Women Practitioners of Medicine in the Middle Ages," *Proceedings of the Royal Society of Medicine, History of* Medicine Section XV, 6, 1922. (Quoted from Charter of Paris II, pp. 257-264.)

6. Thomas Szasz, *The Manufacture of Madness* (New York: Harper and Row, 1970).

7. Jules Michelet, *Satanism and Witchcraft* (Paris, France: The Citadel Press, 1939.)

8. Findley, *op. cit.*

9. *Ibid.*

10. James H. Aveling, *English Midwives, Their History and Prospects.* (London: J. A. Churchill, 1872).

11. Hurd-Mead, *op. cit.*

12. Findley, *op. cit.*, p. 344.

13. Bertha L. Selmon, "History of Women in Medicine," *Medical Woman's Journal,* LIII (March 1946).

14. Richard H. Shryock, *Medicine in America: Historical Essays.* (Baltimore: The Johns Hopkins Press, 1966).

15. John B. Blake, "Women and Medicine in Ante-Bellum America," *Bulletin of the History of Medicine*, Vol. XXXIX, No. 2., pp. 92–123.

2 Sexual Surgery in Late-Nineteenth-Century America

1. R. Caplan, *Psychiatry and the Community in Nineteenth Century America* (New York: Basic Books, 1969), p. 140.

2. N. Dain, *Concepts of Insanity in the United States, 1789–1865* (New Brunswick, N.J.: Rutgers University Press, 1964), pp. 10, 12, 26, 65–66.

3. C. Meigs, Woman: *Her Diseases and Remedies,* 2nd ed. (Philadelphia: Blanchard and Lee, 1851), p. 54.

4. A. Brigham, *Remarks on the Influence of Mental Cultivation and Mental Excitement Upon Health,* 2nd ed. (Boston: Marsh, Capen and Lyon, 1833), pp. vii, 80–81.

5. E. Jarvis, "On the comparative liability of males and females to insanity, and their comparative curability and mortality when insane," *American Journal of Insanity* 7 (1850): 155.

6. I. Ray, *Mental Hygiene* (New York: Hafner Publishing Company, 1968; facsimile of 1863 edition), p. 54.

7. E. Jarvis, "On the supposed increase of insanity," *American Journal of Insanity* 8 (1850): 349

8. I. Ray, "The insanity of women produced by desertion or seduction," *American Journal of Insanity* 23 (1866): 267.

9. B. Barker-Benfield, *The Horrors of the Half-Known Life* (New York: Harper & Row), Ch. 6 and Pt. 3.

10. A. de Tocqueville, *Democracy in America,* Vols. I and II (New York: Random House/Vintage, 1945).

11. D. Meyer, *The Positive Thinkers* (Garden City, N.Y.: Doubleday), pp. 51–56.

12. R. H. Wiebe, *The Search for Order* (New York: Hill and Wang, American Century ed., 1968), pp. xiii, 1, 5–6, 8, 52.

13. A. K. Gardner, *History of the Art of Midwifery* (New York: Stringer and Townsend, 1852), p. 4. (Also published as introduction to Gardner's edition of W. Tyler Smith's *The Modern Practice of Midwifery* [New York: Robert M. DeWitt, 1852].)

14. A. K. Gardner, *Our Children* (Hartford, Conn.: Belknap and Bliss, 1872), p. 210.

15. R. H. Shryock, *Medicine in America* (Baltimore, Md.: Johns Hopkins University Press, 1966), pp. 189–190.

16. R. H. Shryock, *Medicine and Society in America: 1660–1860* (Ithaca, N.Y.: Cornell University Press, Great Seal ed., 1962), p. 147.

17. M. Fishbein, *A History of the American Medical Association* (Philadelphia: W. B. Saunders, 1947), pp. 82–85.

18. H. N. Smith, *Virgin Land* (New York: Random House/Vintage, 1950), Ch. X.

19. G. Vest. In *Up from the Pedestal: Selected Writings in the History of* American Feminism, ed. by A. Kraditor (Chicago: Quadrangle Books, 1968), p. 195.

20. A. K. Gardner, "New York Medical College for Women," *Frank Leslie's Illustrated Newspaper* 30 (April 19, 1870), p. 759.

21. J. Todd, *Women's Rights* (Boston, Mass.: Lee and Shepard, 1867), p. 12.

22. A. K. Gardner, *Conjugal Sins* (New York: J. S. Redfield, 1870), p. 195.

23. H. O. Marcy, "The early history of abdominal surgery in America," *Transactions of the Section on Obstetrics and Diseases of Women and Children of the American Medical Association,* 1909. pp. 248–266,

24. *Transactions of the American Medical Association* 10:31, 1857.

25. A. K. Gardner and F. Barker, "Remarks on puerperal fever," *Transactions of the New York Academy of Medicine,* 1858.

26. T. G. Thomas, *Diseases of Women* (Philadelphia: H. C. Lea), Preface to 1st edition.

27. H. R. Storer, *The Causation, Course and Treatment of Reflex Insanity in Women* (Boston, Mass.: Lee and Shepard, 1871), p. 79.

28. B. Barker-Benfield, *op. cit.*

29. J. M. Sims, *Clinical Notes on Uterine Surgery* (New York: William Wood, 1866), pp. 131–35, 206–207.

30. W. O. Baldwin. In *The Story of My Life,* by J. M. Sims (New York: D. Appleton, 1885), p. 433.

31. J. R. Chadwick, "Obstetrics and gynecological literature, 1876–1881," *Transactions of the American Medical Association* 32:255, 1881.

32. B. Barker-Benfield, "The spermatic economy," in *The American Family in Socio-Historical Perspective,* edited by M. Gordon (New York: St. Martin's Press, 1973).

33. I. Baker-Brown, *On the Curability of Certain Forms of Insanity, Epilepsy, Catalepsy.* (London: Robert Hardwicke, 1866).

34. Meeting to consider the proposition of the Council for the removal of Mr. I. Baker Brown. *Br. Med. J.* 1 (1867), pp. 395–410.

35. L. Tait, "Masturbation," *The Medical News* 53(1): 3, July 7, 1888.

36. J. Bunker, "Surgical manpower: A comparison of operations and surgeons in the United States and in England and Wales," *New. Eng. J. Med.* 282(3): 135–44, 1970.

37. J. Bunker, "When to operate?" *Saturday Review,* pp. 30–31, August 22, 1970.

38. F. S. Norris, "We need women doctors." Letter to the editor, *Washington Evening Star,* December 15, 1970.

39. R. P. Bolande, "Ritualistic surgery—Circumcision and tonsillectomy," New Engl. J. Med. 280(11): 591–597, 1969.

40. J. Klemsrude, "Those who have been there aid breast surgery patients," *New York Times,* February 8, 1971.

41. E. Weiss and O. S. English, *Psychosomatic Medicine,* Ed. 3, Ch. 19. (Philadelphia: W. B. Saunders, 1957).

42. *Maternity Care in the World: Report of a Joint Group of the International Federation of Gynecology and Obstetrics and the International Confederation of Midwives,* (London: Pergamon Press, 1966), pp. 173, 317.

43. T. Jefferson, *Notes on Virginia* (New York: Harper Torchbook, 1964), p. 133

44. A. Myerson, J. B. Ayer, T. J. Putnam, C. E., Keeler, and L. Alexander, *Eugenical Sterilization: A Reorientation of the Problem* (New York: Macmillan, 1936).

45. G. J. Engelmann, "The increasing sterility of American women," *Transactions of the Section on Obstetrics and Diseases of Women and Children of the American Medical Association,* pp. 271–295, 1901.

46. J. Higham, *Strangers in the Land,* (New York: Atheneum, 1968), ch. 6.

47. R. M. Brown, "Historical patterns of violence in America." In *Violence in America,* edited by Gurr and Graham (New York: Signet, 1969), pp. 47–69.

48. R. L. Beisner, *Twelve Against Empire: The Anti-Imperialists,* 1898–1900 (New York: McGraw-Hill, 1968), pp. 45–46

49. D. T. Gilliam, "Oophorectomy for the insanity and epilepsy of the female: A plea for its more general adoption," *Transactions of the American Association of Obstetricians and Gynecologists* 9: 320, 1896.

50. W. Goodell, "Clinical notes on the extirpation of the ovaries for insanity," *American Journal of Insanity* 38: 295, 1882.

51. E. Flexner, *Century of Struggle* (New York: Atheneum, 1968), Chs. 11–13, 15, 16.

52. W. Goodell, *Lessons in Gynecology,* pp. 270–276. Philadelphia: D. G. Brinton, 1879.

53. E. Van de Warker, "The fetich of the ovary," *American Journal of Obstetrics and Diseases of Women and Children* 54: 369, 1906.

54. J. Meyer, "A case of insanity, caused by diseased ovaries, cured by their removal —A phenomenal triumph for operative treatment," *Transactions of the American Association of Obstetricians and Gynecologists* 7: 503–504, 1894.

55. D. C. Brockman, "Oophorectomy for grave functional nervous diseases occurring during menstruation," *Transactions of the Western Surgical and Gynecological Association,* pp. 104–110, 1900.

56. A. P. Dudley, "Results of ovarian surgery," *Transactions of the Section on Obstetrics and Diseases of Women and Children of the American Medical Association,* pp. 188–189, 1900.

57. "Case of excessive masturbation," *American Journal of Obstetrics and Diseases of Women and Children* 6: 294–295, 1873–1874.

58. R. Battey, "Normal ovariotomy-case," *Atlanta Medical and Surgical Journal* 10(6): 323–325, 1872.

59. A. K. Gardner, "The physical decline of American women," *The Knickerbocker* 55(1): 37–52, 1860. (Also appended to *Conjugal Sins,* p. 218. J. S. Redfield, New York, 1870.)

60. R. Battey, "Normal ovariotomy," *Atlanta Medical and Surgical Journal* 11(1): 20–21, 1873.

61. B. S. Dunn, "Conservation of the ovary," *Transactions of the American Association of Obstetricians and Gynecologists* 10: 209–224, 1897.

62. G. J. Engelmann, "Cliterodectomy [sic]," *The American Practitioner* 25: 3, 1882.

63. Transactions of the woman's hospital society, *Am. J. Obstet. Gynecol.* 43: 721, 1901.

64. E. W. Cushing, "Melancholia, masturbation: Cured by removal of both ovaries," In Report of the Annual Meeting of the Gynecological Society of Boston. *J.A.M.A.* 8: 441–442, 1887.

65. A. J. Block, "Sexual perversion in the female," *New Orleans Medical and Surgical Journal* 22(1): 6, 1894.

66. A. Church, "Removal of ovaries and tubes in the insane and neurotic," *American Journal of Obstetrics and the Diseases of Women and Children* 28: 494–495, 1893.

67. Discussion of A. Church's "Removal of ovaries and tubes in the insane and neurotic," *American Journal of Obstetrics and the Diseases of Women and Children* 28: 569–573, 1893.

68. E. H. Pratt, "Circumcision of girls." *Journal of Orificial Surgery* 6(9): 385–386, 1898.

69. W. P. Manton, "The legal question in operations of the insane," *Transactions of the American Association of Obstetricians and Gynecologists* 6: 246, 1893.

70. J. Burnham, "Psychoanalysis and American medicine: 1894–1918." *Psychological Issues* 5(4): 73–81, 1967.

71. A. Hamilton, "The abuse of oophorectomy in diseases of the nervous system," *New York Medical Journal* 57: 180–183, 1893.

72. R. Edes, "Points in the diagnosis and treatment of some obscure common neuroses," *J.A.M.A.* 27: 1077–1082, 1896.

73. R. Edes, "The relations of pelvic and nervous diseases," *J.A.M.A.* 31: 1133–1136, 1898.

74. Warner, Quoted in Report of the Annual Meeting of the Gynecological Society of Boston. *J.A.M.A.* 8: 441–442, 1887.

75. Symington-Brown, Quoted in Report of the Annual Meeting of the Gynecological Society of Boston. *J.A.M.A.* 8: 441–442, 1887.

76. E. A. Praeger, "Is so-called conservatism in gynecology conducive to the best results to the patient?" *Transactions of the American Association of Obstetricians and Gynecologists* 8: 322, 1895.

77. J. Cokenower, "A plea for conservative operations on the ovaries, *"Transactions of the Section on Obstetrics and Diseases of Women and Children of the American Medical Association,* p. 298, 1904.

78. A. Gordon, "Nervous and mental disturbances following castration in women," *J.A.M.A.* 63: 1347, 1914.

79. W. J. Mayo, "Conservation of the menstrual function," *J.A.M.A.* 74(25): 1685, 1920.

80. W. P. Manton, "Mental alienation in women and abdomino-pelvic disease," *Transactions of the Section on Obstetrics and Diseases of Women and Children of the American Medical Association,* pp. 9–20, 1909.

81. Report of the Annual Meeting of the Gynecological Society of Boston. *J.A.M.A.* 8: 441–442, 1887.

82. H. T. Byford, *Manual of Gynecology,* 2nd ed. (Philadelphia: P. Blakiston, 1897), pp. 180–185.

83. J. O. Polak, "Final results in conservative surgery of the ovaries," *Transactions of the Section on Obstetrics and Diseases of Women and Children of the American Medical Association,* p. 340, 1909.

84. H. Kelly, "The ethical side of the operation of oophorectomy," *American Journal of Obstetrics* 27: 208–209, 1898.

85. D. MacLean, "Sexual mutilation," *California Medical Journal* 15: 382–384, 1894.

4 The Birth Controllers

1. Rachel Cowen, "Equador: Birth Controlling the People," *Ramparts,* October, 1971.

2. Louis M. Hellman, Frank N. Beckles, and Philip A. Corfman, "A Five-Year Plan for Population Research and Family Planning Services," *Family Planning Perspectives,* Vol. 3, No. 4, October, 1971.

3. David M. Kennedy, *Birth Control in America* (New Haven: Yale University Press, 1970).

4. Richard Lincoln, "S. 2108: Capital Hill Debates the Future of Population and Family Planning," *Family Planning Perspectives,* Vol. 2, No. 1, January, 1970.

5. *NACLA, Newsletter,* "Population Control in the Third World," Vol. 4, No. 8, December, 1970.

6. Stanley C. Scheyer, "DHEW's New Center: The National Commitment to Family Planning," *Family Planning Perspectives,* Vol. 2, No. 1, October, 1970.

7. J. Mayone Stycos, "Some Minority Opinions on Birth Control," Hastings Center-Institute of Society, *Ethics and the Life Sciences,* June, 1971.

8. Steve Weissman, "Why the Population Bomb is a Rockefeller Baby, *Ramparts,* May, 1970.

PART TWO
4 Have You Ever Wondered about the Male Pill?

1. Interview with A. F. Parlow, in "Major Male Sex Hormone Unraveled," *Science News,* 10 August 1974.

2. R. Rita Arditti, "Women as Objects: Science and Sexual Politics," *Science for the People,* September 1974.

3. B. Seaman, quoted in "Contraceptive Research: A Male Chauvinist Plot?" Sheldon Segal, *Family Planning Perspectives* 4:3, 21–25 (July 1972).

4. Y. Scott Matsumoto, Akira Koizumi and Tadahiro Nohara, "Condom Use in Japan," *Studies in Family Planning* 3:10 (October 1972).

5. L. A. Westoff and Ch. F. Westoff, *From Now to Zero: Fertility, Contraception and Abortion in America* (Boston: Little, Brown and Co., 1971).

6. Philip D. Harvey, "Condoms. A New Look," *Family Planning Perspectives* 4.

7. Michael Briggs and Maxine Briggs, "Oral Contraceptive for Men," *Nature* 252: 584, 585–86, 13 December 1974.

8. Michael Greenfield and William M. Burrus, *The Complete Reference Book on Vasectomy* (New York: Avon Books, 1973), p. 15.

9. Nancy L. Ross, "Sterilization: A Switch from Men to Women." Data from Association for Voluntary Sterilization, *Boston Globe*, 10 July 1973.

10. Joel W. Ager, Harriet H. Werley, Doris V. Allen, Fredericka P. Shea, Harvey Y. Lewis, "Vasectomy: Who Gets One and Why?" *ALPH* 64:7, July 1974.

11. Joann S. Lubin, "The Man's Turn," *The Wall Street Journal,* 29 September 1975.

12. Tien Shun Li, M.D., "Sperm Immunology, Infertility and Fertility Control," *Obstetrics and Gynecology*, October 1974.

13. H. J. Muller, "Human Evolution by Voluntary Choice of Germ Plasm," *Science* 34:643–49, (1961).

14. C. Holden, "Sperm Banks Multiply as Vasectomies Gain Popularity," *Science*, 7 April 1972, pp. 4030–32.

15. Matthew Freund, Ph.D., "The Use of Frozen Semen Banks to Preserve the Fertility of Vasectomized Men," in Lawrence Lader's *Foolproof Birth Control— Male and Female Sterilization* (Boston:Beacon Press, 1972).

16. "Festivals with a Purpose," *War on Hunger* 6(1): 6, 8–9, January 1972; J. Palmer, "The Gujarat State Massive Vasectomy Campaign," Studies in Family Planning 3(8): 186–192 (1972); D. N. Pai, "Indian Vasectomy Campus," in R. M. Richart and D. J. Prager's *Human Sterilization* (Springfield, Illinois: 1972), pp. 5–11.

17. "Off Our Backs," *Liberation News Service,* 30 September 1970.

18. P. R. K. Reddy, "Reversible Contraceptive Action of Testosterone in Males," *Proc. of the Indian Society for the Study of Reproduction and Endocrinology. J. Reprod. Fert.* 38: 227, 249 (1974).

19. N. G. Rothnie and A. J. M. Brodribb, "Pulmonary Embolism in a Man Taking an Oral Contraceptive," *The Lancet,* 6 October 1973, p. 799.

20. Ross, "Sterilization."

21. *Reports on Population/Family Planning,* July 1971. A publication of the Population Council, 245 Park Avenue, New York, N.Y. 10017.

22. Thomas H. Maugh II, "5-Thio-D-Glucose, a Unique Male Contraceptive," *Science* 186:431 (November 1974).

23. Joan Arehart-Treichel, "Sperm Don't Like It Hot," *Science News,* 11 May 1974.

24. J. P. Bennett, "Factors Limiting the Development of New Contraceptives," *J. Reprod. Fert.* 37:487–498 (1974).

6 The Theft of Childbirth

1. Margaret Mead, *Male and Female* (New York: William Morrow, 1975), p. 268.

2. Walter Radcliffe, *Milestones in Midwifery* (Bristol: 1967), p. 81; R. P. Finney, *The Story of Motherhood* (New York: Liveright, 1937), pp. 169–175.

3. Claire Tomalin, *The Life and Death of Mary Wollstonecraft* (New York: Harcourt Brace Jovanovich, 1974), p. 226.

4. Barbara Cross, *The Educated Woman in America* (New York: Teachers College Press, 1965), pp. 37–38.

5. O. W. Holmes, "The Contagiousness of Puerperal Fever" (1843) in *Epoch-Making Contributions to Medicine, Surgery and the Allied Sciences* (Philadelphia, Penn.: 1909).

6. B. Ehrenreich and D. English, *Complaints and Disorders: The Sexual Politics of Sickness* (New York: The Feminist Press, 1973), pp. 26–36.

7. Sylvia Plath, *The Bell Jar* (New York: Bantam Books, 1972), p. 53.

8. H. Speert and Alan Guttmacher, *Obstetric Practice* (New York: McGraw-Hill, 1956), p. 305.

9. Grantly Dick-Read, *Childbirth Without Fear: The Principles and Practice of Natural Childbirth* (1944; New York: Harper and Row Perennial Library, 1970).

10. Pierre Vellay et al., *Childbirth Without Pain* (New York: Dutton, 1968), pp. 18–21; K. D. Keele, *Anatomies of Pain* (Oxford, 1957, Blackwell's Scientific Publications), p. 182.

11. Suzanne Arms, *Immaculate Deception: A New Look at Women and Childbirth in America*. (Boston: Houghton Mifflin, 1975.)

12. Sheila Kitzinger, *The Experience of Childbirth* (New York: Penguin Books, 1973), pp. 17–25.

13. Pierre Vellay, *op. cit.,* p. 28.

14. Shulamith Firestone, *The Dialectic of Sex* (New York: Bantam Books, 1972), pp. 198–199.

15. But not just American hospitals. The Norwegian novelist Cora Sandel describes the sensations of her heroine Alberta, giving birth to her illegitimate child in a Paris hospital at the turn of the century:

> What was happening was inevitable. Outside night lay over the city. . . . Far, far away, in another world lived people she knew who were close to her . . . shades, left behind in an earlier life, incapable of helping her. Nor had they any suspicion of how bitterly forsaken she was in this machine composed of curt, white-clad persons and shining tiled walls, which had her in its clutches and would not release her again until she was transformed, one became two, or until—

Alberta Alone (1939), translated by Elizabeth Rokkan (London: Peter Owen, Ltd., 1965), p. 94.

16. "The Cultural Production of Childbirth" (1974, unpublished), by Brigitte Jordan, Department of Anthropology, Michigan State University.

17. See also N. Fuller and B. Jordan, "Childbirth in a Hammock: Mothers and Midwives in Yucatan" (in Lucille Newman, editor, *The Role of the Midwife in Middle America*, in preparation).

18. Robert Caldeyro-Barcia, MD, director of the Latin American Center for Perinatology and Human Development, and president of the International Federation of Gynecologists and Obstetricians, at a meeting of the American Foundation for Maternal and Child Health, April 9, 1975 ("Some Obstetrical Methods Criticized," by Jane Brody, *The New York Times,* April 10, 1975).

19. Judith Brister, "Vertical Delivery: Childbirth Improved?" in *The Detroit News*, June 1971; *Immaculate Deception*, p. 83.

20. Brigitte Jordan reports, however, that contemporary European delivery tables allow for much greater diversity of position, having a movable backrest, a middle part, and a footend which can be adjusted in various ways. "Routinely, then, pushing is done with the woman in a semi-upright position, hooking her hands under her thighs. Some delivery tables have hand holds (nowhere are a woman's

hands tied down), some have foot supports, but nowhere is the lithotomy position used for routine delivery." (Personal communication, October 1974.)

21. Frederick Leboyer, *Birth Without Violence* (New York: Alfred A. Knopf, 1975) p. 26.

22. "It is generally assumed that the new experience of breathing must be traumatic. It is more likely that delay in breathing associated with prolonged birth provides the traumatic factor rather than the initiation of breathing. My psychoanalytic experience makes me think that it is not necessarily true in all cases that the initiation of breathing is significant." D. W. Winnicott, "Birth Memories, Birth Trauma, and Anxiety" in *Collected Papers* (London: Tavistock Publications, Ltd., 1958), p. 191. Winnicott believes that the normal birth experience is traumaless and that it is fallacious to speak of the "birth-trauma" as a universal experience.

23. Suzanne Arms, *op. cit.,* p. 279.

24. *Ibid.,* p. 103.

25. *Ibid.,* p. 160.

26. *Ibid.,* p. 22.

27. Arms has herself interviewed physicians who express "disenchantment with the whole delivery scene" in the hospital and who, with nurse-midwives, attend home births; the Chicago Maternity Center directed by Dr. Beatrice Tucker delivered 90 percent of its 150,000 births at home. (Since 1973, partly for staffing reasons, it has discontinued home deliveries.)

28. Mary Jane Sherfey, M.D., *The Nature and Evolution of Female Sexuality* (New York: Random House Vintage, 1973), pp. 100–101; Niles Newton, "The Trebly Sensuous Woman," in *Psychology Today,* issue on "The Female Experience," 1973. See also Frieda Fromm-Reichman, *Principles of Intensive Psychotherapy* (University of Chicago Press, 1974), p. 145.

29. Alice S. Rossi, "Maternalism, Sexuality and the New Feminism" in *Contemporary Sexual Behavior: Critical Issues in the 1970s,* ed. by J. Zubin and J. Money (Baltimore, Md.: Johns Hopkins University Press, 1973), pp. 145–171.

PART THREE
6 What Medical Students Learn about Women

1. Barbara Ehrenreich and Deirdre English, *Witches, Midwives and Nurses*. Glass Mountain Pamphlets, Oyster Bay, N. Y.

2. Based on statistics gathered by Dr. Linda Fidell, Associate Professor of Psychology, California State University: Sex Differences in Health Care, American Association for the Advancement of Science, 140th Annual Meeting, San Francisco. In 1972, 40 percent of United States adult female population were prescribed mood-altering drugs. About half of these women manifested symptoms of physical disease.

3. Aileen Adams and Geoffrey Cowan, "The Human Guinea Pig: How We Test New Drugs." *World*, December 5, 1972.

4. Depo-Provera, IUDs, injectable contraceptives, and DES were a few described in Kennedy's Congressional Hearings "Quality of Health Care—Human Experimentation." Hearings, Subcommittee on Health, Committee on Labor and Public Welfare, U.S. Senate, 93rd Congress, Parts la and 3, February 1973.

5. J. R. Willson, M.D.; C. T. Beecham, M.D.; and E. R. Carrington, M.D., *Obstetrics and Gynecology*. 4th edition (St. Louis, Mo.: C. V. Mosby Co., 1971). All quotes in this paper are taken from a 55-page description of women's minds (Chapters 4 and 8, entitled "Psychology and life periods of women" and "Sexual responses of women, dysmenorrhea and premenstrual tension.")

6. Sigmund Freud, "The Economic Problems of Masochism." 1924, *Collected Papers*, Vol. II.

7. R. C. Scott, M.D., *World of a Gynecologist* (London: Oliver and Boyd, 1968).

8. Statistics supplied by C. V. Mosby Publishing Company, St. Louis.

9. Ralph Nader has published in his column "Nader Reports" in *Ladies' Home Journal* that 50 percent of hysterectomies are unnecessary, according to a poll of leading pathologists.

10. Freud, *op. cit.*

11. A. C. Kinsey, et al., *Sexual Behavior in the Human Female* (New York: Simon and Schuster, 1953), p. 582.

12. I. C. Ruben, and Josef Novak, *Integrated Gynecology: Principles and Practice* (New York: McGraw Hill, 1956), p. 77.

13. Langdon Parsons and S. C. Sommers, *Gynecology* (Philadelphia: W. B. Saunders, 1962).

14. Thomas Jeffcoate, *Principles of Gynecology* (London: Butterworth, 1967).

15. E. R. Novak, G. S. Jones, and H. W. Jones, *Novak's Textbooks of Gynecology* (Baltimore, Md.: Williams and Wilkens, 1970).

16. Denslow Lewis, reprinted in the *American Journal of Obstetrics and Gynecology*. by M. H. Hollender, M.D., 1970. p. 108.

17. *Diseases of Women* (St. Louis, Mo.: C. V. Mosby Co., 1926).

18. Germaine Greer, *The Female Eunuch.*

19. L. R. Sillman, M.D., "Feminity and Paranoidism" in the *Journal of Nervous and Mental Disease*, Vol. 143, No. 2, p. 163.

PART FOUR
1 Women Workers in the Health Service Industry

1. J. Weiss, "The Changing Job Structure of Health Manpower." Unpublished dissertation, Harvard University, Cambridge, 1966.

2. National Center for Health Statistics. *Health Resources Statistics: Health Manpower and Health Facilities 1971*. U. S. Department of Health, Education, and Welfare, 1972.

3. S. Health Reverby: "Women's work." *Health-PAC Bulletin* 40: 1–3, April 1972.

4. M. Rosenberg, *Occupations and Values* (Glencoe, Ill.: Free Press 1957).

5. J. Kreps, *Sex in the Marketplace* (Baltimore: Johns Hopkins Press, 1971).

6. V. K. Oppenheimer, *The Female Labor Force in the United States.* Population Monograph Series No. 5, University of California, Berkeley, 1970.

7. H. I. Greenfield, with C. A. Brown, *Allied Health Manpower: Trends and Prospects* (New York: Columbia University Press, 1969).

8. Women's Bureau. *Handbook on Women Workers.* U.S. Department of Labor, 1969.

9. Women's Bureau. *Facts about Women Workers.* U.S. Department of Labor, 1974.

10. P. O. Flaim, and N. I. Peters, Usual weekly earnings of American workers. *Monthly Labor Review* 95(3): 28–38, 1972.

11. Bureau of the Census. *General Social and Economic Characteristics, United States Summary, 1970.* U.S. Department of Commerce, 1972.

12. J. Mitchell, *Woman's Estate* (New York: Pantheon, 1972).

13. J. Ladinsky, "Occupational determinants of geographic mobility among professional workers." *Amer. Sociol. Rev.* 32: 253–264, April 1967.

14. P. D. Smith, *Influence of Wage Rates on Nurse Mobility* Graduate Program in Hospital Administration, (Chicago: University of Chicago Press, 1962).

15. W. Kissick, *Health Manpower in Transition.* U.S. Public Health Service, 1966.

16. L. T. Coggeshall, *Planning for Medical Progress through Education* (Evanston, Ill.: Association of American Medical Colleges, 1965).

17. V. L. Bullough, *The Development of Medicine as a Profession* (Basel and New York: S. Karger, 1966).

18. E. Spieler, "Division of laborers." *Health-PAC Bulletin* 46: 1–2, 4, November 1972.

19. W. A. Nolen, *The Making of a Surgeon.* Simon and Schuster, New York, 1972.

20. V. Cooper, "The lady's not for burning." *Health-PAC Bulletin* pp. 2–3. March 1970.

21. C. Lopate, *Women in Medicine* (Baltimore, Md.: Johns Hopkins University Press, 1968).

22. J. Kosa, and R. E. Cocker, Jr. "The female physician in public health: Conflict and reconciliation of the sex and professional roles." *Sociology and Social Research* 49(3): 294–305, 1965.

23. B. Ehrenreich and D. English, eds. *Witches, Midwives, and Nurses: A History of Women Healers* (Old Westbury, New York: The Feminist Press, 1973).

24. *The Training and Responsibilities of the Midwife* (New York: The Josiah Macy Jr. Foundation, 1967).

25. *The Midwife in the United States,* Josiah Macy Jr. Foundation, New York, 1968.

26. R. Stevens, *American Medicine and the Public Interest* (New Haven: Yale University Press, 1971).

27. E. Levine, "Some answers to the nurse shortage" *Nursing Outlook* 12(3): 30–34, 1964.

28. E. Levine, S. Siegel, and J. De laPrente, "Diversity of nurse staffing among general hospitals." *Hospitals* 35(9): 42–48, 1961.

29. V. Lippard, E. Purcell, eds. *Intermediate-Level Health Practitioners* (New York: Josiah Macy, Jr. Foundation, 1973).

30. S. Reverby, "Sorcerer's apprentice." *Health-PAC Bulletin* 46: 1–2, November 1972.

31. C. A. Brown, "The division of laborers." Allied health professions. *Int. J. Health Serv.* 3(3): 435–444, 1973.

32. B. Ehrenreich and J. Ehrenreich, *The American Health Empire: Power, Profits and Politics* (New York: Random House, 1970).

33. C. A. Brown, "The Development of Occupations in Health Technology." Unpublished dissertation, Columbia University, New York, 1971.

34. W. F. Bowers, *Interpersonal Relationships in the Hospital* (Springfield, Ill.: Charles C Thomas, 1960).

35. W. J. Gershenfeld, "Labor Relations in Hospitals." Paper presented at Emerging Sectors of Collective Bargaining Seminar No. 4, Temple University, Philadelphia, March 28, 1968.

36. "The male-feasance of health." *Health-PAC Bulletin,* March 1970.

37. D. Gaynor, E. Blake, T. Bodenheimer and C. Mermey, "RN strike: Between the lines." *Health-PAC Bulletin* 60: 1–2, 5, September-October 1974.

38. L. Davis, "State of the Union." *1199 Drug and Hospital News,* pp. 20–23, March 1969.

39. "Institutional organizing." *Health-PAC Bulletin* No. 37, January 1972.

40. "Fragmentation of workers: An anti-personnel weapon." *Health-PAC Bulletin* No. 46, November 1972.

41. A. B. Soule, "Trends in training programs in radiologic techology." *Radiol. Technol.* 38: 70–73, 1966.

42. Proceedings of the thirty-ninth annual convention. *Radiol. Technol.* 39: 98, September 1967.

43. V. A. Bergquist, "Women's participation in labor unions." *Monthly Labor Review* 97(10): 3–9, 1974.

BIBLIOGRAPHY

WOMEN'S HEALTH: SOME BASIC READINGS

Corea, Gena. *Women's Health Care: The Hidden Malpractice.* New York: William Morrow & Co., 1977. Nice, useful history of the women's health movement. The basic primer.

Ehrenreich, Barbara and Deidre English. *The Last Romance: Women and Experts.* New York, Anchor Books, 1978.

Frankfort, Ellen. *Vaginal Politics.* New York: Bantam, 1973. Highly recommended.

Seaman, Barbara. *Free and Female: The Sex Life of the Contemporary Woman.* New York: Coward, McCann & Geoghegan, 1972. The book that combined gynecologic liberation, sexual liberation and feminism into one important package. Seaman is right on target with her early attack here on estrogen replacement drugs.

HEALTH CARE: MALE AND FEMALE

Kutlechuck, David. *Prognosis Negative: Crisis in the Health Care System.* New York: Vintage, 1977. Fine basic collection on what's wrong with the national health system. Most of the articles first appeared in the *Health/PAC Bulletin.*

Health Policy Advisory Center (Health/PAC). *The American Health Empire. Power, Profit, and Politics.* New York: Random House, 1970.

HISTORY/HERSTORY

Barker-Benfield, G. J. *The Horrors of the Half-Known Life: Male Attitudes Towards Women and Sexuality in Nineteenth Century America.* New York: Harper Colophon Books, 1976.

Ehrenreich, Barbara and Deidre English. *Complaints and Disorders: The Sexual Politics of Sickness.* New York: The Feminist Press.

Witches, Midwives and Nurses: A History of Women Healers. New York: The Feminist Press. Both pamphlets may be ordered directly from the Feminist Press, Box 334, Old Westbury, N. Y. 11568.

Gordon, Linda. *Woman's Body, Woman's Right.* New York: The Viking Press, 1976. Unique history of the birth-control movement written with a Marxist perspective.

SELF-HELP

Boston Women's Health Book Collective. *Our Bodies, Ourselves.* 2nd ed. New York: Simon & Schuster, 1976. Mindboggling and comprehensive—almost anything a woman would want to know about her body, told in plain, nontechnical language. This book is the first step toward bodily self-awareness.

Our Bodies, Ourselves—Spanish Edition. Boston: BWHBC, 1977. Available through the Collective, Box 192, West Somerville, Mass. 02144. The Collective is making some copies available to groups with limited funds at reduced prices. The copy is much the same as in the English-language edition of the book, but the photographs are of Chicana and Puerto Rican women.

Campbell, Elizabeth and Vicki Ziegler. *Circle One: A Woman's Beginning Guide to Self-Health and Sexuality.* Copies may be ordered from KNOW, P. O. Box 86031, Pittsburgh, Pa. 15221.

Dreifus, Claudia. *Woman's Fate: Raps from a Feminist Consciousness-Raising Group.* New York: Bantam, 1973.

Marieskind, Helen I. "Gynecological Services: Their Historical Relationship to the Women's Movement with Recent Experience of Self-Help Clinics and Other Delivery Modes." Ph.D. dissertation, UCLA School of Public Health, 1976. Obtainable through UCLA.

Rennie, Susan and Kirsten Grimstad. *The New Woman's Survival Sourcebook.* New York: Knopf, 1975.

CHILDBIRTH AND MOTHERHOOD

Arms, Suzanne. *Immaculate Deception: A New Look at Childbirth in America.* Boston: Houghton Mifflin, 1975.

Brooks, Tonya and Linda Bennett. *Giving Birth at Home.* Association for Childbirth At Home, Cerritos, California, 1976. Practical and informational guide by two midwife advocates of home birth.

Haire, Doris, and John Haire. *The Cultural Warping of Childbirth.* Available from the International Association for Childbirth Education, 25 Nottingham Way, Hillside, New Jersey. Mr. and Ms. Haire are home birth crusaders who make a fine scientific case for avoiding hospital maternity rooms.

Rich, Adrienne. *Of Woman Born.* New York: Norton, 1976.

CONTRACEPTION/ABORTION

Calderone, Mary, ed. *Manual of Family Planning and Contraceptive Parenthood.* Baltimore: Williams & Wilkins Co., 1970.

Fleishman, Norman, and Peter L. Dixon. *Vasectomy, Sex and Parenthood.* Garden City, N.Y.: Doubleday and Company, Inc., 1973.

Gardner, Joanne Evans, ed. *Confronting the Enemy.* Pittsburgh: KNOW. This may be ordered from KNOW, P. O. Box 85031, Pittsburgh, Pa. 15221.

Hardin, Garrett. *Mandatory Motherhood: The True Meaning of "Right to Life."* Boston: The Beacon Press, 1974.

Lader, Lawrence. *Abortion II: Making the Revolution.* Boston: The Beacon Press, 1974. The history of the recent struggle for abortion rights by an activist who was at the front lines.

Seaman, Barbara. *The Doctors' Case Against the Pill.* New York: Avon, 1970.

————, and Gideon Seaman, M.D. *Women and the Crisis in Sex Hormones.* New York: Rawson Associates, 1977.

Shulder, Diane, and Florynce Kennedy. *Abortion Rap.* New York: McGraw-Hill, 1971.

MONTHLY BLOOD

Delaney, Janice; Mary Jane Lupton, and Emily Toth. *The Curse: A Cultural History of Menstruation.* New York: Dutton, 1976.

Reitz, Rosetta. *Menopause: A Positive Approach.* New York: Chilton, 1977. Menopause, revised.

Weideger, Paula. *Menstruation and Menopause.* New York: Knopf, 1975. Useful study of psychology, physiology, myth and reality of menstruation.

BREAST CANCER

Crile, George, Jr., M.D. *What Women Should Know About the Breast Cancer Controversy.* New York: Pocket Books, 1974. A maverick physician bucks the cancer establishment to tell us some unpleasant truths. Highly recommended.

Greenfield, Natalee S. *"First Do No Harm . . ."* New York: Two Continents, 1976. A mother tells the true story of her daughter's death. Ms. Greenfield's daughter died in her prime from the birth-control Pill, from malpractice, from male arrogance.

Kushner, Rose. *Breast Cancer: A Personal and Investigative Report.* New York: Harcourt, Brace, Jovanovich, Inc., 1975.

Rollin, Betty. *First, You Cry*. Philadelphia: J. B. Lippincott, 1976. Moving first-person report on one woman's battle with breast cancer.

Winkler, Win Ann. *Post-Mastectomy*. New York: Hawthorn Books, Inc., 1976.

WORKING IN THE HEALTH PROFESSIONS

Ashley, JoAnne. *Hospitals, Paternalism and the Role of the Nurse*. New York: Teachers College Press, 1976. Beautifully written nonfiction about the miseries of nursing.

Campbell, Margaret. *Why Would a Girl Go Into Medicine*? New York: The Feminist Press, n.d. Obtainable from The Feminist Press, Box 334, Old Westbury, N.Y. 11568.

Haseltine, Florence, M.D., and Yvonne Yaw. *Woman Doctor: The Internship of a Modern Woman*. Boston: Houghton-Mifflin Co., 1976.

WOMEN'S HEALTH AT THE WORKPLACE

Hricko, Andrea with Melanie Brunt. *Working for Your Life: A Woman's Guide to Job Hazards*. Berkeley: The Labor Occupational Health Program and Public Citizen's Health Research Group, 1977. Facts on occupational health problems facing women on the job.

PAMPHLETS, BROADSIDES, ARTICLES, ETC.

Coalition for the Medical Rights of Women. *Sterilization Abuse*. A frank, direct booklet giving all the facts on coercive sterilization. Copies may be obtained from the Coalition at 4079 A 24th Street, San Francisco, California 94114.

Curtis, Linda. *A Case of Medical Monopoly: The Tallahassee M.D. Conspiracy*. Mimeographed study sheet about the attempt by a women's clinic to break through the official "doctorhold" on gynecological services in a southern city. Copies may be obtained from the Feminist Women's Health Center, 1017 Thomasville Road, Tallahassee, Florida 23203.

Gray, Nancy. *Chemical Use/Abuse and the Female Reproductive System*. Copies may be obtained from Do It Now Foundation, P.O. Box 4114, Phoenix, Arizona.

Lesbian Health Pamphlet. Obtainable from The Women's Community Health Center, 137 Hampshire Street, Cambridge, Mass. 02139.

Scully, Diana, and Pauline Bart. *A Funny Thing Happened on the Way to the Orifice: Women in Gynecology Textbooks*. A tragi-comic rundown of *why* gynecologists are that way. Obtainable from Pauline Bart, Department of Psychiatry at the Medical Center, P.O. Box 6998, Chicago, Ill. 60680.

CARTOONS

Bulbul. *Dissecting Doctor Medi-Corpse*. Wonderful funnies by a feminist cartoonist about your friendly local Dr. Welby. Obtainable from Arachine Publishing, P.O. Box 4100, Mountain View, Calif. 94040

BIBLIOGRAPHIES

Cowan, Belita, ed. *Women's Health Care: Resources, Writings, Bibliographies*. Write: Belita Cowan, 556 Second Street, Ann Arbor, Mich. 48103.

Ruzek, Sheryl K. *Women and Health Care: A Bibliography*. Write: Program on Women, Northwestern University, 619 Emerson Street Evanston, Ill. 60201.

PUBLICATIONS WITH ARTICLES ON WOMEN'S HEALTH ISSUES

Birth Notes. Newsletter of Association for Childbirth at Home, P.O. Box 1219, Cerritos, Ca. 90701.

Boston Women's Health Book Collective Monthly Packet. Box 192, West Somerville. Mass. 02144.

Feminist Studies. 417 Riverside Drive, New York, New York 10025.

HealthRight Newsletter. 175 Fifth Avenue, New York, New York 10011.

Health/PAC Bulletin. 17 Murray Street, New York, New York 10017.

herSelf. 225 East Liberty Street, Ann Arbor, Michigan.

International Journal of Health Services. c/o Baywood Publishing Company, 43 Central Drive, Farmingdale, New York 11735.

National Women's Health Network Newsletter. P.O. Box 24192, Washington, D.C. 20024.

Majority Report. 74 Grove Street, New York, New York.

The Monthly Extract: An Irregular Periodical. Lolly Hirsch, ed., Box 3488, Stamford, Conn. 06905.

Off Our Backs. 1724 20 St N.W., Washington, D.C. 20009.

Quest: A Feminist Quarterly. P.O. Box 8843, Washington, D.C 20003.

Women and Health. State University of New York, College at Old Westbury, Old Westbury, New York 11563.

CONTRIBUTORS

RITA ARDITTI is a Bay State feminist who, along with several friends, is co-owner of Cambridge's "New Words Bookstore." She's a regular contributor to *Science For the People* magazine, and is working in a doctoral program for the Union for Experimenting Colleges and Universities.

DEBORAH BAKER grew up in Montclair, New Jersey, and has lived in Appalachia for the past eight years. Ms. Baker, who resides in Beckley, West Virginia, is a general assignment reporter for the *Raleigh Register*. Her beat: coal, labor, local government.

G. J. BARKER-BENFIELD is a British-born historian on the staff of the State University of New York at Albany. He obtained his B.A. at Trinity College, Cambridge (England) and his doctorate at UCLA. His book *The Horrors of the Half-Known Life: Male Attitudes Toward Women and Sexuality in Nineteenth-Century America* was published in 1976 by Harper and Row.

CAROL A. BROWN teaches sociology at the University of Lowell and works with the Women's Research Center of Boston, studying the condition of divorced mothers. "I am a member of the usual radical organizations," she says. "And I'm a Marxist-feminist, but that means *feminist*, not sectarian Marxist."

MARK DOWIE is the general manager of *Mother Jones*, a radical mass-circulation magazine published in San Francisco. The author of *Transitions to Freedom*, a book on the problems of ex-prisoners, Dowie is married and the father of four children. He "feels pretty good" about being one of two male writers to be included in this anthology.

CLAUDIA DREIFUS is an author, journalist and lecturer who writes about politics, art, life and all of the aforementioned as they affect women. The author of *Radical Lifestyles* (1970) and *Woman's Fate: Raps From a Feminist Consciousness-Raising Group* (1972), her writings can be found in such diversified places as *McCall's, Rolling Stone, Family Circle, The Progressive, Glamour,* and *The Nation*. She is currently writing her first novel.

BARBARA EHRENREICH and DEIRDRE ENGLISH are feminist pamphleteers and theoreticians. Their two self-published booklets, *Witches, Midwives and Nurses: A History of Women Healers* and *Complaints and Disorders: The Sexual Politics of Sickness* are classics of women's movement literature. They are at present preparing a manuscript on the role scientific "experts" have in shaping women's lives.

ELIZABETH FEE is Irish, and claims descent from a long line of rural female uncertified health practitioners. She has written several articles on science and feminism and is currently completing a study on the history of scientific theories about sex differences. Fee teaches humanities in the School of Health Services, Johns Hopkins University.

ELLEN FRANKFORT is the author of *Vaginal Politics*, a 1972 best seller compiled from her *Village Voice* columns on women and health. She is now working on a book about the problems of women and success.

THE HEALTHRIGHT COLLECTIVE. HealthRight is a women's health education and advocacy organization based in New York City. The Collective publishes pamphlets and a quarterly newsletter, trains organizers, gives "Know Your Body" courses, and provides speakers on women's health issues. Naomi, Pamela, Rachel and the rest of the group can be found at 175 Fifth Avenue, New York, New York 10010.

TRACY JOHNSON is a West Coast free lance whose work has appeared in *The New York Times Magazine, The Village Voice* and *Redbook*.

ROSE KUSHNER'S 1975 book, *Breast Cancer: A Personal History and An Investigative Report* brought national attention to the myriad of unnecessary pains endured by women with breast cancer. She is also the founder and executive director of The Breast Cancer Advisory Center of Kensington, Maryland, a hot line that counsels breast-cancer victims in emergency situations.

DEBORAH LARNED is the associate editor of *womanSport magazine*. Her articles have appeared in *Ms., New Times* and the *HealthRight Newsletter*.

Larned, in her pre-New York life, was the champion speed skater of Northbrook, Illinois.

HELEN MARIESKIND received her doctorate from UCLA's School of Public Health. "Most of my work and research interests are in the organization of women's health services—which was the subject of my doctoral thesis," she explains. Marieskind is the editor and founder of *Women and Health*, an academic journal published by the State University of New York College at Old Westbury. Her writing has appeared in *Social Policy*, the *International Journal of Health Services* and various women's movement publications.

ROSETTA REITZ, author of *Menopause: A New View*, has "interviewed dozens of women experiencing menopause and found that what they were saying and feeling was very different from what the books were saying." She says that her three daughters, all in their twenties, "will have an easy menopause because they already know all about it from my research."

ADRIENNE RICH is a feminist, poet and author of great distinction.

BARBARA SEAMAN is a medical journalist who's published three major works on women's health: *The Doctors' Case against the Pill* (1969), *Free and Female* (1972) and, with her husband Gideon Seaman, MD., *Women and the Crisis in Sex Hormones* (1977). Seaman was cited in 1973 by the Library of Congress as "the American author who raised sexism in health care as a world-wide issue."

JEAN SHARPE, M. D. is a pediatrician in North Carolina, working in a comprehensive care center. She also works in the community on behalf of children and parents, and is active in a local health collective that focuses on the politics of health care.

AMANDA SPAKE is an editor of *Mother Jones*. She was formerly a member of the Newsworks Collective of Washington, D.C., and writes for various national publications on women's health and other political issues. Her book on the dangers of nuclear power, *Abnormal Occurences/Incredible Events*, will be published early in 1978.

KAY WEISS is a women's health activist who holds a master's degree in Public Health. Her writing on women's health issues has appeared in *Ms.*, *Off Our Backs*, and the *International Journal of Health Services*.

VINTAGE POLITICAL SCIENCE AND SOCIAL CRITICISM